Final Cut Pro® 4

Complete Course

Ian David Aronson

WILEY

Wiley Publishing, Inc.

Final Cut Pro® 4 Complete Course

Published by:

Wiley Publishing, Inc.
111 River Street
Hoboken, NJ 07030
www.wiley.com/compbooks

Published simultaneously in Canada

For general information on our other products and services or to obtain technical support please contact our Customer Care Department within the U.S. at 800-762-2974, outside the U.S. at 317-572-3993 or fax 317-572-4002.

Library of Congress Control Number: 2003113976

ISBN: 0-7645-2591-3

Manufactured in the United States of America

10 9 8 7 6 5 4 3 2 1

» Credits

Publisher: Barry Pruett

Project Editor: Cricket Krengel

Acquisitions Editor: Michael Roney

Editorial Manager: Rev Mengle

Technical Editor: Jason Woliner

Copy Editor: John Edwards

Production Coordinators: April Farling,
Maridee Ennis

Layout and Graphics: Beth Brooks, Carrie Foster,
LeAndra Hosier,
Kristin McMullan

Quality Control: John Tyler Connoley,
Susan Moritz, Charles Spencer

Indexer: Ty Koontz

Proofreader: Betty Kish

» Dedication

To Jodi, my better half. I could not have made this book without you.

» Acknowledgments

Thanks to Acquisitions Editor Michael Roney for setting this project in motion and choosing me as the author. I would also like to thank my agent Margot Maley Hutchison at Waterside Productions for putting us in touch.
The editorial team at Wiley made this production a great experience, and I would particularly like to thank Project Editor Cricket Krengel for all her help. I would also like to thank my colleague Bonnie Blake for introducing me to Margot, and for getting the entire process started. Last but not least, I would like to thank Patricia Keeton, Convener of Communication Arts, and Steven Perry, Dean of the School of Contemporary Arts at Ramapo College, for their advice and guidance.

About the Author

Ian David Aronson is a media producer and scholar who lives in New York City. Aronson is director/producer of www.digitaldocumentary.org, a Web site dedicated to advancing the art of online documentary. He is a graduate of the Stanford University Master's Program in Documentary Film and Video, and is an Assistant Professor of Digital Media at Ramapo College.

»Table of Contents

Introduction

Final Cut Pro is a nonlinear editing program that provides you, the editor, with a level of flexibility and control that people only dreamed about a few years ago.

When you edit, you can't really tell how two shots work next to each other until you cut them together. Because older, linear editing systems relied on analog videotape, an editor's options were severely limited. Before the advent of programs like Final Cut Pro, once you put two shots together and cut additional material into the project to create a sequence, even the slightest change to those first two shots would require you to redo each subsequent edit. That means if you spent an entire day editing a five-minute sequence, and then realized you could improve your piece by trimming a half-second of video from your first shot, you were between a rock and a hard place, so to speak. Some people lived with edits they didn't like simply because fixing the edits was too painful, while others spent days on short segments of a much larger production, neglecting everything else.

This agonizing editing cycle is no more. Final Cut Pro is a fantastically powerful editing program that allows you tremendous freedom. This book helps you make the most of it. Final Cut Pro is intuitive enough that you can just sit down with the program and figure things out on your own, but there's a lot more available to you, and that's why this book is helpful.

Final Cut Pro meets the needs of amateur video enthusiasts as well as seasoned, professional video editors. Depending on your level of skill and experience, you can use Final Cut Pro to create a fully functional video project for the first time, to develop and polish a broadcast-quality video master, or even to edit a feature-length film for theatrical distribution. The true power of Final Cut Pro 4 is the depth of its features. You have everything you need to create your project, fine-tune the images and sound, and deliver the finished product. The tutorials in this book walk you through each step of the process and build on one another to give you a comprehensive understanding of Final Cut Pro 4 and the larger world of video editing. Final Cut Pro 4 Complete Course is just that—a complete course.

Is This Book for You?

Yes. Final Cut Pro 4 is deep enough that there's always more to learn, and that's the purpose of this book. If you're a student, a professional editor, an educator who teaches video, or a serious video enthusiast, this book was designed with you in mind.

If you're new to digital video editing, you come at a great time. If you've worked in Final Cut Pro for a while, the new version is a nice step up. This book is a great way to learn from the ground up as well as to explore the new features that the program has to offer.

What's in This Book?

This book is divided into eight parts. But, before you get to the parts, you are introduced to Final Cut Pro with a group of tutorials called the Confidence Builder—it is designed to get you started right away. The following list outlines the layout of this book:

> » "Confidence Builder" is a hands-on, get-your-feet-wet project that introduces you to Final Cut Pro. When you finish, you have an animated video logo, complete with music.

> » **Part I: Course Setup.** This introductory session of the book contains information about Final Cut Pro and this course.

> » "Final Cut Pro 4 Basics" includes an explanation of nonlinear editing, the difference between analog and digital video, FireWire video capture, time code, and nondestructive editing.

» "Project Overview" explains the project you create as you work through this course.

» "General Work Tips and Computer Instructions" explains setups, presets and settings, and basic file management and provides tips on maintaining peak performance.

» **Part II: Getting Started.** This is the first of the tutorials; it gets you started working in Final Cut Pro.

» Session 1, "Starting the Project," includes tutorials to show you how to start a project in Final Cut Pro. You learn how to select and change project settings and editing presets, and how to organize the media you capture and import for a project.

» Session 2, "Assembling a Project," includes tutorials on working with the Timeline and Viewer windows, setting clip length, placing clips in the Timeline, and adjusting clips in the Timeline.

» **Part III: Basic Editing.** This section shows you how to cut a project together.

» Session 3, "Working with Clips," shows you how to edit the length and content of the clips in your project. You learn different editing techniques and tools, and learn to add video and audio tracks to the Timeline.

» Session 4, "Editing Clips," examines different types of edits and the ways different techniques shape your project.

» Session 5, "Transitions, Filters, and Effects," shows you how to add various effects to your video and how to refine each effect to get exactly the results you want.

» **Part IV: Working with Audio.** A cultivated understanding of audio is a major key to success in digital editing. This part shows you how to work with digital audio in Final Cut Pro.

» Session 6, "Preparing Audio Files," teaches you how to craft audio and create an effective sound design using dialog, environmental sound, and music.

» Session 7, "Editing Audio Clips," includes tutorials on the finer points of audio editing, such as equalization, volume settings, and complex audio effects.

» **Part V: Creating and Animating Titles.** Here you learn how to create and animate titles using Final Cut Pro's professional-quality graphics-creation tools.

» Session 8, "Working with Titles," includes tutorials on the creation of a basic title, and the addition of sophisticated animated elements using the new LiveType software that ships with Final Cut Pro 4.

» Session 9, "Creating Animated Credits," shows you how to create titles that move across the screen and how to control them to your exact specifications.

» **Part VI: Adding Transparency and Video Effects.** Final Cut Pro provides the capability to combine layers of video and create Hollywood-quality special effects.

» Session 10, "Using Transparency, Compositing, and Video Effects" includes tutorials on combining different video elements and adjusting properties such as speed, transparency, and scale.

» Session 11, "Using Advanced Compositing Effects and Color Correction" teaches you how to blend multiple layers of video and to adjust the color in your video to broadcast-quality standards.

» **Part VII: Final Edits and Exporting.** This final section takes you through the process of outputting your work in your medium of choice.

» Session 12, "Putting It All Together," shows you how to add complicated speed effects, and to finalize your project and create different versions for different purposes, as well as how to protect yourself from mistakes.

» Session 13, "Deciding on Your Method of Delivery," examines different output options for your project and includes tutorials on preparing your work for delivery via the World Wide Web or for distribution as a DVD.

» Session 14, "Exporting Your Movie Project," includes step-by-step tutorials on exporting a finished videotape or exporting an Edit Decision List that you can bring to an advanced postproduction facility.

Confidence Builder

TOOLS YOU'LL USE
Browser, Viewer, Timeline, Canvas, Video transitions (fades and dissolves), Title 3D generator, Text Color tab, Skew control, Render, Export, Compression.

MATERIALS NEEDED
stylishLogo.mov, backgroundMusic.aif

TIME REQUIRED
40 minutes

The art of editing a good film or video is not simply putting one shot next to another, or clipping out the bad parts so that no one sees your mistakes. Your goal is to create a sequence of material that tells a story. Think of yourself as a chef, turning unedited film and video—the raw ingredients—into a carefully crafted, complex, and flavorful dish. A skilled editor uses sound and images to create a project that engages the audience and creates a worthwhile, satisfying viewing experience. Any good film or video project has an identity. As an editor, it's your job to use visuals and sounds that build on each other to create that identity. An animated logo is a great place to start.

In this tutorial, you make a professional-quality logo that you can attach to your video projects. You've seen these logos at the end of television shows and movies for years. Now you can make your own.

This project introduces you to the fundamental workings of Final Cut Pro: importing media, adding clips to your Timeline, editing, using effects, and exporting. Your finished product is an eight-second video that you design and build from the ground up.

Tutorial

» Building the Basic Project

In this tutorial, you open Final Cut Pro, create a new project, and import some audio clips. To see a finished preview of the video logo that you make in the Confidence Builder, take a look at stylishLogo.mov in the Confidence Builder folder on the CD.

1. **Create a new folder on your hard drive called Final Cut Pro Complete Course.**

   This is where you save the project you create and where you store the media files you copy from the CD that comes with the book.

2. **Open the Final Cut Pro 4 Complete Course CD, and copy the Confidence Builder folder, and its contents, to the folder you just made on your hard drive.**

3. **Open Final Cut Pro. From the desktop, double-click the Macintosh HD icon.**

   When you double-click, a new window opens that displays the contents of your hard drive.

4. **Choose Applications→Final Cut Pro to start the program.**

   If you don't have a video source, such as a DV camera or deck, connected to your computer, Final Cut Pro prompts you to check again or to set the device selection to None. For this book, you don't need an external video device, so just click Continue.

5. **Select DV-NTSC from the Setup For drop-down menu in the Easy Setup dialog box.**

   When you open Final Cut Pro 4 for the first time, the Easy Setup dialog box opens automatically. DV stands for *digital video,* and NTSC is the broadcast video standard used in North America. Final Cut Pro then configures your project for you. Lots of things in life promise to be easy but aren't—the 1040EZ may not live up to its name, but the Easy Setup in Final Cut Pro does.

6. **Click Setup.**

   The dialog box closes, and the DV-NTSC settings take effect.

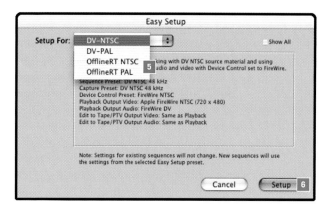

7. **Choose File Import→Files.**

   The Choose a File dialog box opens.

8. **Navigate to the Final Cut Pro Complete Course folder on your hard drive, then to the Confidence Builder folder inside it, and select** backgroundMusic.aif. **Click the Choose button.**

   The .aif file is imported. As you may have guessed from the name, this is the background music for the logo you make.

<NOTE>

AIF stands for Audio Interchange File format, which is a native Mac audio format.

9. **Choose File→Save Project to save your work. Name the file** Company Logo, **and save the project in the Confidence Builder folder on your hard drive.**

   You may not have your own production company, but a logo is a nice beginning, and as an editor, you're entitled to have one.

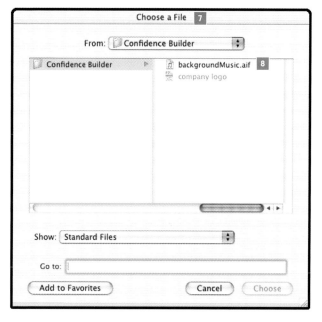

10. **Click the** backgroundMusic.aif **file's icon in the Browser window, hold down the mouse, and drag the audio clip from the Browser window into Tracks A1 and A2 on the Timeline.**
    Because backgroundMusic.aif is a stereo audio clip, it takes up two audio tracks. You can place the file anywhere on Tracks A1 and A2. Once you position the clip in in the Timeline, release the mouse.

11. **Drag your file to the far left of the Timeline so it starts to play at the beginning of your movie.**
    When you drag files from the Browser to the Timeline, they don't automatically snap to the beginning. Click any part of the file you just inserted into your Timeline. As long as your mouse is held down, you can easily slide the file back and forth on the Timeline.

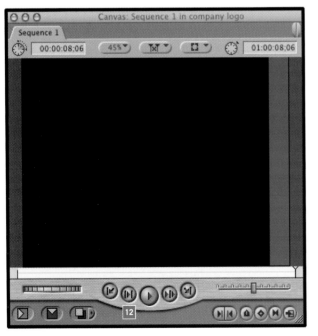

12. **Click the Play In to Out button in the Canvas window.**
    This button appears at the bottom of the Canvas window to the immediate left of Play. You can now hear what your new project sounds like.

13. **Save your project.**
    Congratulations! You just created your first project and made your first edit. Whenever you make a change to the Timeline, even if you just add sound, it's considered an edit. This is a small start, but you're on your way.

< T I P >

If you think it takes too long to use the File menu to save the project, you can always just press ⌘+S.

Tutorial
» Creating Titles to Go with Your Audio

Final Cut Pro has great graphics tools, and you have complete control over each detail. Best of all, Final Cut Pro automatically generates video clips from the graphics that you create, so you can easily edit graphics into your movies. In this tutorial, you create two titles and add them to your Timeline. The first title has the name of your production company; the second displays your slogan.

1. **Click the Video Generators button in the Viewer, and select Title 3D from the menu.**
   A new window opens. This is the Title 3D control window, and it contains a flashing cursor where you can type in your text.

   <NOTE>
   If you closed your company logo after saving it, open it now and repeat this step so you're working on the same project. As the course goes on, it's a good idea to leave things open for the next tutorial when you finish the preceding one.

2. **Type the name of your company in the Title 3D window.**
   The name of the production company that I use in this example is team 1002 productions. To make the text appear on different lines, press Return after each word, just as you would do in a word processing program. If you don't have a name for your production company, you can make one up. Your last name, followed by the word *Productions* is a safe bet (for example, Aronson Productions).

   <TIP>
   If you have a love interest, create a version of this movie with his or her name in at least one of the titles. A project like this can earn you lots of points.

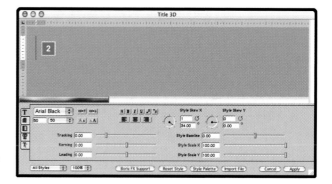

3. **Highlight the text you entered in Step 2, and select a font from the font pull-down menu.**
   Final Cut Pro previews your title in the Title 3D window.

4. **With your title still highlighted, select a size from the point size pull-down menu.**
   In the example, I use Arial Black, size 50.

   <TIP>
   You don't have to choose from one of the options Final Cut Pro provides; you can type your own size directly into the size field.

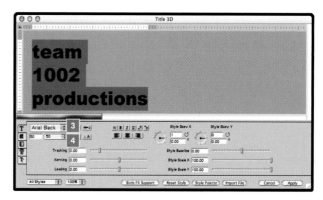

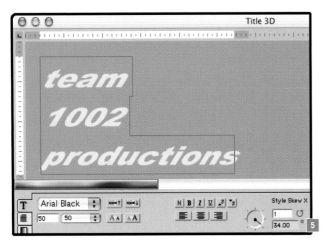

5. **Adjust the Style Skew X dial to 34 degrees.**

   This leans your text to the right and gives it a dynamic, action-movie style. If you feel like experimenting, you can lean your text in the opposite direction, or even skew it upside down.

6. **Click the Text Color tab.**

   The bottom half of the Title 3D window changes, and a new set of controls appears. These controls allow you to set the color of your title. Give your title a color that matches the name. For example, if you use a bold, assertive name, choose a bold and assertive color.

7. **Click the Style Color field, and the Colors dialog box opens. Select Crayons from the List pull-down menu in the Colors dialog box.**

8. **Choose the color you want to work with—this example uses Mercury—and click OK.**

   When you click OK, the Colors dialog box closes and Final Cut Pro applies your selection to the highlighted text, changing the color.

9. **Click Apply in the Title 3D window to create your first title.**
   Your new title opens as a video clip in the viewer and is ready for you to cut into your project.

<NOTE>
The checkered background indicates transparency.

<NOTE>
You can use different colors for different words. However, if you use too many colors, your text can start to look ugly. If you make only one word a different color, it really stands out.

10. **Drag the title from the Viewer onto Track V1 of your Timeline.**
    Drag the clip all the way to the left so it starts at the beginning of the Timeline. Now it's time to make a new title with your company slogan.

11. **Click the Video Generators button again, and select Title 3D, as you did before in Step 1.**
    A new Title 3D window opens.

12. **Type in your slogan, highlight it, and set the font and point size.**
    Final Cut Pro defaults to the same font, point size, and color you used in your last title. This helps to create a unifying theme, but if you want to use different settings, go for it.

13. **Click Apply again to create your second clip.**
    The new clip opens in the Viewer, replacing the last clip. Once you place a clip in the Timeline, it becomes a part of the project, so don't worry—you haven't lost your first title even though it no longer appears in the Viewer. You're now ready to place the new clip in the Timeline—but hold on, there's no room. You need to edit.

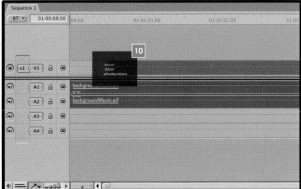

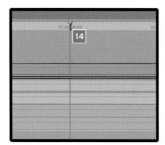

14. **Drag the position indicator back to about 01:00:04;00.**
This is where the music changes from many instruments to one instrument. This is also where you want to transition from your title to your slogan. As you navigate through your sequence by clicking and dragging the small yellow triangle at the top of the position indicator, you hear the music playing. This is called *scrubbing*. You can scrub until you find the exact location that you want.

<NOTE>
If 01:00:04;00 seems like a strange number, don't worry. You learn more about timecodes later in the book.

15. **Move your the cursor to the end of the video clip on Track V1, and notice how the cursor changes shape from a single arrow into a vertical bar with arrows pointing left and right.**
This indicates you can make the clip longer or shorter by clicking the beginning or end of the clip and dragging it to the left or right. Dragging the end of a clip to the left, toward the beginning of the Timeline, makes the clip shorter. Dragging the end of a clip to the right makes the clip longer.

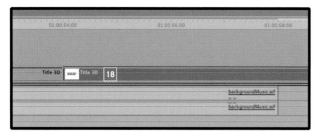

16. **Click the end of the clip, and drag the end of the clip back to the position indicator.**
The video clip snaps into place. You just shortened it.

17. **Click the Play In to Out button in the Viewer to see what your edit looks like.**

18. **Drag your slogan from the Viewer onto Track V1, directly to the right of your first title.**
Notice how your slogan is too long and extends past the end of the music? You have to edit.

19. **Drag the position indictor back to the spot where the music ends (about 01:00:07;15).**
Ending the video just as the sound drops out adds some finesse and can make your project look really cool.

20. **Drag the end of the video clip with your slogan to the left so it snaps to the position indicator.**

21. **Save your project.**

22. **Press Home on your keyboard to take your position indicator to the beginning (or simply drag it back), and press the Spacebar to play your full sequence.**
It's a great feeling when your work starts to take shape, isn't it? In this tutorial, you created and polished two video titles. You added them to the Timeline and adjusted their start and end points.

Tutorial

» Adding Fades and Transition Effects

At this point, your project is basically ready to go. You have sound and picture, and you edited them together. By adding some subtle effects, you can polish what you have and make something that you can be really proud to show off. (Go ahead, strut your stuff—you can be modest later.)

1. **Click the beginning of your first title.**
   When you preview your movie, this first title starts out "up full," or fully visible. If you fade the title up from invisible to visible, it makes your project more elegant, and it demonstrates a higher degree of technical sophistication.

2. **Choose Effects→Video Transitions→Dissolve→Fade In Fade Out Dissolve.**
   Final Cut Pro fades your video in evenly over the first second of your movie.

3. **Scroll through the clip using the arrow keys, or by dragging the position indicator, to preview the transition you just added.**
   You won't be able to play the sequence until you render it at the start of the next tutorial, but scrolling through will give you a good idea of what the transition looks like. Normally, a dissolve fades one clip out as the other fades in. Because you applied a transition to the first clip in the movie, there was only one clip to work with. Next, you apply a transition that dissolves from the first title to the second.

4. **Click the edit where your first title meets the second title.**

5. **Choose→Effects→Video Transitions→Dissolve→Dip to Color Dissolve.**
   This effect quickly fades out your company logo, briefly displays a black screen, and then fades your company slogan in.

6. **Scroll through the clip using the arrow keys, or by dragging the position indicator, to preview the transition you just added.**
   Can you see a theme starting to take shape? You have nice fades at the beginning and the middle, and then a hard cut at the end. To be consistent, you can fade the video out at the end, too, but it's nice to give the audience something unexpected. In this business, a subtle surprise can go a long way.

7. **Save your project.**

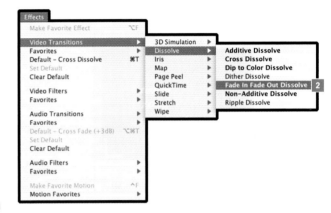

Tutorial
» Rendering and Exporting: The Final Steps

Your first movie is almost ready for its worldwide premiere. When you built titles for your company name and slogan, Final Cut Pro created video clips you could play on the Timeline. In the old days—meaning the era before the release of version 4—you had to render these clips before you could play them back. *Rendering* is the process in which a computer generates a video file for full-speed playback. A few years ago, rendering took a tremendous amount of time and gave video editors a great excuse to take breaks. Now, Final Cut Pro features real-time rendering, so you can immediately play back your work and preview the changes you make without interrupting your workflow. This is a big improvement, unless of course you miss taking breaks. However, before you can export the file as a video clip to share with your friends and loved ones, you need to render the sequence you just made.

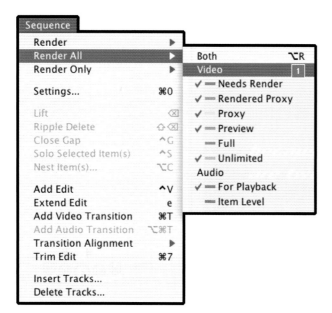

1. **With your project open, choose Sequence→Render All→Video.**
   Final Cut Pro now generates high-quality video files from the titles that you created. That may, in fact, be the easiest thing you do all day. Now you're ready to export.

2. **Choose File→Export→Using QuickTime Conversion.**
   The Save dialog box opens. Most computer users have a QuickTime player installed on their system, so if you save the movie as a QuickTime file, most people can enjoy your work.

3. **Click Options.**
   The Movie Settings dialog box opens, allowing you to choose specific settings that create a compact, high-quality digital video file.

4. **Click the Settings button in the Video panel.**
   The Compression Settings dialog box opens.

5. **In the Compression Settings dialog box, choose Video from the pull-down menu.**
   Video files take up lots of memory and are hard for computer processors to handle. Running a video-editing program like Final Cut Pro takes substantial computer power, and compressing your video makes it easier to watch on computers that aren't as powerful.

6. **Set the Quality slider to Best.**
   This setting determines the image quality of your movie. Best looks really good, and of the available options, is the closest in appearance to broadcast-quality video. The Best setting also produces the heaviest file—that is, a file that takes up the most memory. Setting the slider to Medium or Least uses less memory but also lowers the picture quality, so images appear blocky or "pixilated."

7. **Choose a Frames per second setting of** 30, **and click OK to close the Compression Settings dialog box.**
   Using a setting of 30 here ensures your video plays back smoothly. A lower frame rate, such as 15, results in a smaller file, but the video looks "jerky" and fades don't look smooth.

8. **Click the Size button in the Movie Settings dialog box to open the Export Size Settings dialog box. Select the Use custom size option.**

9. **Set the width to** 360 **and the height to** 240. **Click OK to close the Export Size Settings dialog box and apply your settings to the file.**
   The natural size for digital video files is 720 pixels by 480 pixels. Exporting your video at a smaller size generates a much lighter file (a file that takes up much less memory) and probably won't freeze a computer with a slower processor.

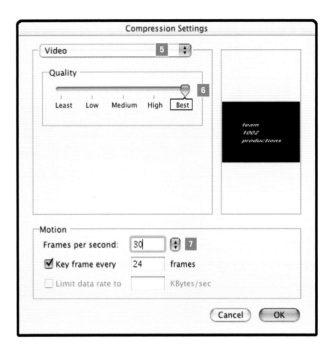

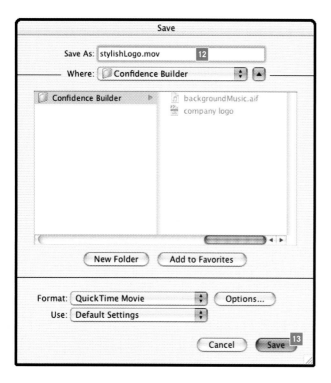

10. **Deselect the Prepare for Internet Streaming check box in the Movie Settings dialog box.**
Streaming is something addressed later in the book, but for now, you do not want to use this option.

11. **Click OK to close the Movie Settings dialog box.**
Now you're ready to export.

12. **Name your QuickTime file by entering a name in the Save As field of the Save dialog box.**
I named the example stylishLogo.mov. You can name your file anything you want; just make sure the filename ends in .mov. Without the .mov file suffix, users may not be able to watch the video. Take a look at the finished sample, stylishLogo.mov, on this book's CD, to review what the project should look like.

13. **Navigate to the Confidence Builder folder on your hard drive, and click Save.**
Once the file is ready, you have a short clip you can be proud of. In this tutorial, you exported a completed QuickTime movie and specified the quality, frame rate, and image size. Each of these items is fundamentally important in digital video. Your completed logo is now available for you to use in future productions or to distribute via CD or the Internet.

< N O T E >
The amount of time needed to export your file depends on the amount of RAM installed in your computer, your computer's processor speed, and the settings you choose. The more powerful your computer, the faster the export. Higher image-quality settings and higher frame rates demand more from your computer and take longer to process.

< N O T E >
The filename extension .mov identifies the file as a QuickTime movie that can be played back with the QuickTime player.

Part I:
Course Setup

Final Cut Pro 4 Basics

How Nonlinear Editing and Final Cut Pro Have Changed the Editing Process

As recently as the late 1990s, video was linear. To get to the end, you first had to watch the beginning and then the middle. If you were editing, you had to finish one sequence before doing any work on the next. Edits were permanent. If you went back and changed something in the beginning, you could easily ruin everything that came after it. This inspired fear in some and bravado in others. (A friend once told me about a particularly macho editor who put a bumper sticker on his car which reads "Real editors don't hit Preview.")

Today, we live in much happier times because Final Cut Pro lets you make changes to your edits and leave the material around them intact. In addition, Final Cut Pro gives you the ability to replace a few frames of video, an entire shot, or even a whole sequence. You can shape your video to fit your vision without fear of having to redo everything if you decide to make even a small change.

Final Cut Pro also provides a level of organization that would satisfy the keenest hunger for order (picture Felix Unger editing a movie). You can group your clips into clearly labeled bins and divide your clips into subclips. Even editors who were devoted to cutting and splicing 16mm or 35mm film on a mechanical flatbed editing system have migrated to digital nonlinear editing because it's so much easier to keep track of everything. Film editors would cut and splice pieces of a film print, and hang the leftover frames, called *trims,* on a hook. There were so many trims that people would hire an assistant editor to keep track of them, and more often than not, trims would still get lost—or even worse, turn up on the bottom of someone's shoe. With Final Cut Pro, the cutting room floor is much neater.

Nonlinear video editing is frame-accurate. Video is measured in hours, minutes, seconds, and frames (approximately 30 frames per second). Final Cut Pro lets you place a specific frame of video exactly where you want it.

Final Cut lets you import digital video directly into your computer system, and then edit the video in an entirely digital process. You can easily create different versions of a project for different purposes, safely experiment with a wide variety of effects and transitions, and you can even finish your project and ensure it conforms to broadcast quality standards. The current version, Final Cut Pro 4, allows you to dynamically mix audio tracks in real time, generate sophisticated animated titles, and export finished products for distribution via the Internet, CD-ROM, DVD and, of course, videotape.

With Final Cut Pro, you can revise and polish your work until you're 100 percent satisfied (or at least until your client thinks you're the best editor on the planet). You have exact control over how things appear in your show and meticulous command of each shot's beginning and end, down to a fraction of a second. Digital video and Final Cut Pro have changed the way that people edit.

What's the Difference between Analog and Digital Video?

For years, analog video was all that existed, and analog video is much harder to edit than digital video. I often begin a semester by asking students the difference between analog and digital media. People come up with a variety of answers, usually having something to do with "digital is better," but in reality, the difference is digital media is the product of a computer: Sound and images are recorded as binary information—a collection of 1s and 0s. Analog media, in contrast, uses a mechanical process to record and play back audio and video. Once media becomes information that can be stored and edited on a computer, the media becomes much easier to work with. Think of how easy it is to cut and paste text in a word processing program and how hard it would be to shift paragraphs around a printed page using a typewriter, a pair of scissors, and some Elmer's glue. It would still be possible, and people wrote great works of literature long before the invention of Microsoft Word, but the process was a lot messier.

Part of the ease of nonlinear editing comes from random access. Digital media allows you to get to any section of recorded material at any time, which makes editing much faster. Compare opening a thick volume of text to a bookmarked page versus slogging through 5,000 words to reach the same paragraph. Nonlinear editing is possible because digital media allows you to access specific information with the click of a mouse. Digital technology permits nonlinear editing and analog doesn't, because the two forms of media process, store, and handle information differently.

Analog videotape uses a physical process to play back sound and images. The tape runs across a playback head, and the videotape deck converts the electro-magnetic signal on the tape into sounds and images. If you play a tape often enough, it wears out. If you put the tape too close to a magnetic field, such as a video or sound monitor, you can erase parts of the tape. Cheap tape is often less reliable and has a shorter life span than higher-quality tape. Even the best video-tapes suffer a loss in quality as they age because the physical material starts to decay. (The analog tape that you worked so hard to record and edit just doesn't last forever.)

Digital media doesn't employ a physical process. Instead, digital video stores sound and images as a series of instructions. Computers read the instructions and reproduce the sounds and images you record exactly the same way each time. Once you capture and store these instructions on your hard drive, you can play back the same material repeatedly without a loss in quality or damage to the original. If you make a backup copy, your material survives even if your computer crashes or your hard drive fails.

Because digital media uses computer instructions instead of a physical process, you can make an infinite number of backup copies, easily transfer media from one computer to another, and capture material from the camera with no loss in quality.

FireWire Video Capture

Have you ever made a cassette copy of a record album? (You do remember record albums, right?) The cassette would never sound as good as the record, and if you made another cassette from your cassette copy, the second cassette would sound even worse. There's a loss in quality each time you get farther away from the original. Each copy is referred to as a *generation,* and the strength of the analog signal breaks down more with each generation.

Digital media doesn't break down the same way. Because it's saved as computer information, each copy is identical to the original. In fact, duplicate copies of digital videotapes are often called *clones.*

When you record to digital videotape, your camera stores the video as digital information. Once it's copied to your hard drive, this information can be shared and reproduced as easily as any other digital file. The trick is getting the material into your computer. In the early days of digital video editing, there was rarely a way to get the digital information directly from the camera to the editing system. Even people with expensive, high-tech digital editing systems often used an analog connection to capture footage shot on digital tape. As you can imagine, there was a de facto loss in quality. If the editor doing the capture was good, the quality loss was barely noticeable, if anyone could see it at all. However, if the editor didn't know what he or she was doing, there could be real problems. At best, this method created an inconvenient extra step.

Macintosh computers now come with FireWire ports as standard equipment. FireWire, called IEEE 1394 in non-Mac computers, is a digital interface that lets you connect your computer to a video source and capture the information on your videotapes with no loss in quality. Once you have the information stored on your hard drive, it's exactly the same as what's on your tapes, which you can then archive as backup copies.

Because Macs ship with FireWire ports already installed, connecting your computer to digital video equipment is as simple as plugging one end of a FireWire cable into the computer and the other into your deck or camera. FireWire connections are much faster than other interface types, such as USB, and also allow you to control a camera or deck through your computer. You can also use a FireWire connection to transfer media between your computer and an external hard drive, which can easily expand your storage space by a few hundred gigabytes.

Analog Video Capture

FireWire capture ensures that the material on your hard drive is identical to the information on the original tape. Analog video capture is another ballgame—basically it's a rerecording. There are three basic types: component, composite, and S-video.

Professional analog cameras (yes, people still use them and they're very good) record in *component video*. The component signal breaks video color and brightness information into three parts, or components, which hold up well in editing. If you've ever seen news crews walking around with big video cameras, they're most likely shooting component video, such as BetaSP.

The consumer video signal (what you see on your TV or VCR at home) is called *composite video.* This is essentially a compressed version, or composite, of the professional signal. The quality is not as good and breaks down more easily.

Somewhere between composite and component is *S-video*, which is found in higher-end analog consumer products. Before digital video and FireWire became common, people used S-video for sophisticated home editing systems.

Analog video capture involves a rerecording of your source material into a digital format and requires the use of waveform and vector scopes to ensure good quality. The tutorial files in this book are delivered as digital media, so analog capture isn't explored in detail in this book. Digital video acquisition is discussed further in Part II. If you are interested in more detailed information on analog capture, I suggest reading *Final Cut Express and Final Cut Pro 4 Bible* (published by Wiley Publishing, Inc.).

SMPTE Timecode

The random access that makes nonlinear editing possible is based on timecode. *Timecode* identifies the exact position of each piece of video and is written in hours, minutes, seconds, and frames—for example, 01:15:20;05 means one hour, 15 minutes, 20 seconds, and 5 frames. When you transfer media from your camera to the hard drive of your computer via FireWire, you capture the audio and video information along with the timecode.

Not all analog media contains timecode. Professional analog video—such as the Beta cameras and decks that are used by news crews—uses timecode, but the standard home VCR does not.

Timecode is what makes nonlinear editing frame-accurate, and without timecode, nonlinear editing just doesn't work. The hours:minutes:seconds;frames timestamp that is on a video tape is always the same, regardless of what deck you play the tape on. When you capture digital video in Final Cut Pro, the software asks you to enter an identifying name or number for each tape. Final Cut Pro stores the tape name and the timecode information for all the material that you capture so that you can identify each piece of audio and video, down to $\frac{1}{30}$ of a second, and access it instantly. Final Cut Pro also generates timecode when you edit clips together into a sequence. You can use this timecode to create an Edit Decision List (EDL), which you can bring to a postproduction house for completion as a film print, a sophisticated broadcast-quality digital Beta, or a high-definition master tape.

There are two types of timecode: drop frame and non-drop frame. Broadcast television signals operate at a slightly different speed than a clock, so a program's length in timecode may differ slightly from its actual length in hours and minutes. To compensate, drop frame timecode drops, or skips, frames at regular intervals to conform the length of a program to a standard broadcast clock. Drop frame timecode is written with a semicolon between the seconds and frames (01:15:20;05) while non-drop frame is written with a colon between the seconds and frames (01:15:20:05). Before computerized editing systems, editors worked with non-drop frame timecode because it was easier to calculate. Final Cut makes drop frame timecode much easier to work with. NTSC, the broadcast video standard for North America, uses drop-frame timecode, as do the video files on this book's CD-ROM.

Nondestructive Editing

When you create a sequence in Final Cut Pro, you're not actually cutting the media files, or even editing them. You're instructing the computer to find particular pieces of video on your computer's hard drive and to play them back in a specific order. This is called nondestructive editing.

Nondestructive editing with Final Cut Pro takes the pressure off of you as an editor, and opens up a whole world of opportunities. Not sure if something will work? Go ahead and try it out. If you're not happy with the results, press ⌘+Z or choose Edit→Undo. Because you're not actually changing the media files, you can experiment without irreversible consequences. If only the rest of life were that simple.

Storing Media

When you set up your Final Cut Pro system, you tell the computer where to store the media you capture. You can change the setup for each project you create, and you can make changes while you're working on a project. Your media files and the editing instructions, called *project files,* can be stored on the same hard drive or in different locations. Media files take up large amounts of memory, but project files are small enough that you can easily save backup versions to a Zip disk. This also allows you to save different versions of a project. For example, you can save one version as a director's cut and make another, shorter version for television broadcast. I create a different version of my project files each time I make a major change, so if I don't like the way something works out, I can just go back to the older version. I also make backup copies of my files so my world won't come to an end if my computer crashes. Making backups may seem like an unnecessary precaution, but believe me, it's not fun to lose something you've spent a long time working on. You know how it never rains when you bring your umbrella, but it pours as soon as you leave it at home? Save yourself a headache, and back up your project files. The worst thing that can happen is you'll have some added peace of mind.

System Requirements

Final Cut Pro 4 requires a Macintosh computer with a PowerPC G4 processor and an AGP (Accelerated Graphics Port) graphics card. The software also requires the following items:

- » 350MHz or faster processor
- » 384MB RAM; 512MB is recommended for real-time effects
- » DVD-ROM drive
- » 6GB audio/video–rated hard drive; 20GB or larger is recommended
- » Mac OS X v10.2.5 or later
- » QuickTime 6.1 or later

System Configurations

Editing systems are configured based on the needs and resources of each editor. A Final Cut Pro system requires a way to capture media, a computer to edit and process the media, at least one monitor to view the program, and a means to output the media in a format that is accessible to the audience. Depending on the type of project, the medium of distribution, and the project budget, editing systems can be configured differently.

The bare-bones system

Each Final Cut editing system must have at least a source deck to play back the recorded tape. You can use your camera, but if you use a dedicated deck instead, your camera lasts longer. The system then requires a connection from the source deck to the Mac. For digital video, a FireWire connection is the best and easiest way to go. Analog video requires a digital-to-analog converter. It is a given that every system also needs a monitor. And, because computers generally have monitors attached to them, many people stop there. However, the only way to judge what a program looks like on TV is to view it on a TV monitor.

Computer monitors and video monitors process images differently. A computer monitor uses *pixels,* or tiny squares, to create images. Video monitors and television sets use lines of resolution, which are horizontal lines. Because the two processes differ, video may not look the same on a computer monitor and on a TV screen. To avoid surprises, editors often connect a dedicated video monitor to their Final Cut Pro systems, make their edits using the computer screen, and then evaluate the results on the video monitor.

The videotape system

Exporting the completed project as a videotape requires a record deck, which can record the video signal output of the Final Cut Pro system. Editors on a tight budget often use the same digital video camera for their source deck and their record deck. Editors with greater means may use a VHS or Super VHS (S-VHS) deck to record a composite analog version of their work as well, and professional editors often output a component analog version of their project to a BetaSP deck, or a component digital version to a DigitalBetacam deck. Analog output requires a digital-to-analog converter.

Editors working at the really high end may not output directly to tape from their system in any format. Instead, an editor with even the most basic Final Cut Pro system can output an EDL to take to a postproduction house as a computer file. Working with the postproduction facility staff, the editor can use the EDL to assemble video from the original source tapes into a super-high-quality program, which is then output as a DigitalBetacam master tape or even as high-definition video for broadcast or eventual transfer to a film print. Few editors have DigitalBetacam or HD decks connected to Final Cut Pro systems, because the decks cost more than the down payment on a nice house.

DVD output

Just as digital media has changed the way people edit, it's changing the way people watch video. The consumer DVD player is making its way into homes at twice the rate of the VCR, according to the *New York Times Magazine,* and who do you know that doesn't have a VCR? Even after digital editing had become the method of choice, editors were still converting their work back into an analog format (videotape) to reach their viewers. With the advent of DVD technology, editors can now output and distribute their work as digital media, adding interactive features and maintaining stunning image and sound quality. The Mac you use to run Final Cut Pro may already contain a DVD burner, called a SuperDrive. If it does, try it out; you may be happy with the results.

Using the Program for the First Time

Final Cut Pro requires the current versions of Mac OS X and QuickTime. Even if you just bought a brand new machine, you may still need to update the operating system before you can install Final Cut Pro. The Final Cut Pro 4 installer checks your system software before installing the application, and if the installer doesn't find the version of OS X that it's looking for (v10.2.5 or later), it doesn't install anything. Take a minute to check your system software before you try to run the Final Cut Pro installer.

Tutorial

» Check the System Software

Before you attempt to install Final Cut Pro 4, you can easily check to see if your computer meets the criteria as listed in the System Requirements section earlier in this chapter. In particular, you want to be sure you have the proper operating system installed—Mac OS X v10.2.5 or later.

1. **Click the Apple icon in the upper-left corner of your screen, and select About This Mac from the pull-down menu that appears.**
   A new window opens that displays your operating system version (for example, 10.2.6), the amount of RAM that's installed in your computer, and the processor speed.

2. **Click the red button in the upper-left corner to close the window.**
   If you have an older operating system, or need a later version of QuickTime, you can update your software in the next tutorial.

Tutorial
» Update the System Software

If you check your system software and find that something's missing, don't panic. Macs ship with a built-in software update, in this tutorial you learn how to use it. If you check your system and find that you don't need to update anything, you can skip this tutorial.

1. **Click the Apple icon in the upper-left corner of your screen, and select System Preferences from the pull-down menu.**
   The System Preferences window opens.

2. **In the System row, click Software Update.**
   The Software Update dialog box opens.

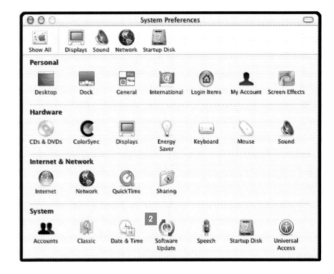

3. **With the Update Software tab active, click the Check Now button.**
   If you are currently connected to the Internet, Software Update checks to see whether updates are available for the software on your computer. A new Software Update dialog box opens listing the new versions of your software. By default, items in the list appear with a check mark in the Install column, meaning that they install themselves when you click the Install button.

<NOTE>
If you don't have an Internet connection, Software Update doesn't work. Instead, contact AppleCare or your local Apple retailer to see if any software you might need is available on disk.

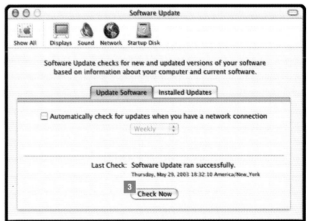

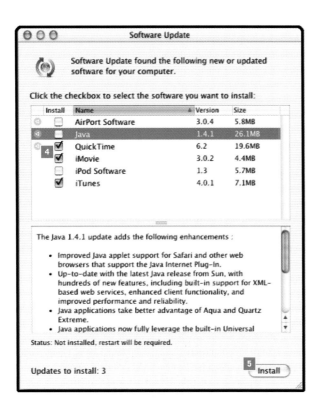

4. **In the Install column, deselect anything that you don't want to update.**

   Deselected items are not installed.

5. **Click the Install button.**

   Your Mac automatically downloads and installs the new versions of the software.

Final Cut Pro comes with a Read Before You Install document on the installation DVD. This document is worth the time it takes you to read it, and can save you some headaches if you actually do read it before you install anything.

Before you install QuickTime and Final Cut Pro, connect and turn on your video source deck or camera so that the software can detect the equipment that you use to capture video.

Final Cut Pro offers you a world of options. A few years ago, only a handful of professionals had access to this level of quality, and it was extremely expensive. Nonlinear editing systems in 1999 routinely cost more than $60,000. Now you have one on your desktop, and it's much more powerful that those from just a few years ago.

In the words of a famous New York sportscaster, "Let's go to the videotape."

Project Overview

This book is a hands-on, tutorial-based course intended for students, educators, and even hard-core, professional filmmakers. If you've been working with Final Cut Pro for a while, you can use these tutorials to build a new repertoire of skills and techniques, or you can use the book to firm up your existing knowledge base before you branch out further. If you're new to Final Cut Pro—or to nonlinear editing in general—you can use this course to build a new skill set from the ground up.

Understanding the Project Story

Editing can make or break a documentary. Editing is always important in any film or video genre, but because so much of documentary production is unscripted, it's up to a good editor to pull everything together. A documentary is an editor's moment to shine. This moment is yours. Using this book, you create a 90-second preview for *Sonia Williams, Photographer,* a documentary about an up-and-coming young photographer. You need to grab the audience's attention from the start and engage each viewer for the length of the preview. The CD that accompanies this book contains all the media that you need to create a highly produced, tightly edited portfolio sample. Final Cut Pro gives you the ability to execute complicated edits and richly textured composite effects. As you complete each step-by-step tutorial, you take the preview from an idea to a reality, and at the end of each tutorial session, you have tangible evidence of your newfound expertise.

Sonia Williams is a photographer based in New York City. She documents daily life in the city's public places, working in the tradition of Helen Levit, Garry Winnogrand, and Walker Evans. Evans took a series of photographs on the New York City subway and noted that even in crowded public places, when people think no one is watching, their facial expressions are as unguarded as when they're looking in a mirror. Williams looks for similarly candid moments in her work, and in this sample project, you see her on the street in SoHo, camera in hand, exploring the world in visual terms.

Sonia Williams, Photographer is a documentary about Williams's work and her photographic technique. The documentary contains observational footage of Williams in action as well as interview material in which she describes her influences, interests, and appreciation for the photographic possibilities of Lower Manhattan. Cut together in a dynamic, multilayered style, the documentary brings the photographer's work to life with a unique blend of sound, personality, and digital effects. Your preview lets the audience know this is something they can't miss.

Developing the Project

As you develop your editorial technique, you also develop this preview sample from a basic assembly to a sophisticated, carefully edited finished product. Each stage of the project corresponds to a specific stage of this book. The book's stages break down as follows:

» **Project creation and assembly:** This includes creating a new project, customizing your project settings, importing video into Final Cut Pro, and organizing your video clips.

» **Basic editing:** This means trimming the clips and shaping them into a sequence. You also work with transitions from one clip to another.

» **Working with audio:** Good audio is just as important as good visuals. This project takes you step by step through editing dialog, adding original music, and managing your overall sound design.

» **Creating and animating titles:** Final Cut Pro offers a full-featured title generator that allows you to make static, rolling, and crawling titles. This book not only shows you how to create each kind of title but also explains the differences between them and gives you tips on how to use them.

» **Adding transparency and video effects:** As the editor, you have total control. You can use the sleekest, slickest effects to trick out your video, or gently manipulate and change your material for an elegant, understated effect.

» **Final edits and exporting:** Once you're ready to share your work with the world, this course takes you step by step through the process of making your file into a videotape, a DVD, or a broadcast-quality master.

Working with Tutorial Files

Think of this book as one-stop shopping. The CD contains a folder called Tutorial Files, and everything you need is there: professionally shot video, original music, and ambient sound, just waiting for you to create a project worth watching.

Before you work on the tutorials, copy the files to your computer. You can make a new folder, or you can copy the files on the CD into the Final Cut Pro Complete Course folder that you created in the Confidence Builder. The simplest way to do this is to select the items on the CD and drag them into the folder on your hard drive.

Each session has its own project file, and each session builds upon the previous one. When you're finished with this book, you'll know how to edit a project from the first frame to the last, using the latest tools and a full spectrum of Final Cut Pro effects.

General Work Tips and Computer Instructions

Understanding Setups, Presets, and Settings

Video editing is a technically intensive endeavor, requiring a dizzying array of choices, specifications, and standards. Final Cut Pro offers you the option of an Easy Setup, which configures everything for you. Final Cut Pro also allows you to specify exact, individual settings based on the particular needs of your project. As your skills advance, you can customize your project at the most fundamental levels by using settings and presets, or you can configure the whole project in one step by using a predefined setup.

A *setting* adjusts an individual, basic element of your Final Cut Pro project, such as the size of your video image or the number of frames that appear each second. There are separate settings for video and audio.

A *preset* is a group of settings that you assign together to control an aspect of your project. For example, a Capture Preset defines the way that Final Cut Pro captures material from a video source, and a Sequence Preset controls the way video is processed in your Timeline. A Device Control Preset determines how your computer communicates with and controls the media source you capture information from, such as a video camera. Presets control video and audio settings at the same time.

An Easy Setup defines Capture Presets, Sequence Presets, and Device Control Presets as a group, so instead of defining each setting, you can define the specifics of your whole project at once.

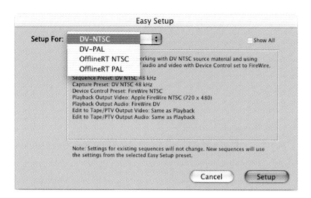

When you first open Final Cut Pro 4, you're prompted to choose an Easy Setup (which you may remember from the Confidence Builder). The first item in the Easy Setup dialog box is the Setup For drop-down menu. The most common video format for people who use Final Cut Pro is DV-NTSC, so that's the default choice. DV stands for digital video, and NTSC is the video standard for North America. A description of the setup appears below the drop-down menu, and below that is a listing of the settings that the Easy Setup applies to your project.

For the work you do with this book, the DV-NTSC setting is all you need and, in fact, is probably the setting that you will use most of the time with Final Cut Pro. You can change your Easy Setup at any time, but you don't need to unless you change the type of video equipment that you work with or the type of projects that you work on. For example, if you started working with tape shot by an overseas production crew for European broadcast, you need to change from NTSC, the North American standard, to PAL, which is the European broadcast standard.

Basic File Management

Final Cut Pro lets you decide where to save your media files and your project files. *Media files* are the raw files you capture from a camera or other source.

Your *project files* are the instructions Final Cut Pro uses to assemble the media into clips and sequences. When you make an edit in Final Cut Pro, you're not actually changing the media files; you're just changing the instructions for how the media files should be played back.

The place where your media files are stored is called the *scratch disk.* When you capture or import media, Final Cut Pro uses your scratch disk as the destination folder. If you have only your computer's hard drive and no external drives are connected to your editing system, your computer's hard drive is the only option for your scratch disk. However, if you have more than one hard drive, Final Cut Pro recommends setting the secondary drive (the one that doesn't have Final Cut Pro installed on it) as a dedicated scratch disk.

You can save your project files anywhere on your hard drive, just like you can save a word processing document in a specific folder or create a new folder to help you keep track of things. Keeping track of your project and media files is called *file management,* and it is more important than most people think. For your project to function, you need to know where all your files are at all times, and the computer also needs to know these locations. If you move your project files from one folder to another, you need to update the project files so they can locate and play back the associated media files. This book does not require you to move your media files, which should save you some gray hairs. Reconnecting media files and project files can confuse even the most organized and experienced editor.

Maintaining Peak Performance

There's an old joke that if you ask 10 Yankee fans the same question, you get 12 different answers. Computer maintenance inspires an equal diversity of opinion; everyone you talk to tells you something different. Just about the only thing people agree on is that video files consume tremendous amounts of storage space. Five minutes of DV-format video takes up more than a gigabyte of space on your hard drive. To put that in perspective, when I bought a snazzy new Powerbook in 1997, the entire hard drive stored only 750MB, and people were impressed with that.

In addition to your project and media files, Final Cut Pro also creates render files when it needs to generate video from the titles and effects in your project. If you create more than one version of our project, you have even more files. Storing and processing video files tax your computer. A good maintenance strategy aids your computer's performance and makes editing much easier. Follow these tips to optimize the performance of your computer:

» Turn off other programs before starting Final Cut Pro. Your computer has a finite amount of RAM, so it can only do so many things at one time. Even if you have a lot of RAM and a super-hefty processor, memory-hungry programs such as Microsoft Word and Photoshop don't need to be open at the same time you use Final Cut Pro. These additional programs slow your computer's performance.

» Writing video files to your hard drive entails moving a great deal of information and can easily fragment your disk. A computer stores files as chunks of information. On a clean hard drive, a computer stores large chunks together, making the information easy to access. As the hard drive gets full, fewer large spaces are available, so the computer breaks up large files and places them into fragments of open space on the hard drive. Because the files are spread throughout the drive, it takes more time for the computer to read them, slowing down performance. To avoid fragmentation, some editors partition their hard drive (so that the computer reads the drive not as one large drive but as several smaller drives) and always capture video to the same partition. This saves the remainder of the hard drive from being used to write and rewrite large files. For this book, you don't need a dedicated video capture partition, but it's something to think about for the future.

» All the files for this course fit on a 700MB CD, so they're not that big, and because they're delivered on CD, you don't need to capture anything; you can just import them as already created files. If you use an external hard drive to store your media files for this book or another project down the line, make sure the drive can transfer information to the computer quickly enough to play back video. DV-format playback requires a sustained transfer rate of 3.6MB per second. A lower transfer rate causes video to hang up or stutter when you try to play it back. Zip drives and CD drives don't work for capture or playback because they don't transfer data fast enough.

More information on partitioning a hard drive is available in Mac Help. And, Final Cut Pro Help contains extensive information on the use of external hard drives for video capture and storage.

Part II:
Getting Started

Session 1
Starting the Project

Session Introduction

When you open a new project, you lay the foundation for your movie. The editing process starts long before you place one shot next to another or add your first transition. Editing starts as soon as you create a new project in Final Cut Pro.

In this session, you learn how to start a new project and adjust the settings and presets to fit the particulars of your media. You also learn how to import media and organize the media into clips and bins. Everything you need to complete this session is included on the accompanying CD. In this session you access the files on this CD and copy them to your hard drive. This session also discusses how to use Final Cut Pro's Log and Capture function to add names and descriptions to segments of videotape and capture them to your hard drive.

TOOLS YOU'LL USE
Audio/Video Settings dialog box, Sequence Presets tab, Browser window, Log and Capture window, Choose a File dialog box

MATERIALS NEEDED
Company Logo project file you created in the Confidence Builder, Session 1 video clips (from the Session 1 folder in Part II)

TIME REQUIRED
90 minutes

Tutorial
» Changing Settings and Editing Presets

This course uses standard DV-NTSC video, so you don't need to change any video settings. However, this book uses CD-quality audio for the music, which contains slightly less information than audio that's recorded by a DV camera. This tutorial shows you how to change the audio settings for a project to CD-quality. Once you make these changes, you can leave them in place for the remainder of the book.

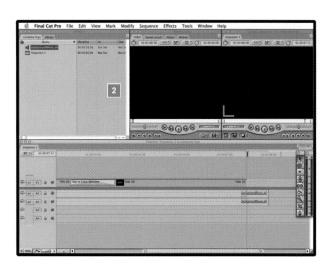

1. **From the desktop, double-click Macintosh HD to open a window that displays the contents of your hard drive.**

2. **Choose Applications→Final Cut Pro to start the program.**
   When Final Cut Pro starts, it automatically opens any project that was on-screen when you last exited the program.

< N O T E >

If you had the Company Logo project open from the Confidence Builder when you last exited Final Cut Pro, the program automatically opens the Company Logo project so you can continue working on it. Because changes you make to the settings don't take effect until you open a new project, you can leave the Confidence Builder open for now without damaging it.

3. **Choose Final Cut Pro→Audio/Video Settings....**
   The Audio/Video Settings dialog box opens, displaying a summary of the Sequence, Capture, and Device Control Presets that are defined by the Easy Setup.

Choosing an Initial Setup

When you opened Final Cut Pro for the first time and chose Easy Setup, the application was configured to work with NTSC video material and 48-kHz digital audio, and all the settings were defined accordingly. (Part IV: Working with Audio explains digital audio in detail and clarifies terms like 48kHz.) These settings are now the default settings for any new project that you create in Final Cut Pro. Any changes you make to your settings apply only to subsequent projects, not to projects that you already completed or even to projects that you have open at the time you make the changes. As a result, you don't have to choose a setup each time you open the program or each time you create a new project. You also don't need to change the setup unless you decide to work in a different format—for example, use a different type of video than you've used before.

4. **Click the Sequence Presets tab.**

   The Audio/Video Settings dialog box changes to show you a list of all the available presets and a summary of each one. To change the audio settings, you need to edit the current Sequence Preset, which is selected when the dialog box opens.

5. **Click Duplicate.**

   A copy of the preset opens in the Sequence Preset Editor dialog box.

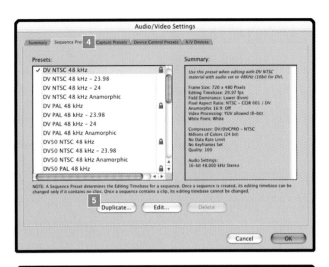

6. **Name the new preset** Final Cut Pro 4 Complete Course.

   You use this preset for the remainder of the book, so be sure you give it a name that you can easily recognize. The text in the Name field is highlighted when the dialog box opens, so anything you type replaces the name DV NTSC 48 kHz Copy. Once you name the preset, it shows up in the list of available presets in the Audio/Video Settings dialog box.

7. **Click in the Description field, and change the description to** Use this preset when editing with material from the Final Cut Pro 4 Complete Course CD.

8. **In the Audio Settings panel, select 44.100 from the Rate pull-down menu.**

   This changes the audio settings to CD-quality.

9. **Click OK to close the dialog box and create a new preset.**

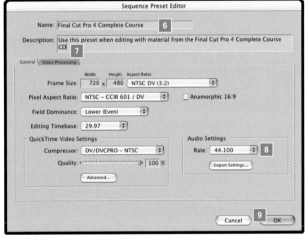

10. **Click the Summary tab in the Audio/Video Settings dialog box.**

    To use the preset you just created, you need to select it from the Sequence Preset pull-down mennu.

11. **Click the Sequence Preset pull-down menu and select Final Cut Pro 4 Complete Course.**

    The new setting applies to sequences that you create in future projects.

12. **Click OK to close the window.**

    In this tutorial, you learned how to access the Audio/Video Settings dialog box and create a new default Sequence Preset with modified audio settings. Leave Final Cut Pro open for the next tutorial.

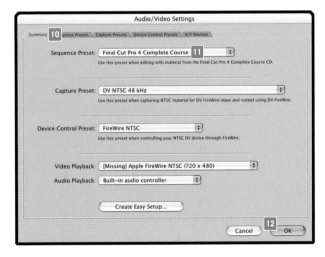

< N O T E >

The significance of 44.100 and 48.000 are both explained in detail in Part IV: Working with Audio.

Tutorial

» Opening a New Project

Final Cut Pro allows you to work on more than one project at a time. The Confidence Builder project was probably open when you last exited Final Cut Pro, so it opens along with the application. By default, the Confidence Builder project also stays open when you open a new project. Older video editing programs only allowed an editor to open one project at a time, which meant that any files that were associated with another project were out of reach. Opening multiple projects is great if you have different projects underway for more than one client, or if you want to edit more than one version of the same project. This can be helpful when working on a large project over an extended period of time. For now, closing the project makes your work easier. This tutorial teaches you how to open a new project and close the last project you worked on. If you closed Final Cut Pro since you finished the last tutorial, you need to open it now.

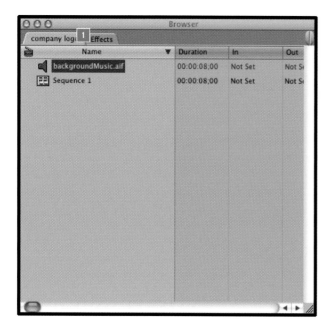

1. **In the Browser window, click the Company Logo tab (or the tab with the name of your most recent project).**
   This ensures the correct project is selected.

<NOTE>
If the Company Logo project doesn't open with the application, Final Cut Pro may present you with an untitled project (most likely named Untitled Project 1) or your most recent project. You can follow the first two steps of the tutorial with either project.

2. **Choose File→Close Project to close the project.**
   The Timeline and Canvas windows both close. Because no project is open, there is nothing for the windows to display.

3. **Choose File→New Project to open a new project.**
   A new Canvas opens, along with a new, blank Timeline. A tab named Untitled Project appears. Any work that you do now becomes a part of this new project.

4. **Choose File→Save Project As to save the new project.**
   The Save dialog box opens.

5. **Navigate to the Final Cut Pro Complete Course folder you created for the Confidence Builder. Click Final Cut Pro Complete Course in the list of folders which appears in the Save dialog box.**
   The Save dialog box changes to show you the contents of the folder.

6. **Click the New Folder button at the bottom of the Save dialog box to create a new subfolder for your new project.**
   The New Folder dialog box opens.

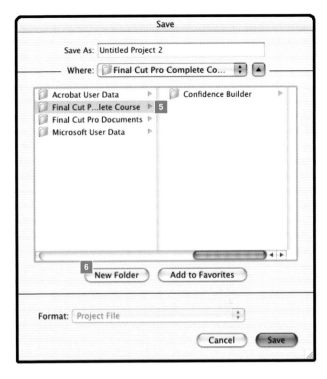

7. **Highlight the words untitled folder, and type** Part II.
   You named the new folder Part II. (When you highlight the text, anything that you type replaces what is highlighted.)

8. **Click Create.**
   The Save dialog box changes to show you the contents of your new, empty folder.

9. **In the Save As field, name your new project Camera Closeups.**

10. **Click Save to save the project and close the dialog box.**
    In this tutorial, you learned how to close an existing project to make editing a new project easier and to prevent unintended changes, how to open a new project, and how to save the new project in a new folder.

< N O T E >
The Camera Closeups project uses the Final Cut Pro 4 Complete Course Sequence Preset that you created in the previous tutorial.

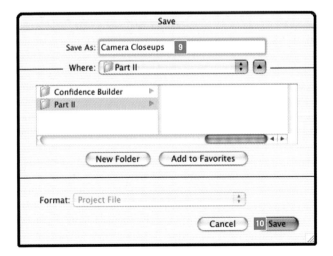

Discussion

The Importance of Organization and File Management

When you work with computer files, few things are more important than organization. Just as you need to know where all your files are so you can find them, your computer needs to keep track of each file's location so it can access the audio or video information that's contained in each file.

Because Final Cut Pro stores the project files and the media files separately, this location information is especially important. Final Cut Pro keeps track of media files by using relative file paths. This means Final Cut Pro remembers the location of a media file relative to the location of the project files. If the relationship between the files changes—for example, you move the media files but the project files stay in the same place—Final Cut doesn't know where to find the audio or video information and displays a message in the Canvas that the media is offline or unavailable.

This relative location is often described as the file hierarchy—which file is inside which folder, and which folder is inside which other folder. Maintaining this hierarchy is essential. So is ensuring the relationship between files does not change. Large film and video productions have an assistant editor (some very large projects have several editors) in charge of file management. The assistant editor's full-time job is to make sure all media is accounted for and available to the editor at all times. If the media becomes unavailable, the editor can't edit. If you work on your own without an assistant, the responsibility falls to you. Keeping a fastidious eye on every file in your project may seem overly cautious, but in the long run, it allows you to spend more time editing and less time fixing mistakes.

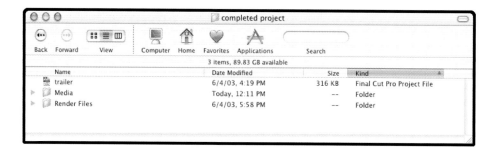

Discussion
Logging and Capturing Digital Video

Final Cut Pro's Log and Capture function allows you to select video clips, add names and descriptions, and using a FireWire connection, capture video and audio directly from the source deck with no loss in quality. The best part of Log and Capture is you can bring in a batch of clips, complete with names and time-code information. Once the clips come in, they're ready for you to edit and easy to keep track of. When you use Log and Capture, the clips also contain the name of the tape from which they were captured. The tape name lets you easily recapture the clips if files are lost or damaged and lets you create an Edit Decision List (EDL) if you want to take your project to a high-end postproduction facility to create a high-definition master tape or a film print.

You access the Log and Capture function by connecting your computer to a video source and then choosing File→Log and Capture.

Reel numbers

When you open the Log and Capture window, or change tapes in your source deck, Final Cut Pro prompts you to enter a reel number, which is a name for the source tape. Clear and distinct numbers are important, especially if your project has material from more than one tape. An easy-to-maintain system for reel numbers starts with 001 for your first tape, uses 002 for the second, 003 for the third, and so on. This allows you to use 999 separate tapes (almost 500 hours of material if you use half-hour tapes) without duplicating a reel number and throwing off your

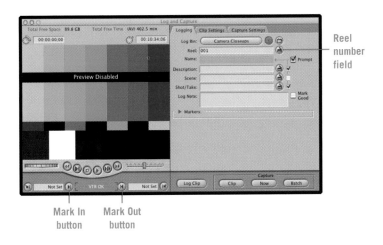

Reel number field

Mark In button   Mark Out button

system. To keep track of which tape number goes with which tape, I write the three-digit reel number on the tape label as soon as the tape comes out of the camera. Professional video cameras allow you to set different start timecodes for each tape that you record, which is another way of identifying tapes. High-end consumer cameras, such as the Canon XL1, which are used by many professionals, don't let you set different start timecodes, so each tape you record has the same timecode. If you duplicate reel numbers in your project, you can easily have tapes with the same number and the same timecode, which confuses Final Cut Pro. If you give each tape a clear and unique number, you avoid problems.

Log clip versus capture clip and capture now

When material comes in from the field, the first thing that you should do is log the tape. This creates a record of what's on each tape and where each important element is within that tape. In the days of analog video, logging meant sitting down with a sheet of paper and writing down the timecode numbers of where different shots started and ended. For example an editor creating a log on paper might have come up with a list like this:

> Log Sheet Tape #024
>
> 01:15:21;03 – 01:17:06;19—Exterior, supermarket and parking lot
>
> 01:17:06;20 – 01:19:01;05—Wide shot, supermarket checkout line

A detailed log might even contain comments about different shots, such as "out of focus" or "good action."

The producers and editorial staff would then sit down with the log and decide which shots to assemble into the finished project.

Final Cut Pro allows you to automate the logging process. Using the controls in the Log and Capture window you can review the material on each tape, mark individual sections you'd like to import, add a name and comments to each section. Automating the capture process using Final Cut Pro is much easier than writing up a list of timecode locations for various shots, and can save you tremendous amounts of time. Best of all, once you log your tape, Final Cut Pro allows you to automate the import process—you can simply select the list of clips you just logged and set Final Cut Pro to batch capture the entire group.

When you open the Log and Capture window, the window displays a full set of logging and device controls. The left half of the window displays a preview of the tape you're logging, along with a set of device controls that let you play, pause, and fast forward through the tape. The left half of the window also contains marking controls that let you set In and Out points for each clip. As you review the material on a tape, you can mark portions to import as clips, and then click the Log Clip button to store the information.

Once you log clips on a tape, you then capture the material. You can log an entire tape and automate Final Cut Pro to capture all the clips at once, by pressing the Batch button in the Capture panel. You can also capture individual clips one at a time by logging a clip and pressing the Clip button in the Capture Panel. Editors working with Final Cut also have the option of pressing the Now button in the Capture panel, to capture the information on a tape without logging. The function of each of the buttons in the Capture panel is described in detail below.

Capture Clip uses the In and Out points that you specify to immediately capture the clip's video to your scratch disk. This function is similar to Log Clip, except that instead of storing the timecode and name information to capture a group of clips at one time, this function captures each clip as you identify it rather than in a group.

Capture Now captures currently playing video as it feeds into the computer. You can use this feature to capture an entire tape at once and break the tape into clips later. You can also use this feature to capture material from a source deck that is not controlled by a computer or does not have DV timecode, such as an older 8-mm camera or even a VHS deck.

Capture Batch is not available until you highlight a clip or group of clips—for example, the clips you created by using Log Clip. Once you highlight a group of clips and click Batch, Final Cut Pro captures the video for each clip to your scratch disk. During the batch process, if the clip was logged from a tape with a different reel name than the tape that's currently in the source deck, Final Cut Pro prompts you to change tapes. You can also use the Capture Batch function if you encounter severe problems with your media and need to recapture. You may never need to replace your media files, but if you do, using Capture Batch is infinitely more pleasant than having to start from scratch.

Tutorial

» Importing Digital Video

In this tutorial, you import video clips from the CD supplied with this book. The process is similar to importing an audio file, which you did in the Confidence Builder, and is the process you use to import video files from the CD for remaindner of the course. Before starting this tutorial, start Final Cut Pro and open the Camera Closeups project you created in the last tutorial. Make sure to close the Log and Capture window, if you opened it in the previous discussion.

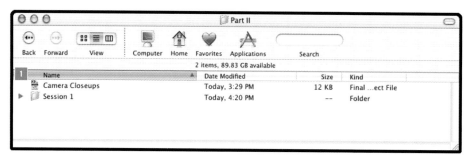

1. **From the Finder, open the FCP Complete Course CD and copy the Session 1 folder into the Part II folder you created during the preceding tutorial.**

2. **In Final Cut Pro, choose File→Import→Files.**
   The Choose a File dialog box opens.

3. **Navigate to the Session 1 folder you just copied to your hard drive.**

<TIP>

You can Shift+click the files to select more than one file at a time. Hold down Shift as you select files, and select as many files as you want.

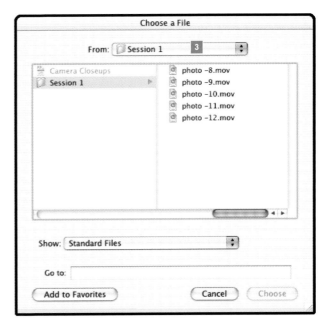

4. **Select all five files in the Session 1 folder** (photo -8.mov, photo -9.mov, photo -10.mov, photo -11.mov, **and** photo -12.mov).

5. **Click Choose to import the files and close the dialog box.**
   Each file appears as a clip in the Browser and is ready for you to edit into your project. You just imported five video clips, which you turn into your first video sequence later in the course.

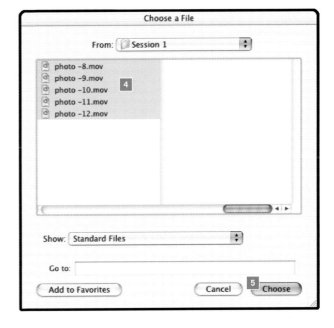

Tutorial

» Organizing the Project Contents into Clips and Bins

Now that your project contains a few video clips, it's time to organize them by content. Because you only have five clips, it's easy to keep track of everything. Organizing the clips into bins makes keeping track of the clips easier as you import more clips for this project and is good practice for when you work on larger projects that may use dozens, or even hundreds, of clips. You can create and name as many bins as you need to organize your material. The bins you create become part of your project files and are not stored as separate folders on your hard drive. If you delete a bin, the media files for any clips inside the bin are not deleted from your hard drive.

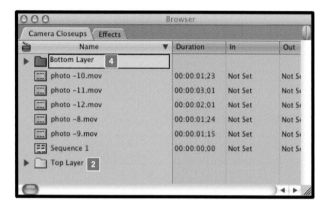

1. **With the Camera Closeups project selected, choose File→ New→Bin.**
   A new bin appears in the Browser window, inside the selected project. When the new bin appears in the Browser, Final Cut Pro gives it a default name (Bin1, Bin5, and so on). Changing the bin name makes it much easier to remember what's inside each one.

<TIP>
The default name for the bin is highlighted when the new bin appears in the Browser window, so any text you type replaces the bin's default name.

2. **Name the Bin** Top Layer**, and press Return.**
   Once you press Return, the bin's name is no longer high-lighted, and Final Cut Pro organizes the items in the Browser, including the new bin, in alphabetical order.

<NOTE>
The term *bin* comes from 16- and 35-mm film editing, when editors would hang a film clip on a numbered hook in a bin. To find clip number 16, the editor would look on hook number 16 in the bin. Bins work essentially same way in Final Cut Pro, but allow you more flexibility.

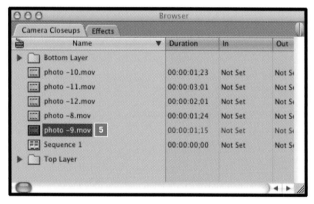

3. **Create another bin by pressing ⌘+B.**
   Both methods of creating a bin lead to the same result; you can choose which works best for you.

4. **Name the new bin** Bottom Layer **and press return.**

5. **Select** photo -9.mov **in the Browser, and drag it into the Bottom Layer bin.**

6. **Select the remaining clips** (photo -8.mov, photo -10.mov, photo -11.mov, **and** photo -12.mov), **and drag them into the Top Layer bin.**

   To select multiple clips at a time, you can Shift+click them, just as you can in the Finder.

7. **Save the project.**

   In this tutorial, you arranged the imported clips in the Camera Closeups project into two bins that you created. You labeled the bins according to their contents, making file management much easier.

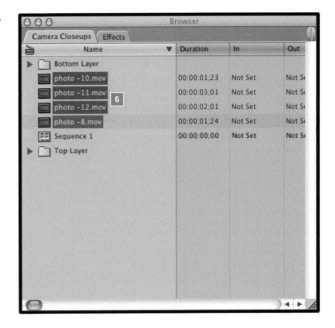

» Session Review

This session introduced you to working in Final Cut Pro 4. It included tutorials on creating and editing new project settings and opening new projects. The session also showed you how to import clips of video and organize the clips into bins, which you learned how to create. This session also examined the importance of file management and provided an overview of the Log and Capture function.

The Final Cut Pro Complete Course folder you created on your hard drive should now contain a Confidence Builder folder and a Part II folder. The Part II folder should contain a subfolder named Session 1, which holds the clips for your Camera Closeups project. As the course develops, you import additional audio and video material and organize it into an increasingly complex project.

Use the following questions to help you review what you learned in this session. The answer to each question is located in the tutorial or discussion noted in parentheses.

1. Do you need to choose a new setup whenever you open a new project? (See Tutorial: Changing Settings and Editing Presets.)

2. You adjust the audio settings for a project using which dialog box? (See Tutorial: Changing Settings and Editing Presets.)

3. If you adjust the audio or video settings in Final Cut Pro, will the changes alter projects that are open when you make the adjustments? (See Tutorial: Changing Settings and Editing Presets.)

4. Does opening a new project automatically close existing projects? (See Tutorial: Opening a New Project.)

5. Why does Final Cut Pro sometimes open a project automatically? (See Tutorial: Opening a New Project.)

6. Does Final Cut Pro automatically keep track of file locations if you move your project files? (See Discussion: The Importance of Organization and File Management.)

7. What is file management? (See Discussion: The Importance of Organization and File Management.)

8. Why is it important not to duplicate reel names? (See Discussion: Logging and Capturing Digital Video.)

9. What is the difference between Log Clip and Capture Now? (See Discussion: Logging and Capturing Digital Video.)

10. How do you select more than one video file for import at the same time? (See Tutorial: Importing Digital Video.)

11. What are the two ways of creating a new bin to organize your media? (See Tutorial: Organizing the Project Contents into Clips and Bins.)

12. How do you move audio or video material into a bin? (See Tutorial: Organizing the Project Contents into Clips and Bins.)

Assembling a Project

Session Introduction

In the preceding session, you created a new project and learned how to adjust the default settings and presets for subsequent projects. You also imported a group of clips, which you assemble into your first sequence in this session. In this session's tutorials, you work with the essential editing tools of Final Cut Pro, opening individual clips in the Viewer, setting the length of each clip, and placing the clips into the Timeline. When you finish this session, you'll have a handle on the basic editing functions of Final Cut Pro and a deeper understanding of the way experienced editors transform raw video into the finished products people watch at the movies and on television.

TOOLS YOU'LL USE
Browser window, Viewer window, Timeline window, Add Marker button, Mark In button, Mark Out button, Play In to Out button, Close Gap command

MATERIALS NEEDED
Session 1 video clips (from the Session 1 folder in Part II on the FCP Complete Course CD), Camera Closeups project file from Session 1

TIME REQUIRED
90 minutes

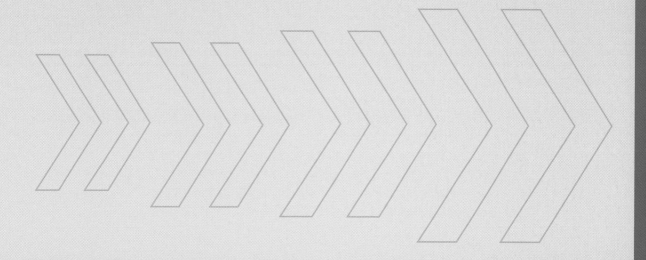

Discussion

Planning Your Structure Before You Cut

Measure twice, cut once. Don't paint yourself into a corner.

There's an obvious correlation between good planning and good results, and the cost of mistakes is tangible—if you cut a piece of wood in the wrong place, you can't just press ⌘+Z to fix the problem. In the virtual world, especially when it comes to digital editing, planning is just as important, but people often overlook its importance. Planning the structure of your project before you start to edit saves you aggravation, and also saves you time.

Paper edit. If you go into an editing room, it's not uncommon to see a large bulletin board filled with index cards. Each card represents a clip and has a description of a shot or some lines of transcribed dialog. The editor places one card next to another on the bulletin board to approximate placing one shot next to another in the finished film or video. This is called a *paper edit.* The editor can easily rearrange the cards to get an idea of which clips work well next to other clips and which order yields the best results. Index cards can be arranged and rearranged far more easily than actual clips, so the paper edit allows a filmmaker to experiment without consequence. A good paper edit takes time, but in the long run, makes editing much faster, because it gives the editor an idea of how things should look before he or she starts to cut.

Assembly. The next step in a large editing project is to assemble the shots according to the paper edit. Clips and sequences always look different on-screen than they do on paper, so the assembly provides the editor with a fuller picture. The goal of the assembly is not to create a finished piece, but to create an early, functional version that the editor can develop and polish. It's bulky and longer than the finished piece, and generally unrefined. Film and video editing entails continually reworking the material and revising editorial decisions to arrive at the finished product. There are a number of stages in between the assembly and what you show to the public, including the rough cut, which starts to look like the final product, and the fine cut, which is an "almost there" version that just needs some tweaking.

Even after you make an assembly or a rough cut, you can still go back to your paper edit to see how things look if you rearrange some shots. Moving a few index cards around on your bulletin board may save you hours of work at your editing station. The ease with which you can make revisions in Final Cut Pro makes it tempting to start editing on the computer right away, but a little planning goes a long way before you choose File→New→Project.

Tutorial
» Working with the Browser, the Viewer, and Clips

Now that you have created a new project, imported some video, and divided the clips into bins, you're ready to start building your project. This tutorial shows you how to open and watch the clips you imported into your project.

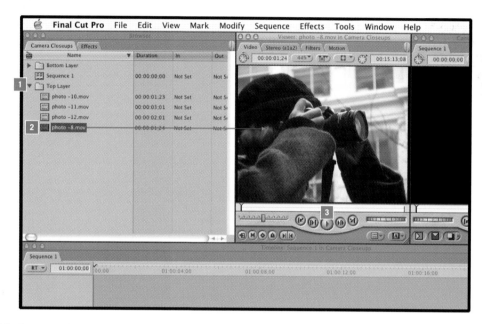

1. **Click the triangle to the left of the Top Layer bin in the Browser.**
   This lists the Top Layer bin's contents: photo -8.mov, photo -10.mov, photo -11.mov, and photo -12.mov.

2. **Double-click** photo -8.mov **to open the clip in the Viewer.**
   The first frame of video in photo -8.mov appears in the Viewer window, which was previously black.

3. **Click the Play button in the Viewer to watch the clip.**
   The clip plays in the Viewer from beginning to end.

< TIP >

You can open a bin in a new window by double-clicking the bin's icon. Some editors find bins easier to manage if each bin opens in its own window; others prefer not to have too many windows open at the same time. The method you use depends on your working style. To close a bin that has opened in its own window, click the Close button in the upper-left corner of the window.

< TIP >

You can change the contents of a bin at any time by dragging clips from one bin to another.

4. **Double-click** photo -10.mov **in the Browser.**

   The new clip opens in the viewer window, replacing photo -8.mov. Only one clip can appear in the Viewer at a time, so opening photo -10.mov in the Viewer automatically closes photo -8.mov.

5. **Click the Play button in the Viewer window to watch** photo -10.mov.

   You have now viewed two of the clips that you work with in this session.

   In this tutorial, you learned how to open a bin and how to open the bin's contents in the Viewer. Leave photo -10.mov open in the Viewer for the next tutorial.

Tutorial

» Using Markers and In and Out Points

Shortening a clip is one of the most basic and most important tasks in editing. When raw footage comes out of the camera, each shot is almost always too long. In fact, a good director and a good camera operator work together to give the editor extra material. Having extra material at the head and tail (beginning and end) of a shot leaves an editor with options and room to make adjustments. In this tutorial, the head of photo -10.mov needs to be trimmed. You adjust the length of a clip to make it fit.

1. **Click the Play button to watch the clip** photo -10.mov **in the Viewer.**

   Notice how the image bounces around in the frame at the beginning of the shot? In this tutorial, you change the length of the shot so the audience doesn't see the image bounce.

2. **Drag the playhead in the Viewer window to 00:00:00;16.**

   The timecode field in the upper-right corner of the Viewer displays the current timecode location of the playhead.

<NOTE>

The timecode field in the upper-left corner of the Viewer shows the length of the clip.

<TIP>

You can bring the playhead directly to a specific timecode location by typing the timecode into the field in the upper-right corner of the Viewer.

3. **Click the Add Marker button in the Viewer so you can easily return to this frame in the clip.**

The frame at 00:00:00;16 appears slightly more than one-half second after the clip starts, which is after the camera has stopped shaking. When you click the Add Marker button, a small yellow marker appears on the Viewer's Timeline.

<TIP>

You can also add a marker by pressing M.

4. **Play the clip in the Viewer again.**

The clip plays from the marker you just added to the end of the clip. There is some slight camera movement (called a *camera bauble*), but it's not nearly as jarring as the movement at the beginning of the shot, and it adds to the character of the clip. You can now set the In and Out points for the clip so only the part you want appears in the sequence.

5. **Click the Mark Out button in the Viewer.**

Because the playhead is already at the end of the clip, it's easier to set the Out point first. The Mark Out button sets the current location of the playhead as the Out point, or end, of the clip. A small triangle with a vertical line next to its left side appears on the Viewer's Timeline; this is the Out point symbol.

6. **Choose Mark→Previous→Marker.**

   This brings the playhead back to the marker you added in Step 3.

7. **Click the Mark In button to set the In point for the clip.**

   A triangle with a vertical line on its right side appears in the Viewer's Timeline. The area in the Timeline to the left of the In point turns gray. The portion of the Timeline between the In and Out points remains white, indicating this is the portion of the clip that will appear in a sequence.

8. **Click the Play In to Out button in the Viewer.**

   The clip plays from the In point you set in the previous step to the Out point you set in Step 5.

9. **Save your project.**

   In this tutorial, you learned how to use markers and how to set In and Out points to define the beginning and end of a clip. You also used the playhead and timecode field to navigate the Viewer Timeline.

Tutorial
» Working with the Timeline Window

The Timeline is a graphical representation of your project from start to finish. Your project begins at the left of the Timeline and plays out to the right. It's called a Timeline because as you move through it from left to right, you're moving through your project from start to finish. When you place a clip in the Timeline the clip appears in the sequence in the same order it appears in the Timeline.

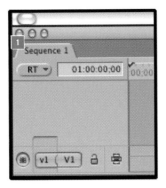

1. **Close the Timeline window by clicking the Close button in the upper-left corner of the window.**
   The Timeline window disappears.

2. **Open the Timeline window by choosing Window→Timeline.**
   The Timeline window reopens. Clips placed in the Timeline window are not removed when the window is closed, so if you ever close the Timeline unintentionally, don't worry.

<TIP>
You can toggle the Timeline from open to closed—and back to open again— by pressing ⌘+3.

3. **Increase the track height by clicking the largest bar in the Track Height Control.**
   All the tracks on the Timeline become taller. Final Cut Pro allows you to place audio and video clips on different tracks on the Timeline. Increasing the track height allows you to see more detail on the Timeline once you start to add clips.

4. **If you don't see scroll bars to the right of your Timeline, hide the Tool palette by choosing Window→Tool Palette.**
   The Tool palette disappears. If you can see the scroll bars already, you can skip this step and go directly to step 6.

<TIP>
If you increase the track height to the highest setting, you can't see all the tracks at once. To see additional tracks, you have to scroll vertically through the Timeline display using the scroll bar or arrows at the right of the Timeline.

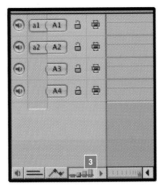

5. **Hide the audio meters by selecting Window→Audio Meters.**
   The audio meters disappear, revealing two vertical scroll bars on the right side of the Timeline window that allow you to scroll vertically through the Timeline window to see tracks that are currently not displayed.

6. **Click the vertical scroll bar arrow in the lower-right corner of the Timeline window to scroll down and display Tracks A3 and A4.**
   Audio Tracks 3 and 4 are now visible, instead of audio Tracks 1 and 2. In this tutorial, you learned how to open and close the Timeline window, change the track height, and scroll through different tracks.

<NOTE>
The Timeline window is easy to close accidentally. Knowing how to open it again, helps to lower your anxiety level.

Tutorial
» Placing Clips in the Timeline

There are many ways to place clips on the Timeline and combine them into a sequence. In later sessions, you learn about different types of edits and keyboard shortcuts. This tutorial introduces you to placing clips on the Timeline by dragging clips from the Browser window and performing an insert edit.

1. **Select** photo -10.mov **from the Top Layer bin in the Browser and drag it into Track V1 in the Timeline.**

   The clip appears on the video and audio Timelines. This shot ultimately becomes the second-to-last clip in the sequence, so you don't need to place the clip at the very left end of the Timeline.

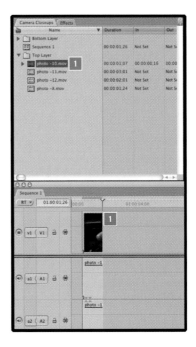

Dragging a clip to a specific location

Later in this tutorial, you add another clip earlier in the sequence—to make the process easier, place photo -10.mov at least 2 seconds from the start of the Timeline to avoid overlap and confusion. When you drag a clip into the Timeline, you can place the clip at any location you want. To ensure your clip is at least two seconds from the start of the sequence, use the Timeline ruler that runs across the top of the Timeline. Aligning the start of clip halfway between the start of the sequence and 01:00:04;00 on the timecode ruler is an easy way to estimate a good location. Once you've placed your clip in the Timeline you can easily reposition the clip by clicking it once to select it, and dragging the clip to the left or right to move it to an earlier or later location on the Timeline.

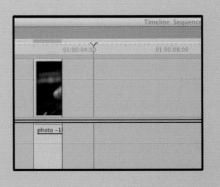

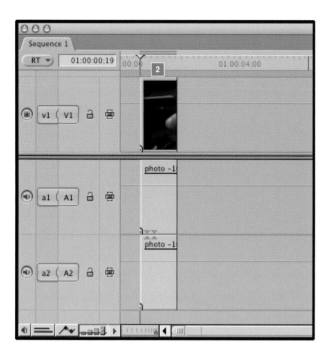

2. **Drag the playhead to the head of the clip on the Timeline.**

   Notice how the playhead snaps to the beginning and end of the clip whenever you place it nearby.

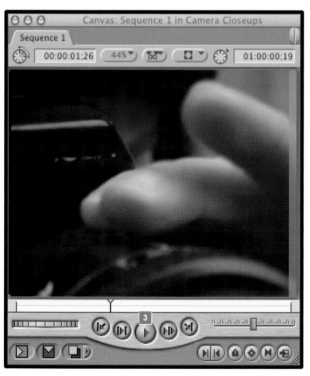

3. **Click the Play button in the Canvas window.**

   The material in the Timeline plays in the Canvas window, starting from the location of the playhead. The clip photo -10.mov plays from the In point that you set earlier to the Out point at the end of the clip.

4. **Select** photo -11.mov **in the Browser and drag it into the Timeline, to the immediate right of** photo -10.mov.
   The new clip snaps into position against the right side of photo - 10.mov, which was already there. Be sure that they don't overlap. If it looks like the clips could overlap as you add photo -11.mov to the Timeline, move it to the right before releasing the mouse.

5. **Drag the playhead back to the start of** photo -10.mov.

6. **Click the Play button in the Canvas window.**
   The first clip plays in the Canvas, immediately followed by the second clip. You just created your first sequence.

7. **Select** photo -8.mov **in the Browser and drag it into the Timeline, to the left of the first clip in your sequence.**
   The new clip appears at the beginning of the Timeline. When you placed photo -10.mov two seconds into the Timeline in step 1, you conveniently left space to add photo -8.mov. Final Cut Pro leaves a space after the first clip, but that's okay. You adjust this in the next tutorial.

8. **Save the project.**
   In this tutorial, you learned how to place clips in the Timeline to create your first sequence. In the next tutorial, you polish the sequence to remove the space between the first two clips and adjust the length of the first and last clips.

Tutorial
» Adjusting Clips in the Timeline

Your timeline now contains three of the four clips from the Top Layer bin. In this tutorial, you add the final clip from this bin, close any gaps on the Timeline, and trim the tail (ending) of the last clip.

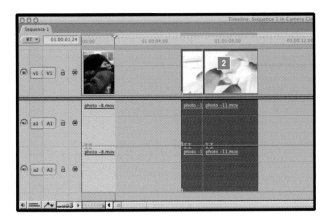

1. **Shift+click** photo -11.mov **and** photo -10.mov, **the last two clips in the Timeline, to select both at the same time.**
   The clips appear highlighted in the Timeline.

2. **Drag the selected clips to the right.**
   Both clips move together, increasing the space between the first and second clips.

3. **Click the Play In to Out button in the Canvas window.**
   The first clip plays, followed by the other two clips in the Timeline after a pause. The only clip in the Top Layer bin that does not yet appear in the sequence is photo -12.mov, which you insert into the gap inthe Timeline in the next step.

<TIP>

A gap in the Timeline does not need to be an exact size to accommodate a clip. To be on the safe side, drag the clips that appear to the right of the gap a little farther to the right to make extra space.

4. **Drag** photo -12.mov **from the Browser into the gap between the first two clips in the Timeline.**
   All four clips appear in the Timeline, with a small gap before and after the second clip.

<TIP>

You can close gaps in a sequence by positioning the playhead inside the gap between two clips and choosing Sequence➜Close Gap. Final Cut Pro closes the gap by shifting all subsequent clips (everything that appears in the sequence after the playhead) to the left. You can also close the gap by pressing Control+G.

5. **Select** photo -12.mov **in the Timeline, and drag it to the left until it snaps into place alongside** photo -8.mov, **the first clip in the Timeline.**

< T I P >

When you work with large sequences, small gaps may be hard to locate. To find gaps in a Timeline track, bring the playhead to the beginning of the sequence and choose Mark→Next→Gap. The playhead advances to the start of the next gap. You can then use the Close Gap command.

6. **Click** photo -10.mov **in the Timeline to select it, and Shift+click** photo -11.mov **so that both are selected together.**

7. **Drag the two clips to the left until they snap alongside the first two clips in the Timeline, with no gap in between.**

8. **Click the Play In to Out button.**
   All four clips play, one after another, with no pauses in between. The only thing left to do is trim the tail of the last clip in the sequence.

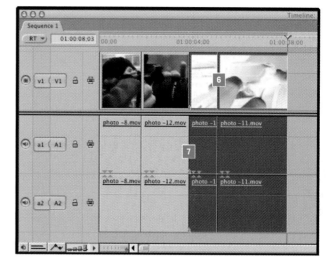

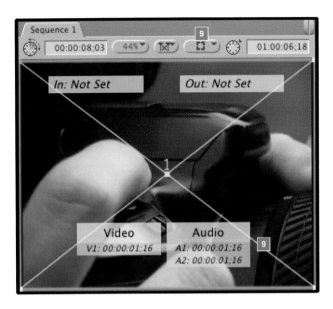

9. **Click the View button in the Canvas, and choose Show Overlays from the menu that appears.**

   When Show Timecode Overlays is selected, Final Cut Pro displays the source timecode of the frame that appears in the window.

10. **Drag the playhead in the Timeline to the left until the video timecode overlay for Track V1 in the Canvas displays 00:00:01;16.**

    This is the last frame of the clip in the sequence that you create. At this point, the clip is about 1½ seconds longer than it should be.

11. **Place your cursor over the end of the last clip in the Timeline, and drag the end of the last clip to the left until it snaps to the playhead.**

    You just shortened the clip.

12. **Save the project.**

13. **Click the Play In to Out button to view your sequence.**

    The sequence plays in the Canvas and ends at the shortened tail of the last clip.

    In this tutorial, you learned how to reposition and trim clips in the Timeline.

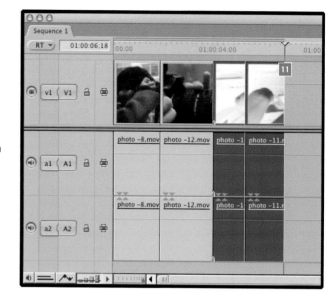

Discussion

What Is a Sequence, and How Do You Build a Good One?

At the most basic level, a *sequence* is a group of clips placed together. When you place a series of clips in the Timeline, you build a sequence. In the larger scheme of things, a sequence is the elemental building block of any film or video—each one tells its own story, and together, a string of sequences forms a complete and nuanced motion picture.

When people talk about a memorable scene in a movie, they're referring to a good sequence. The positioning of each shot, each sound, and each editorial cut has been carefully orchestrated by an editor. Just like a delicious cake doesn't magically pop out of the oven by itself, a good sequence doesn't happen just by chance—an editor massages and finesses the raw material until it works together seamlessly.

The payoff from a good sequence is obvious: You produce a viewing experience that stays with the audience long after they finish watching your project. The downside to a bad sequence is just as evident: The audience's attention shifts to something that doesn't work (a badly timed edit, a shot that's out of focus, or a distorted audio clip), and people stop focusing on your story. Once your viewers' attention shifts away from your story, it's always hard to get it back, and sometimes it's impossible. Spend as much time on each sequence as you need to make sure everything works.

When I was in film school, a professor wisely pointed out that a series of good shots doesn't improve the quality of a bad shot placed next it; instead, the bad shot brings everything else down with it. There's no substitute for revision. Place your shots in the Timeline, and try different combinations until you're 100 percent satisfied. Even then, come back to the same sequence a day or two later to see if it still holds up. Final Cut Pro makes it easy to trim the length of your clips and move them around the Timeline to see what combination works best. Once your project is finished, you can show it to audiences for years to come. Spend some extra time on each sequence to make sure your work is something you're proud of.

» Session Review

This session covered the assembly of a new project. You began the session with a series of raw clips and learned how to open them in the Viewer, define the clips' length using In and Out points, and drag the shortened clips to the Timeline. This session also included lessons on adjusting clips, changing their positions and trimming their lengths in the Timeline.

Your project's Timeline now has a series of clips you can play from beginning to end as a sequence. It's a short and simple sequence, but a sequence is the basic building block of any editing project—and this first sequence is an important step.

Use the following questions to help you review what you learned in this session. The answer to each question is located in the tutorial or discussion noted in parentheses.

1. Why do many professional editors use index cards before they make their first edit in Final Cut Pro? (See Discussion: Planning Your Structure Before You Cut)

2. What are two ways to see the contents of a bin? (See Tutorial: Working with the Browser, the Viewer, and Clips)

3. Once you select a clip in a bin, how do you play the clip in the Viewer? (See Tutorial: Working with the Browser, the Viewer, and Clips)

4. When you reach the end of a clip in the Viewer, how do you return to a marker you placed at an earlier frame? (See Tutorial: Using Markers and In and Out Points)

5. What button do you use in the Viewer to play a clip from its In point to its Out point? (See Using Markers and In and Out Points)

6. If the Timeline window is not visible, how do you open it? (See Tutorial: Working with the Timeline Window)

7. How do you scroll vertically to see additional tracks that are not currently visible in an open Timeline? (See Tutorial: Working with the Timeline Window)

8. Can you reposition a clip you place in the Timeline? (see Tutorial: Adjusting Clips in the Timeline)

9. How do you trim the end of a clip in the Timeline? (see Tutorial: Adjusting Clips in the Timeline)

10. What are the three ways to close a gap between clips in the Timeline? (see Tutorial: Adjusting Clips in the Timeline)

11. Can Final Cut Pro play a sequence that contains gaps? (see Tutorial: Adjusting Clips in the Timeline)

Part III:
Basic Editing

Working with Clips

Session Introduction

In the preceding session, you organized clips into bins, added clips to the Timeline, and edited clips in the Timeline and in the Viewer. In this session, you continue to manage and edit clips by creating subclips from larger video files and adding additional audio and video tracks to the Timeline. Just like you can organize your clips into bins, you can place video and audio clips on specific tracks to create complicated sequences and effects. Final Cut Pro gives you a tremendous amount of control as you make editing decisions. The techniques in this session help you manage that control more thoroughly.

TOOLS YOU'LL USE
Timeline window, Browser window, Viewer window, Mark In button,
Mark Out button, Go to Previous Edit button, Go to Next Edit button,
Edit Marker dialog box, Insert Tracks dialog box

MATERIALS NEEDED
Session 3 folder, Camera Closeups project files

TIME REQUIRED
90 minutes

Discussion

Using File Management Strategies

No one doubts the importance of organization in a film or video project—if you can't find a shot, you can't use it, so it's of no value to you regardless of how good the material is. It takes time to organize your material, and it takes time to maintain a high level of organization, especially as you revise your project and it becomes more complicated. Your project takes a lot more time, however, if you can't find what you need.

You can organize your media files as you capture and import them, or you can bring your files in as large chunks of information and organize them later once they're on your hard drive. Either way, a good file management strategy is essential to your project.

File management is all about making sure you have access to the media files you want when you want them. Everyone agrees that file management is important; the question is how to best go about it. There are as many different organizational strategies as there are editing styles and personality types. Final Cut Pro gives you the ability to break large, complex video projects into small, manageable clips to which you can add labels and descriptions. This makes it much easier to keep track of things, especially if you identify each shot and make each shot its own clip. For example, in the preceding session, you placed four different closeup shots of Sonia Williams into the Timeline. Because each shot was saved as a separate clip, you could easily edit and adjust each shot on its own.

There are two fundamental strategies you can use when organizing your material into clearly labeled clips. The first is to bring separate shots of video into your editing system one by one as individual clips. The other way is to bring the material in as large, unedited chunks that you then break down shot by shot into individual clips. Each strategy has its advantages and disadvantages.

Strategy A: Bring your media in shot by shot

You can log each shot in Final Cut Pro's Log and Capture window, using Log Clip, and then batch-capture all the shots at once. This process was discussed in detail in Session 1. Logging each shot can take much longer than the actual length of the tape. For example, it could take more than 2 hours to log a 60-minute tape, but you have to do it only once. After you log the tape, Final Cut Pro captures the media as separate clips that are easy to identify and work with.

This is a front-loaded approach—that is, your workload is heavier at the beginning stage when you log the material. After you finish the logging, the process becomes very simple. Final Cut Pro batch-captures on its own with minimal supervision; you basically just change tapes and let the software do the work.

Advantages: By organizing and capturing the material at the same time, you free yourself to focus on editing, instead of trying to find a particular shot in a big mass of tape. You can also filter out bad parts, skipping over sections of problem tape that don't add to your project but would take up space on your hard drive if you captured them.

Disadvantages: You can damage the tape by rewinding and fast forwarding through the same spot repeatedly while you decide where to set the In and Out points for the clips you want to capture.

If you don't capture enough extra material (called *handles*) at the head and tail of each clip, editing can be more difficult, especially if you decide to revise an edit or add a transition.

If you don't capture something, it doesn't become a part of your project. You may realize down the line that some raw footage you never captured would have been the best part of your show. (Although this is unlikely, it could happen.)

Strategy B: Bring your media in all at once

Another file management strategy uses Capture Now to acquire large chunks of video, possibly even an entire tape, at one time. You can use the Capture Now function to capture long stretches of material as one large clip. Once the material is in the computer, you can then carefully go through and divide the large chunks of video into individual subclips. Each subclip then appears in the Browser window as a separate clip, annotated with as much detail as you would like to enter.

Advantages: Because you're capturing large chunks of tape without rejecting anything, you can be sure that everything you shot winds up on your hard drive.

Disadvantages: Everything that you shot winds up on your hard drive. Tape that you capture may contain obvious mistakes or clearly unusable material you know you're never going to use. Bad tape takes up just as much room on your hard drive as good tape, and any time you saved by not logging your tape may now be lost filtering out and deleting unusable material.

Once the capture is completed, you still have to spend time sifting through captured material before you can edit. Because you haven't identified where each shot begins and ends, you still have a fair amount of work to do before you can start cutting your project together.

Tutorial

» Making Subclips

As noted in the previous discussion, making subclips could turn out to be one of the more useful file management techniques you come across. At some point, you'll probably find yourself with a large video clip that would be much easier to work with if you could break it into individual shots. Creating a subclip does not change the media files of the original master clip or delete any video; it just makes a selected part of the master clip easier to find. The video clip provided as part of this tutorial is a good example. The media file named a_lot_of_tourists.mov contains video that you can use as two separate clips, once you break the file into subclips. This tutorial shows you how to create these subclips.

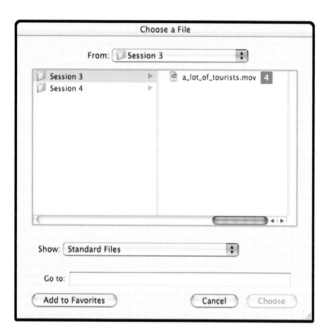

1. **Drag the Part III folder on the FCP Complete Course CD into the Final Cut Pro Complete Course folder on your hard drive.**
   If you closed Final Cut Pro or the Camera Closeups project after completing the last session, please open the program and/or the project now.

2. **Choose File→Import→Files to open the Choose a File Window.**
   The window opens to the Session 1 folder because that's the last folder you opened to import files.

3. **Navigate to the Part III folder and open the folder named Session 3.**

4. **Double-click the a_lot_of_tourists.mov file to import the file into the Browser.**
   The file is intentionally too long. Instead of containing one shot of video to use as one clip, it contains two shots for you to break into two different subclips.

5. **Double-click a_lot_of_tourists.mov in the Browser to open it in the Viewer.**

6. **Click in the Current Timecode field in the Viewer, enter 00:00:02;20, and then press Return.**

This advances the playhead in the scrubber (the Viewer Timeline) to the last frame of the first shot.

<TIP>

You can also click the Current Timecode field in the Viewer and just enter 220. Final Cut Pro interprets your entry as two seconds and 20 frames.

7. **Click the Mark Out button to mark the Out point of what becomes the first subclip.**

The Out point symbol appears inthe Timeline and the frame.

<TIP>

Once the playhead is positioned, you can also set the Out point of a clip by pressing O.

Out point symbol

8. **Click the Go to Previous Edit button in the Viewer to return the playhead to the start of the file.**

9. **Click the Mark In button to mark the In point of what becomes the first subclip.**

   The In point symbol appears on the Timeline and in the frame.

<TIP>

You can set an In point at the current playhead location by pressing I.

10. **Choose Modify→Make Subclip.**

    A subclip named `a_lot_of_tourists.mov Subclip` appears in the Browser. When the subclip first appears, its name is highlighted in the Browser so that any text you type replaces the current name once you press Return.

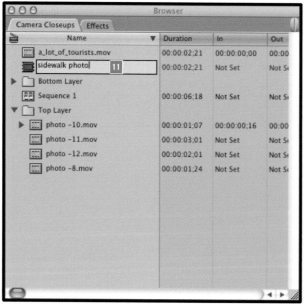

11. **Name the subclip** sidewalk photo**, and press Return.**

12. **Save the project.**

    In this tutorial you set in and out points in a clip, and used them to create a subclip. The subclip is much shorter than the original master clip, and as a result is much easier to work with.

Tutorial
» Adding a Named Marker

In the previous tutorial, you created a subclip by marking the In and Out points in the Viewer. You can also create a subclip using a marker. The first step is to add a marker and give the marker a name, which is what you do in this tutorial.

1. **Click the Go to Next Edit button in the Viewer to bring the play-head back to the Out point of the first subclip (00:00:02;20).**

2. **Advance to the next frame of video in the Viewer by pressing the right-arrow key once.**

The Viewer displays the first frame of the next shot.

3. **Click the Add Marker button.**

The Viewer displays a new marker, in this case named Marker 1.

< T I P >

You can also add a marker by pressing M.

4. **Click the Add Marker button again to open the Edit Marker dialog box.**

   Because you already created a marker in this location, Final Cut does not add another to the exact same spot, but instead opens a dialog box.

5. **Type** Standing Spin **in the Name field to name the marker.**

   Later in this session, you use this marker to create a new sub-clip. Naming the marker according to the contents of the clip makes it much easier to keep track of and work with later on.

<NOTE>

The default name of the marker, Marker 1, is highlighted when the Edit Marker dialog box opens, so anything you type replaces the default name.

6. **Click OK to close the Edit Marker dialog box.**

   The new name for the marker, Standing Spin, now appears in the Viewer. In this tutorial, you learned how to insert a marker and give it a custom name.

Tutorial
» Extending a Marker to a Specific Duration

Now that you added a named marker to a media file, you can set the marker's duration. In this case, setting the duration allows you to turn the marked area into a subclip. You can also use a marker with a duration to get an idea of what something of a specific length looks like in your project. For example, you can visually judge the length of a section of voice-over that you may add to your project, or you could proportionally measure the length of a piece of music relative to the length of the project as a whole.

1. **Drag the playhead in the scrubber to the last frame of video in the shot, which is at 00:00:05;24.**

< T I P >

You can also navigate to the last frame of video by entering the timecode 00:00:05;24 directly in the Current Timecode field in the Viewer and pressing Return.

2. **Choose Mark→Markers→Extend.**
   This extends the marker from its current frame to the location of the playhead.

3. **Choose Mark→Previous→Marker to return to the first frame of the marker.**
   Returning to the first frame allows you to open the Edit marker dialog box in the next step.

< T I P >

To return to the previous marker using the keyboard, hold down Shift and press the up-arrow key. To advance to the next marker, hold down Shift and press the down-arrow key.

4. **Press M to open the Edit Marker dialog box.**
   The dialog box displays a duration of 00:00:03;03 (3 seconds and 3 frames) for the marker. Before you set the duration in this tutorial, the marker displayed a duration of 00:00:00;00.

< T I P >

You can also extend a marker to a specific duration by typing the duration directly into the marker's Duration field. This is useful if you wanted to know, for example, where a 3-minute, 35-second song would begin and end relative to other media if you placed it in a sequence.

5. **Click OK to close the dialog box.**

6. **Save the project.**
   In this tutorial, you extended the duration of a marker to match the length of a shot.

< T I P >

You can add a new marker and open the Edit Marker dialog box in one step by shift-clicking the Add Marker button.

Tutorial

» Turning a Marker into a Subclip

The Standing Spin marker you created in the previous two tutorials begins in the first frame of the shot and ends in the last frame. In this tutorial, you create a subclip from the marker. The new subclip contains the entire shot (and nothing else), making it easy to edit into your project.

1. **In the Browser, click the triangle next to the a_lot_of_tourists.mov clip.**
   The Browser changes to show any markers in the clip.

2. **Select Standing Spin.**
   Because you only added one marker to the clip, Standing Spin is the only marker you can choose. If you had created other markers, they would appear as well.

3. **Select Modify→Make Subclip.**
   Final Cut Pro creates a subclip named Standing Spin from 'a_lot_of_tourists.mov Subclip. The default name comes from the name of the marker you created and the name of the master clip in which the marker was placed.

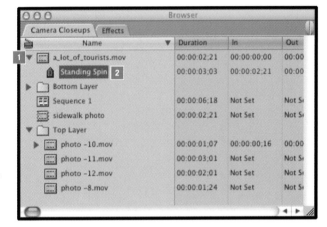

< T I P >

You can also make a subclip from a selected marker by pressing ⌘+U.

4. **Rename the subclip by selecting the name in the Browser and typing Standing Spin.**
   The shorter name is much easier to read.

5. **Save the project.**
   In this tutorial, you created a subclip from a marker. The subclip contains an entire shot from start to finish. Eventually, you turn this subclip and the subclip that you created earlier into a sequence and add transitions.

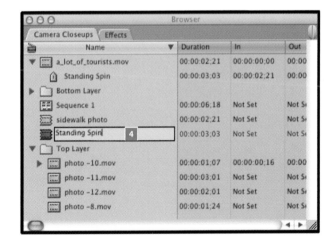

Tutorial
» Adding Video Tracks to the Timeline

In Session 2, you created a simple sequence from the four clips that you placed in the Top Layer bin. In the finished project, these clips occupy the top half of the screen, while an additional video track plays in the bottom half. Playing back more than one layer of video at a time requires an additional video track, which you add to your sequence in this tutorial. First, you rename the sequence so that it's easier to manage.

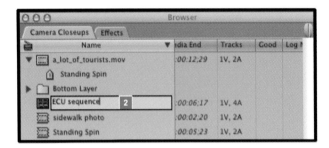

1. **In the Browser, click the name Sequence 1 (not the icon) to select the text, and then click it again so the name of the sequence is highlighted.**

2. **Type** ECU sequence **to rename the sequence.**
   An ECU is an *extreme closeup*. At this moment, you only have one sequence in the project. Naming the sequence makes file management easier when you add other sequences and files later on.

3. **Click the tab labeled ECU sequence in the Timeline to make sure the sequence is selected.**
   If the Timeline isn't selected, you can't complete the next step. If you have another sequence open in the Timeline and that sequence is accidentally selected instead of the ECU sequence, the change you make in the next step applies to the wrong sequence.

4. **Select Sequence→Insert Tracks.**
   The Insert Tracks dialog box opens.

5. **Type** 1 **in the Video Tracks field.**
   This adds one video track to your sequence.

6. **Select the Before Base Track option button to add the track beneath the existing video track.**
   This allows you to create a sophisticated multilayered sequence later in the book.

7. **Click OK to close the window and add the track.**
   A new video track is added to the sequence Timeline. The new, blank video track is labeled V1 because it's the first, or bottom, video layer.

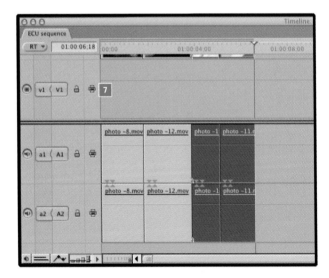

Tutorial
» Adding Audio Tracks to the Timeline

You just finished adding a video track to the sequence currently displayed on the Timeline. In this tutorial, you add audio tracks. The process is basically the same as adding video tracks. You add two tracks to accommodate stereo audio.

1. **Select Sequence→Insert Tracks.**
   The Insert Tracks dialog box opens.

2. **Type 2 in the Audio Tracks field to insert two new audio tracks.**
   Keep the After Last Track option button selected; this is the default. Final Cut Pro inserts the new tracks below the original four audio tracks that are currently displayed in the Timeline.

<NOTE>
When you open a new project in Final Cut Pro, the Timeline automatically contains one video track and four audio tracks.

3. **Click OK to close the dialog box and add the tracks.**
   The Timeline does not appear to have changed. Because the audio tracks you added come after the tracks that are currently in the Timeline, Tracks A1 and A2 still show in the current display.

4. **Save the project.**
   In this tutorial, you added two audio tracks to the Timeline, for a total of six audio tracks. These tracks accommodate two tracks for each video clip, two tracks of stereo music, and two tracks of additional dialog or effects.

<NOTE>
Stereo audio uses two tracks, one for the left channel and one for the right channel. DV cameras generally record in stereo, so most of the time, you use stereo audio in your projects.

See and Hear the Difference: Audio versus Video Tracks

Although the process of adding audio and video tracks is almost identical, the two types of tracks function in very different ways once they are added to your project. Multiple audio tracks play at the same time. If you have six different audio clips on six different tracks, you can hear them all together. The advantage of using more than one track is you can combine different sound elements, such as music, dialog, and ambient sound, while controlling each individually. You can make one louder than another or start one a fraction of a second before the next.

Video tracks also play together when more than one appears in the Timeline, but only the track at the top is visible. Imagine a stack of papers on your desk. The top paper is visible, so it obscures the others. Video tracks in Final Cut Pro operate the same way. You can apply effects and you can control opacity levels to make more than one video track visible at one time. This creates really cool compositing effects, but the top track blocks your view of the other video tracks unless you take specific steps. If you've worked with layers in Photoshop, you'll notice that video tracks in Final Cut Pro work the same way.

» Session Review

This session addressed different ways to manage your files, ranging from carefully bringing in each clip individually to capturing large sections of tape and sorting out the clips later. You learned how to make subclips from a larger clip by setting the In and Out points in the Viewer and by creating a marker. You also learned how to add video and audio tracks to the Timeline and how to navigate through sequences and clips, as well as through the Timeline itself.

The following are some questions to help you review the information in this session. The answer to each question is located in the tutorial or discussion noted in parentheses.

1. What is the difference between logging individual clips on a tape and using the Capture Now function? (See Discussion: File Management Strategies)

2. How does the choice of logging individual clips or capturing an entire tape shape your file management strategy? (See Discussion: File Management Strategies)

3. Does creating a subclip change the original media file (which is also called the master clip)? (See Tutorial: Making Subclips)

4. What keyboard shortcut can you use to set an Out point at the playhead's current location? (See Tutorial: Making Subclips)

5. How do you create a marker with a name other than the default (Marker 1, Marker 2, and so on)? (See Tutorial: Adding a Named Marker)

6. Instead of creating a marker and extending it to the current playhead location, how would you create a marker with a specific duration? (See Tutorial: Extending a Marker to a Specific Duration)

7. The keyboard shortcut you use to create a subclip from the In and Out points in the Viewer is the same as the shortcut used to create a subclip from a selected marker. What is the keyboard shortcut? (See Tutorial: Turning a Marker into a Subclip)

8. How do you change the Browser display to list the markers in a particular clip? (See Tutorial: Turning a Marker into a Subclip)

9. If you add a video track before the base track, does the video track appear above or below the current video track in the Timeline? (See Tutorial: Adding Video Tracks to the Timeline)

10. If you have audio clips in the same timecode location on multiple audio tracks, which clips are audible when you play the sequence? (See Tutorial: Adding Audio Tracks to the Timeline)

11. If you have video clips in the same timecode location on multiple video tracks, is the video on each track equally visible? (See Tutorial: Adding Audio Tracks to the Timeline)

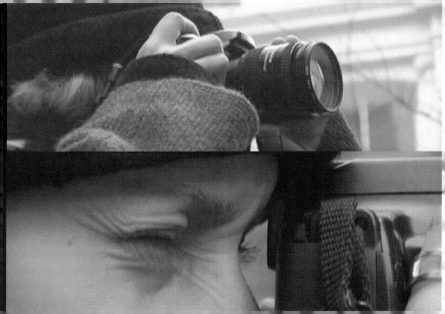

Session 4
Editing Clips

Session Introduction

In this session, you move beyond the basics of assembling a sequence and begin to work with more advanced types of edits. This session examines the way editing shapes the overall tone of your project and teaches you how to use different editing techniques to achieve different results. Dragging a clip from the Viewer into the Timeline produces one type of edit, and using the edit buttons in the Viewer can produce others. You can also assign video and audio from the Viewer to specific tracks in the Timeline to craft intricately textured combinations of audio and video. Once you've finished your first round of edits (called your *first pass*), you can go back and revise your work, fine-tuning each edit until it works exactly the way you want it to. Final Cut Pro lets you take full advantage of the potential of nonlinear digital video editing, and this session gets you started.

TOOLS YOU'LL USE
Timeline window, Browser window, Viewer window, Mark In button, Mark Out button, Mark Clip function, Insert edit, Overwrite edit, Replace edit, Fit to fill edit, Ripple edit, Track Visible button, Source control, Destination control

MATERIALS NEEDED
Session 3 sequences you created and the accompanying media files, Session 4 folder (which includes tourists_interview.mov)

TIME REQUIRED
120 minutes

Discussion

How Editing Determines the Feel of Your Project

Editing determines not only how each shot in your project is cut together, but it also determines the pacing, the rythym, and even the style of your show. One of the best, and most memorable edits I ever saw is part of a French film called *When the Cat's Away.* The protagonist takes a vacation, and you momentarily see her on-screen swimming in the ocean. She takes a deep breath, and just as she starts to relax, the editor cuts to the next sequence, showing her back in daily life. The edit works not only to move the story forward, but it also makes a larger statement—as soon as you start to relax and enjoy your vacation, it's time to go back to work.

Another brilliantly edited sequence appears in *The Graduate,* where the editor cuts back and forth between between Dustin Hoffman jumping into the family swimming pool and jumping into bed with Mrs. Robinson. The editor cuts the two separate actions together so smoothly that it's hard to tell where one action stops and the other begins. This editing style highlights the larger theme of the movie—Hoffman's character is an innocent student who is spending the summer with his parents and at the same time is having an affair with a married woman. The two parts of his character are hard to separate, and their intersection (on the screen and in the story) is what makes the film so entertaining to watch.

A graduate school professor once told my class to always be searching for metaphors in our editing. Asembling a sequence by placing one shot next to another gets you from Point A to Point B, but skillfull editing adds to the impact and depth of your story just as much as conflict, character development, or witty dialog. Creativity doesn't end when the director stops rolling the camera. As the editor, you have the power to create something really great. Make the most of the opportunity with each cut.

Discussion
Managing Destination Controls and Locking Tracks

So far, you've added all your video clips to the same track (V1) and all your audio to Tracks A1 and A2. In the previous session, you added additional video and audio tracks to the Timeline. In this session, you learn how to use the additional tracks. You can use different audio and video tracks together to create complicated effects, and you can use multiple tracks to organize the media in your sequences. The key is managing each track so that each clip appears where you want it to in the Timeline. Assigning a Destination track allows you to specify which track is the destination for an audio or video clip that you add to the sequence. (Earlier versions of Final Cut Pro used Target tracks to perform a similar function.) You can also lock a track to prevent yourself, or anyone else editing your project, from accidentally making changes. Once a track is locked, nothing can be added, removed, or modified.

Destination controls

Tape-based editing systems use a source deck and a record deck. With these systems, an editor plays material on the source deck and records the segments that he or she wants onto the record deck. The Source and Destination controls in Final Cut Pro work in much the same way. The source is the material in the Viewer, and the destination is the track you specify in the Timeline.

The Source and Destination controls are located at the far left end of the Timeline. The Source control contains a lowercase letter and a number (for example, v1 for video or a1 for audio) that represent a video or audio track of the clip that is currently displayed in the Viewer. The Destination control contains a capital letter and a number (for example, V1) that represent a track in the sequence Timeline. Aligning the Source and Destination controls allows you to determine the placement of audio and video in the Timeline—because there's more than one track, there's more than one possible destination.

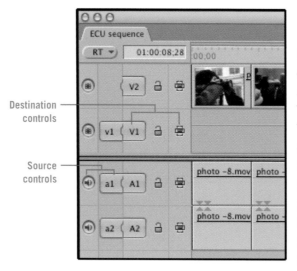

In this illustration, the video Source control is aligned with Track V1 and the audio Source controls are aligned with Tracks A1 and A2 in the left side of the Timeline. This means when an editor executes a command using one of the edit keys—for example, insert edit, the video is placed on Track V1 and the audio is placed on Tracks A1 and A2. The source clip contains one video track and two audio tracks. As the editor, you choose a destination for each track.

You can also use the Source and Destination controls to add audio to a sequence without adding an accompanying video track (or to add video without adding any audio tracks).

This illustration demonstrates a new example. The audio Source control is connected to Destination Tracks A1 and A2, but unlike the previous example, the video Source control has been disconnected. Because the video Source control is disconnected, an insert edit adds audio to Tracks A1 and A2, but it does not add any video to the sequence.

If you make changes to Source and Destination controls but then decide that you want to return to the default state, you can Control+click the area at the far left of the Timeline (between the destination controls and the track lock controls) and choose Reset panel from the pop-up menu that appears.

Locking tracks

Each track in a sequence contains a locking control you can use to prevent modifications. This means that nothing can be added or removed, and you can't accidentally change your track. Material on locked tracks plays back along with the rest of your sequence, so locking a track does not make the track invisible or hidden.

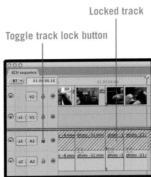

Toggle track lock button

Locked track

A locked track appears on the Timeline with diagonal lines running through it. By default, a track is unlocked. To lock a single track, click the Toggle Track Lock button for that track. To unlock the track, click the Toggle Track Lock button again.

In the figure, Track A1 is locked, so even though audio Source Control a1 is aligned with audio Destination Control A1, an insert edit does not add audio to the track.

Video added on V1

Audio added on A2

However, an insert edit adds video to Track V1 and audio to Track A2 because both tracks are unlocked. The locked track, A1, remains unchanged. Use the following actions to lock various tracks:

» To lock all video tracks in a sequence, press Shift+F4.

» To lock all audio tracks in a sequence, press Shift+F5.

» To lock all the audio or video tracks in a sequence except one, press Option and click the Lock Track control for the track you want to keep unlocked.

Tutorial
» Using the Edit Buttons Instead of Dragging Clips

As you have probably noticed by now, the most obvious way to add a clip to a sequence is to drag the clip from the Browser into the Timeline. You select the clip in the Browser, drag it to one of the tracks in the Timeline, and the clip becomes a part of your sequence. You can't really get too much more obviouis, but obvious might not be everything you want. The Canvas contains three edit buttons you can use to perform more advanced editing functions that not only insert material into the Timeline but also over-write or replace current clips. Once you get comfortable using the edit buttons and their keyboard shortcuts, you may decide using the edit buttons is even easier than dragging material into the Timeline.

1. **Choose File→New→Sequence to create a new sequence in the Timeline.**

   A new sequence appears in the Browser window.

2. **Name the sequence** houston clips**, and press Return.**

   The two subclips you created in the last session show Sonia Williams on Houston Street. In this tutorial, you add these subclips to the Timeline. Creating a new sequence allows you to work without interfering with earlier edits.

3. **Double-click the houston clips icon in the Browser to open the sequence.**

   A new, blank sequence opens in the Timeline, along with a blank Canvas and Viewer.

4. **Double-click the sidewalk photo subclip icon in the Browser.**

   The subclip opens in the Viewer.

5. **Click the Insert Edit button in the Canvas.**

   Final Cut Pro inserts the entire clip into the Timeline. Because the audio Source controls are aligned with Tracks A1 and A2, audio is added to those audio tracks.

<TIP>

The keyboard shortcut for the Insert Edit function is F9.

<NOTE>

When you work with an insert edit, the playhead is the default insertion point. Because no In or Out points were set in the Timeline, the playhead's location in the first frame of the sequence became the insertion point.

6. **Double-click the icon for the Standing Spin subclip to open the subclip in the Viewer.**

7. **Press F9 to add Standing Spin to the Timeline.**

   This is an alternate way of creating an insert edit. The Standing Spin subclip inserts into the Timeline at the playhead's current location, just after the sidewalk photo subclip.

8. **Save the project.**

   You performed two insert edits, without dragging a clip into the Timeline, using the Insert Edit button in the Canvas and the keyboard shortcut F9.

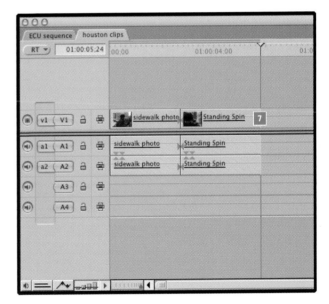

Tutorial
» Using an Insert Edit

Each edit button in the Canvas allows you to perform a different type of edit. In this tutorial and the three that follow, you add clips to a sequence using different types of edits to gain a better understanding of each type of edit. You start with an insert edit, which adds material to the Timeline without damaging audio or video clips that you already placed in the sequence. The houston clips sequence contains two shots of video. You add a third clip to the sequence between the two clips that are already on the Timeline. Because you use an insert edit, Final Cut Pro does not erase or overwrite material in the sequence but instead moves the second clip to make room for the clip you add.

1. **Select File→Import→Files, and navigate to the Session 4 folder in the Final Cut Pro Complete Course folder on your hard drive.**

2. **Open the Session 4 folder, and double-click `tourists_interview.mov` to import the clip.**
The `tourists_interview.mov` clip appears in the Browser.

3. **Double-click the `tourists_interview.mov` icon to open the clip in the Viewer.**

4. **Click the Go to Previous Edit button in the Canvas to move the playhead between the first and second clips.**

   The default insertion point is the location of the playhead. This is the location where the next clip is inserted.

<NOTE>

The Go to Previous Edit button is the farthest left button in the row containing the Play button.

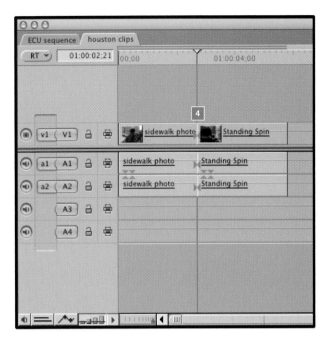

5. **Click the Insert Edit button in the Canvas.**

   Final Cut Pro inserts the clip that's currently displayed in the Viewer, tourists_interview.mov, into the sequence at the playhead's current location. Final Cut Pro does not erase or overwrite the adjacent clip. Instead, the length of the sequence extends to accommodate the recently added clip, and the clip that was already in the Timeline was moved to the right.

6. **Save the project.**

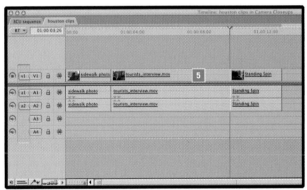

Tutorial

» Using an Overwrite Edit

An overwrite edit allows you to add material to a sequence without extending the sequence's length. Instead of shifting material in the Timeline, an overwrite edit adds a clip in place of current material—it overwrites what is already there. In this tutorial, you perform an insert edit and then an overwrite edit to see the difference between the two.

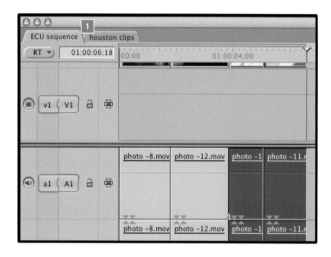

1. **Click the ECU sequence tab in the Timeline to ensure the sequence is open and selected.**

   The Timeline displays the sequence that you created in the previous session.

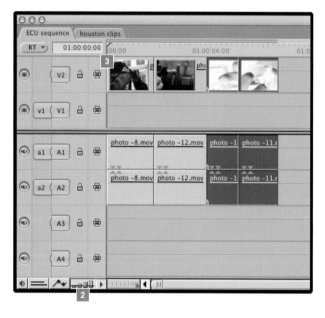

2. **If you can't see more than one video track in the Timeline, click the Toggle Timeline Track Height control so both video tracks are visible at the same time.**

3. **Move the playhead to the beginning of the sequence.**

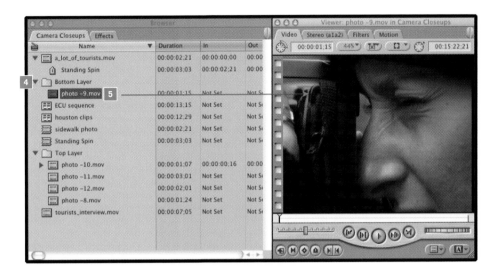

4. **In the Browser, click the triangle next to the Bottom Layer bin icon to open the bin, if it is not already open.**
   The Browser displays the contents of the bin, photo -9.mov.

5. **Double-click** photo -9.mov **to open the clip in the Viewer.**
   Your goal is to insert the video from photo -9.mov into Track V1 without adding audio to the sequence and without shifting the location of any of the clips.

6. **Click the Source Controls a1 and a2 to disconnect them from Tracks A1 and A2.**
   This ensures you won't add audio to the sequence in your next edit. Source Control v1 is aligned with Track V1, so an edit adds video to Track V1 at the playhead's current location, the beginning of the sequence.

7. **Click the Overwrite button in the Canvas.**
   Final Cut Pro adds photo -9.mov to the Timeline, overwriting the blank space at the beginning of Track V1. If there had been a video clip in the track, Final Cut Pro would have overwritten enough of the media in the Timeline to accommodate the clip you just added.

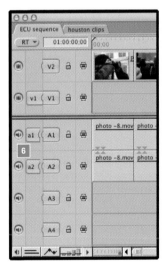

<TIP>
The keyboard shortcut that you use to perform an overwrite edit is F10.

8. **Save the project.**
   In this tutorial, you learned how to perform an overwrite edit, inserting material onto the Timeline without shifting the locations of any clips. When you made the overwrite edit, Final Cut Pro overwrote the blank space at the insertion point in the track.

<NOTE>
If you had performed an insert edit instead of an overwrite edit, Final Cut Pro would have placed the video from photo -9.mov at the head of Track V1 and would have inserted blank space into the other tracks, extending the sequence to the right. To see how this works, undo the edit you made in Step 7 and try using an insert edit instead. When you finish experimenting, undo your changes.

Tutorial
» Using a Replace Edit

Imagine that you just added photo -9.mov to the Timeline as an overwrite edit, and the director of the project walks into the room and asks you to keep the length of the shot the same but using different contents. The shot should start and end in the same place on the Timeline but should contain the video from the sidewalk photo subclip, beginning just before the photographer raises the camera to her eye. This change is easy to make with a replace edit, which makes you look really sharp to the director. The replace edit is a specialized type of overwrite edit that quickly replaces an entire shot with another shot that you open in the Viewer. Additional material in the Timeline is not changed during a replace edit—the selected clip is replaced, and nothing else is changed.

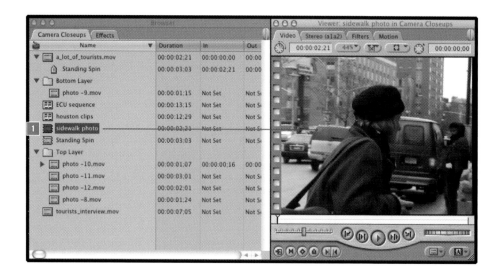

1. **Double-click the sidewalk photo subclip in the Browser to open it in the Viewer.**

When you perform a replace edit, whatever frame the playhead is on in the Viewer becomes the frame that sits wherever the playhead is in the Timeline—the rest of the footage is filled in, both before and after the playhead. Any In or Out points that you specified in the source clip are ignored.

2. **Advance the playhead to frame 00:00:00;26 in the Viewer.**

   This is the frame just before the photographer raises the camera, and it becomes the first frame of the new clip.

3. **Bring the playhead in the Timeline to the beginning of the first shot.**

   A replace edit replaces the shot that begins at the playhead's location in the Timeline.

4. **Check to make sure the audio Source controls are disconnected and that the video Source control is aligned with Track V1.** If the audio Source controls remain connected you will change the audio in the sequence as well as the video.

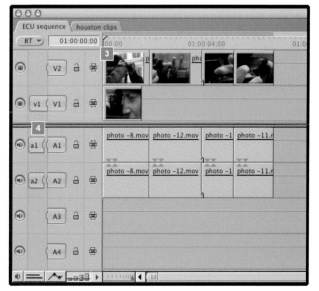

5. **Click the Replace Edit button in the Canvas.**
   Final Cut Pro replaces the clip photo -9.mov with video from the sidewalk photo subclip. The frame of video at the playhead's current location in the Viewer becomes the first frame of video in the new clip.

   <TIP>
   The keyboard shortcut for a replace edit is F11.

6. **Click the Visible icon at the far left end of the Timeline to make Track V2 invisible.**
   The track appears shaded. The video you replaced is hidden behind Track V2. To see Track V1 play in the Canvas, you need to make Track V2 invisible.

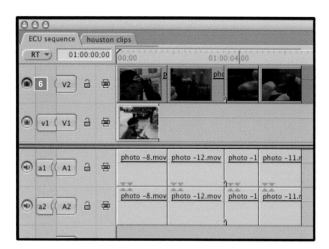

7. **Play the sequence in the Canvas.**
   The video you replaced in Track V1 plays in the Canvas, and then the window goes black because there's no more video on the track.

8. **Click the Visible icon again to make Track V2 visible.**
   The track appears on the Timeline with no shading.

9. **Save the project.**
   In this tutorial, you easily replaced a shot on the Timeline with video from another clip without disturbing any other tracks. The director who decided to test your technical abilities is now impressed with your skill. But wait, there's more . . .

Tutorial

» Using a Fit to Fill Edit

Your imaginary director has returned to the room after a cup of coffee and is freshly invigorated by the caffeine. The director tells you to use the first shot but asks that you stretch it out to play under all four shots of video that are already on Track V2. It's no problem; you are unflappable. You use the fit to fill edit.

The fit to fill edit is an important type of overwrite edit and is especially helpful when you want to fill a long space with a short clip. You select a section of your sequence Timeline and then use media from a clip in the Viewer to fill the space. Final Cut Pro slows down or speeds up the shot, extending or shortening the length of the clip to fit the space you select.

1. **Double-click the photo -9.mov clip in the Browser to open the clip in the Viewer.**

2. **Bring the playhead to the first frame on the Timeline, and click the Mark In button in the Canvas.**
   The In point symbol appears in the upper-left corner of the Canvas window.

<TIP>
You can also return to the beginning of the sequence by typing 01:00:00;00 in the Timeline's timecode field, or by pressing the Home key.

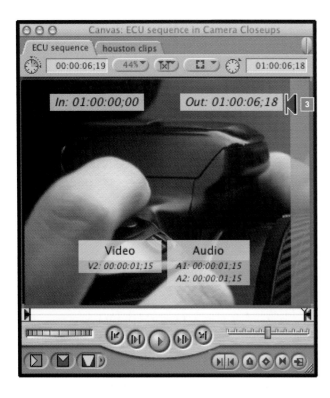

3. **Bring the playhead to the last frame on the Timeline, and click the Mark Out button in the Canvas.**

   The Mark Out symbol appears in the upper-right corner of the Canvas. You have now selected the entire length of the photo -9.mov sequence.

4. **Click and hold the Replace Edit button, and select Fit to Fill from the pop-up menu that opens.**

   Fit to Fill is the second button from the left in the popup menu and looks like a green envelope. Once you select it, Fit to Fill takes the place of the Replace Edit button in the Canvas.

   <NOTE>

   To restore the Replace edit button to the Canvas window, hold down the Fit to Fill button and select Replace from the pop-up menu that appears.

5. **Click the Fit to Fill button in the Canvas.**

   Final Cut Pro adds photo -9.mov to Track V1 in the Timeline and stretches it to fill the area between the In and Out points. The clip appears in the Timeline with (23%) next to its name. This means the clip has been slowed to 23 percent of its original speed to fit the space available.

6. **Set Track V2 to invisible, and bring the playhead to the start of the sequence.**

   Making V2 invisible allows you to see the Fit to Fill edit you added to V1.

7. **Click the Play In to Out button in the Canvas.**

   The clip you just added plays smoothly at a reduced speed.

8. **Make Track V2 visible again.**

9. **Save the project.**

   In this tutorial, you marked In and Out points before using a fit to fill edit to stretch a short clip of video to fill the length of the sequence.

Tutorial
» Performing Three-Point Edits

When you make an edit, you can specify In and Out points in the clip, In and Out points in the Timeline, or a combination of both. The combination is called a three-point edit. For example, if you set In and Out points in a clip and then set an additional In point where you want to insert the material into your Timeline, you're using three edit points. In this tutorial, two of the points specify how much of the source clip is used, and the third specifies where the clip appears in the sequence.

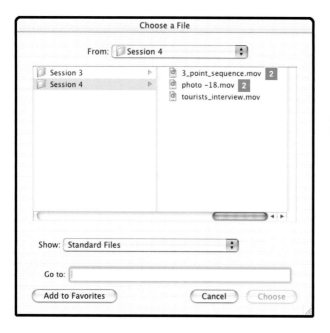

1. **Select File→Import→Files.**
   The Choose a File dialog box opens.

2. **Select** 3_point_sequence.mov **and** photo -18.mov **clips from the Choose a File dialog box. Click choose to import the clips.**

< T I P >
If you shift+click clips, you can import them together.

3. **Select File→New→Sequence.**

   A new sequence appears in the Browser.

4. **Name the sequence** three point.

5. **In the Browser, double-click the three point sequence to open it.**

   Three point is a new sequence. Because you have not yet added anything for them to display, the Timeline, Canvas, and Viewer are all blank.

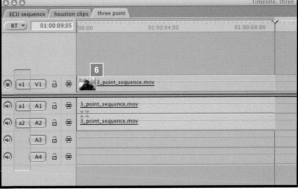

6. **Drag the** 3_point_sequence.mov **clip from the Browser onto the existing tracks of the Timeline at the beginning of the new sequence.**

7. **Double-click the** photo -18.mov **clip in the Browser to open the clip in the Viewer.**

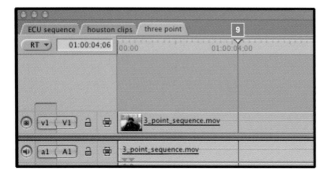

8. **Select Mark→Mark Clip.**

   The Mark Clip function sets an In point in the first frame of the clip and an Out point in the last frame.

9. **Bring the playhead in the sequence Timeline to 01:00:04;06.**

   This is the timecode location where you add a clip to perform your first three-point edit.

10. **Select Mark→Mark In to set an In point in the sequence.**

    You have now set three points—an In point and Out point in the clip, and an In point in your sequence. When you perform an edit, Final Cut Pro adds the selected portion of the clip to your sequence, placing the first frame at the In point in the Timeline.

<NOTE>

Because you placed In and Out points in the first and last frames of the clip, the entire clip is added to the Timeline.

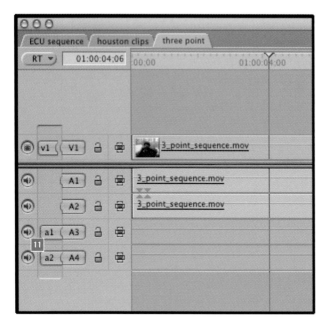

11. **Drag Source Control a1 to align with Destination Track A3, and align Source Control a2 with Destination Track A4.**

    This imports the audio into your sequence without interfering with the audio on Tracks A1 and A2.

12. **Click Source Control v1 so it is disconnected from Track V1.**

    This allows you to place additional audio in your sequence without adding video. The next edit you perform is an over-write edit, so adding material to the wrong track could unintentionally erase material that's currently in your sequence.

13. **Click the Overwrite Edit button in the Canvas.**

    Final Cut Pro adds the audio tracks from the clip in the Viewer to Tracks A3 and A4 on your Timeline. You just completed your first three-point edit.

<NOTE>

If you had placed In and Out points around a shorter section of the clip, only the material in that shorter section would have appeared in the Timeline.

14. **Click the Play In to Out button in the Canvas.**

    You hear the interview clip, along with the ambient sound.

15. **Save the project.**

    In this tutorial, you added material to the Timeline based on two points you set in the Viewer and a third you placed in the sequence Timeline. You also aligned Source Controls a1 and a2 with Destination Tracks A3 and A4, directing audio from the clip in the Viewer to Tracks A3 and A4 in the Timeline.

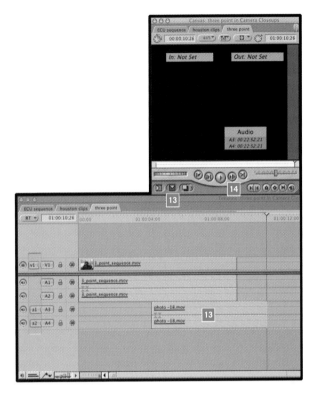

Tutorial
» Refining Your Edits

Editing is a process of revision. Much like wood carving, you make your first pass, cut away a layer, and then return to cut some more. By the time you finish, all the excess has been trimmed away, and all the edges have been smoothed. After you cut a sequence together, come back to it a day or so later and look at it as critically as you can. You may find an edit that you were perfectly happy with but now want to improve. In this tutorial, you revise edits in the ECU sequence that you created in Session 3. Rather than rebuilding the entire sequence, you can make some small changes that revise the timing and pacing of two shots and make the whole sequence work infinitely better.

1. **Click the ECU sequence tab in the Timeline.**
   The sequence you created earlier comes into view.

2. **Click the Play In to Out button in the Canvas to view the entire sequence.**
   Be sure Track V2 is visible so you can watch the four clips on the top video track. The third clip is much shakier than any of the others. You need to tighten some edits to make the camera movement less noticeable and to improve the overall feel of the sequence.

3. **Choose Window→Tool Palette to make the Tool palette visible.**
   The Tool palette contains a variety of tools you can click on to perform various editing functions.

4. **Click the Roll tool, and hold it down.**
   An additional tool menu extends from the Tool palette.

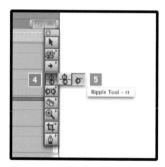

5. **Click the Ripple Tool icon, just to the right of the Roll tool.**
   The Rippple tool appears in the Tool palette. The Ripple tool allows you to edit the head or tail of a shot, without altering the In or Out points of the shot next to it and without creating a gap between shots. In the following steps, you use the Ripple tool to trim the head of the shaky closeup.

Leave in Only Your Best Tape:
You've Got To Kill Your Darlings

I had another graduate school professor who said that all films are 25 percent too long. Her point being any film or video project, no matter how well edited, can always be tighter. The professor who said we should always be searching for metaphor also said to "send the orphans down the river" when it was time to excise our favorite shots. The shots you enjoy the most as a director or editor may do nothing for the audience. Even worse, the wrong combination of shots may significantly weaken your project.

Walter Murch (editor of *The English Patient, The Godfather*, and other similarly acclaimed films) notes in his book *In the Blink of an Eye* that filmmakers in the editing room often maintain too

much of an emotional attachment to events that happened when they were shooting. As a result, when they review their footage, the filmmakers see "around the edge of the frame," and instead of watching what's on-screen, they relive the process of capturing the shot. You may have carried a heavy camera and tripod up the side of a mountain to get the perfect establishing shot—and damn it, you're going to use it! The viewer, however, doesn't know the history of your material. To the audience, it's just a shot, and if the shot doesn't move your audience, it isn't worth all that much to your project.

Don't be afraid to cut. It may hurt now, but you'll be glad later.

6. **With the Ripple tool selected, click the left side of the third shot in the Timeline.**

   The Ripple tool selects the head of the clip (including audio and video).

<N O T E>

If you click the right side of a shot, you select the tail.

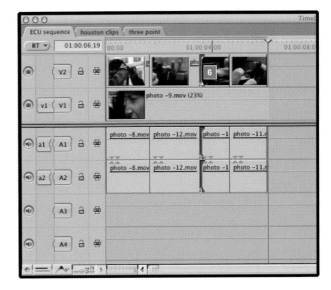

7. **Hold down the mouse, and drag the head of the clip slowly to the right until the timecode display of the incoming clip in the Canvas reads 00:00:01;03, and then release the mouse.**

   This action trims 17 frames (slightly more than a half-second) from the head of the third clip in the sequence. The shots on either side of the clip remain unaltered. The last clip now appears 17 frames earlier but is otherwise unchanged. The only other difference in the sequence is the clip on Track V1 now extends past the end of the last shot on Track V2.

8. **Click the Selection tool in the Tool palette.**

   The cursor changes from the Ripple tool back to an arrow.

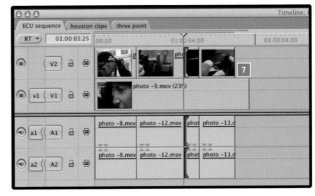

Working with the Ripple Tool

The Canvas changes to show the last frame of the previous (or outgoing) clip on the left and the first frame of the current (incoming) clip on the right. As you drag the head of the clip with the Ripple tool, you change the In point of the incoming clip. Final Cut Pro displays the frame where you moved the In point as well as the timecode. An additional timecode display in the Timeline shows the number of frames you have trimmed from the clip. The benefit of working with the Ripple Tool is it enables you to edit one shot in your sequence, without changing the length of the shots before or after. This becomes especially valuable once you've spent time arranging a series of shots, and want to make a change only to one. In step 7 you used the Ripple tool to shorten the third clip in the sequence, but did not change the content of adjacent clips in the Timeline.

9. **Select the end of the shot on Track V1, and drag it to the left until it snaps into place flush with the rest of the clips.**

   All tracks in the sequence now end in the same frame. The ripple edit shortened Tracks V2, A1, and A2. You manually trimmed the tail of the shot on Track V1.

10. **Click the Play In to Out button in the Canvas to view the sequence.**

    Shortening the third clip by a half-second makes the sequence much more dynamic because the viewer does not expect a sudden change in tempo.

11. **Save the project.**

    In this tutorial, you used the Ripple Edit tool to shorten a shot without changing the length of the shots that came before or after it in the Timeline. The fit to fill edit you added needed to be shortened as a result. You did this by moving the end of the clip with the Selection tool. You also removed a slight technical flaw from the sequence that took away from the overall strength of the project.

» Session Review

This session examined the ways you can edit clips in the Timeline and the way editing shapes the feel of your project. In the final tutorial of the session, slightly trimming one clip changed the entire feel of the sequence, altering the rhythm and pace of everything around it. You learned how to assign and manage Destination tracks to control where you inserted media, and you added clips to the Timeline using several different types of edits. You can now decide if your edits should replace material in your sequence or extend the sequence, leaving existing clips untouched. You also learned how to perform three-point edits, setting two edit points in the Viewer and one in the Timeline (or vice versa) to precisely control what you add to a sequence and where it appears.

The following questions can help you review what the course covered in this session. The answer to each question is located in the tutorial or discussion noted in parentheses.

1. How do you determine what track an edit is applied to? (See Discussion: Managing Destination Controls and Locking Tracks)

2. How do you use the Source controls to add audio to a track without adding video? (see Discussion: Managing Destination Controls and Locking Tracks)

3. One way to perform an insert edit is to drag a clip from the Browser into the Timeline. How can you execute the same type of edit using an edit button in the Canvas? (See Tutorial: Using the Edit Buttons Instead of Dragging Clips)

4. When you work with an insert edit, using the keyboard or an edit button, what is the default insertion point inthe Timeline? (See Tutorial: Using the Edit Buttons Instead of Dragging Clips)

5. When you use an insert edit to add a clip between two existing clips inthe Timeline, what happens to the last clip already in the Timeline? (See Tutorial: Using an Insert Edit)

6. If you perform an overwrite edit on a section of the Timeline that already contains video and audio material, what happens? (See Tutorial: Using an Overwrite Edit)

7. What makes the replace edit valuable? (See Tutorial: Using a Replace Edit)

8. How would a fit to fill edit help you if you wanted to use a clip in a space that was too long or too short? (See Tutorial: Using a Fit to Fill Edit)

9. What are the three points in a three-point edit? (See Tutorial: Performing Three-Point Edits)

10. When you trim the head or tail of a shot with the Ripple tool, what happens to the shots before and after it in the Timeline? (See Tutorial: Refining Your Edits)

Transitions, Filters, and Effects

Discussion: Straight Cuts or Snazzy Effects: Choosing a Visual Style and Sticking to It

Tutorial: Adding Transition Effects to Video

Tutorial: Adding Transition Effects to Audio

Tutorial: Editing and Tweaking Transitions Until You're Satisfied

Tutorial: Creating and Exporting Stills from Video Clips

Discussion: Understanding Real Time, Rendering, and the Difference

Session Introduction

In the previous session, you used a series of different edits to construct a complicated sequence using multiple tracks of audio and video. So far, you've used a series of straight cuts—edits that end one clip and begin the next, with no type of transition in between. In this session, you add transitions to the beginning and ending of each track, and then edit the transitions to change the shape and feel of the sequence. As the sequence becomes more elaborate, your ability to control the audience's viewing experience increases substantially. Sometimes, however, less is more. This session examines the techniques of adding and adjusting transition effects to your work, offers strategies to limit the time you need to spend rendering so you can spend more time editing, and examines when you should use visually arresting transitions and when you should just let a cut be a cut.

TOOLS YOU'LL USE
Timeline window, Browser window, Canvas window, , Push Slide video transition, Cross-fade audio transition, Transition Editor, Transition duration settings, Transition angle attributes, Roll Edit tool, Export Still Image function, TIFF Options dialog box, Render Control settings

MATERIALS NEEDED
ECU sequence you created in Session 3 and modified in Session 4, and the associated media files

TIME REQUIRED
90 minutes

Discussion

Straight Cuts or Snazzy Effects: Choosing a Visual Style and Sticking to It

Final Cut Pro offers a broad array of transitions and effects, from simple fades and dissolves that gradually replace one shot with another to high-tech, 3D "cube spins" and other visual transformations designed to make a viewer's jaw drop. Of course, you also have the option of keeping your edits simple. You don't need to use transition effects; you can just cut straight from the end of one clip to the beginning of the next. It all comes down to what type of visual style works best for your project. Depending on the subject—and your target audience (as well as the desires of your client)—you can choose an understated approach using edits so subtle no one notices the cuts you make. Or, if you're a fan of sci-fi action movies, you may want an over-the-top editing style, using every technique and effect available to you. What's most important is choosing a style that works for you and for the piece—and sticking to it.

If you use an understated style for most of your movie, an elaborate transition in one of your final sequences may totally disrupt the flow of your project. Even if the transition is technically flawless, your audience could be so surprised to see the way one shot dissolves to the next that they continue to marvel at your transition long after it's finished—and don't pay any attention to the rest of your work.

Similarly, if you have an impressive display of visual effects each time you change from one shot to the next, your viewer will expect you to maintain the effect level at each transition. If you don't, the one straight cut in your movie may stand out so much it becomes a problem.

Even the most outrageous movies are presented with remarkably few changes in the types of transitions they use. As the editor, you get to decide what approach works best with your material. Once your audience gets comfortable with your visual style, they will expect it to continue for the length of the film—especially if they like it.

Tutorial
» Adding Transition Effects to Video

Straight cuts are great. More often than not, the beginning of one shot works nicely against the end of end of another. However, there are times when your project needs a transition effect to spice things up or to smooth out some rough edges. In this project sample, the clips in the top half of the ECU sequence slide in from the right, and after they play, slide out to the left. In this tutorial, you add and modify a transition effect to make the video slide across the screen as it plays. In Session 10, you scale the clips so that you can see both tracks of video at the same time, but for now, you only add the transitions. For this tutorial, and the rest of the session, you need the ECU sequence that you created in Session 4. If you closed Final Cut Pro or the Camera Closeups project, make sure both are open now.

1. **Click the head of the first shot on Track V2 of the ECU sequence.**
   Final Cut Pro highlights the left edge of the clip's icon in the Timeline to show you it's selected. Notice how Final Cut Pro also selects the audio on Tracks A1 and A2. This happens because the video and audio tracks for this clip are linked; anything you apply to one track also applies to the others.

2. **Click the Link Selection control in the upper-right corner of the Timeline so it changes from green to black.**
   This unlinks the selections, allowing you to select a video track without selecting the accompanying audio, or vice versa.

3. **Choose Edit→Deselect All.**
   The left edge of the video and audio clips are no longer high-lighted, which means they're no longer selected. You can now select only the video clip.

4. **Click the left edge of the first clip on Track V2 to select it.**
   The head of the video clip highlights—and nothing else.

5. **Choose Effects→Video Transitions→Slide→Push Slide.**

A *slide* is a type of transition that moves a clip of video across the screen so the clip appears to be sliding. Final Cut Pro adds a transition icon to the Timeline at the head of the first clip in the sequence. A red line appears over the icon, which means you must render the effect before you can play it back. You render the file later in this tutorial. First you need to modify the transition.

<NOTE>

Rendering, as you may remember from the Confidence Builder, is the process of generating new video files that contain an effect or other changes you've made to your video clips.

6. **Press the right-arrow key to scroll through the sequence one frame at a time and preview the effect.**

Each frame plays in the Canvas, allowing you to preview the transition. The transition must be rendered before it can play back at full speed. By default, the Push Slide transition moves a clip onto the screen from the bottom up. In the finished project, however, the clip moves onto the screen from the right, so you need to make some changes.

7. **Double-click the Transition icon on the first clip.**

The Transition Editor opens in the Viewer. This set of controls allows you to adjust the settings of a transition so it appears exactly the way you like.

<TIP>

You can also preview a transition by dragging the playhead back and forth through the shot.

8. **In the Angle field, type** 270 **and press Return.**

This sets the incoming clip to move across the screen from the right, which is what you want. The default angle setting is 0, which moves the clip up from the bottom of the screen.

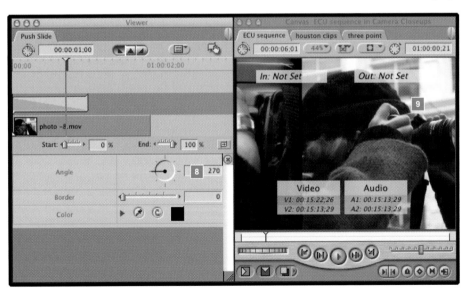

< T I P >
You can also change the angle of the transition by moving the Angle dial.

9. **Scroll through the transition in the Canvas by using the arrow keys to preview the change you just made.**

< N O T E >
The default length for a transition in Final Cut Pro is 1 second (30 frames). You can lengthen or shorten a transition by entering a new length in the Duration field in the upper-left corner of the Transition Editor. You can also change the duration by dragging the ends of the Transition icon in the Timeline to the right or left, making the transition longer or shorter.

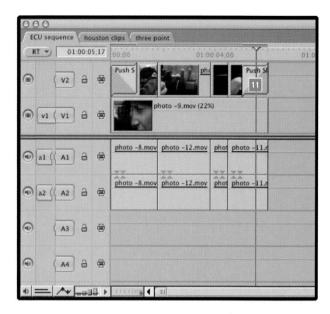

10. **Select the tail of the last clip on Track V2.**
    Final Cut Pro selects the right edge of the clip.

11. **Choose Effects→Video Transitions→Slide→Push Slide to add a Push Slide to the end of the last clip.**

12. **Press the right-arrow key or drag the playhead to scroll through the sequence one frame at a time and preview the effect.**
    Because you placed the transition at the tail of the clip, Final Cut Pro slides the clip off the screen to the top, which is the default setting.

13. **Double-click the Transition icon at the end of the last clip.**
    The Transition Editor opens in the Viewer window. To match the first clip in the sequence, you need to edit the transition to move the clip off screen to the left.

14. **Type** 270 **in the Angle field, and press Return.**

15. **Scroll through the transition in the Canvas by using the arrow keys or by dragging the playhead to preview the change you just made.**
    The clip now moves off screen to the left, in the same direction to which the first clip entered.

16. **Save the project.**
    In this tutorial, you applied a transition effect to the beginning of the first clip in the sequence and to the end of the last clip. You also edited the parameters of each transition, changing the way the effects are applied.

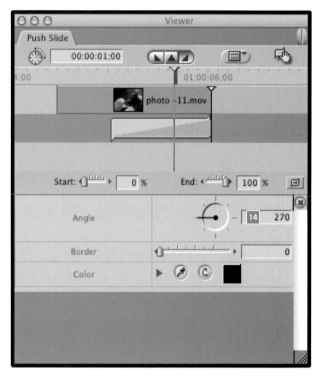

Tutorial
» Adding Transition Effects to Audio

The audio for the ECU sequence starts at full volume and continues at the same level for the duration of the sequence, including the ending. When you add video transitions to a sequence, it's a good idea to add audio transitions to go with them. You don't have to use the same transitions, but your sequence is improved when the audio and video work well together. In this tutorial, you add a fade to the beginning and ending audio in the sequence.

1. **Click the head of the first audio clip on Track A1 in the sequence.**
   Final Cut Pro selects the head of the audio in Tracks A1 and A2 together because they're both part of the same source clip.

2. **Choose Effects→Audio Transitions→Cross Fade (0dB).**
   Final Cut Pro adds a Transition icon to the head of the first audio clip in the sequence. A cross fade gently lowers the volume of the outgoing clip while raising the volume of the incoming clip. Because the selected clip is the first clip in the sequence, there's no outgoing clip, so the audio increases from silent to full volume.

<NOTE>
The difference between the menu choices Cross Fade (0dB) and Cross Fade (+3dB) only comes into play when fading from one clip to the next. Choosing Cross Fade (0dB) fades one clip up from 0 to full volume, while the other clip simultaneously fades from full volume down to 0. At the point where they intersect, both clips are at half volume, so there's a dip in the sound. Choosing Cross Fade (+3dB) compensates for this dip by raising the sound level at the point where the clips intersect so the sound stays at full volume for the length of the transition.

3. **Click the Play In to Out button in the Canvas to preview the audio transition.**
   The audio plays, but the video does not. Audio files require much less information and are relatively easy for Final Cut Pro to process, so they don't require rendering before you can play them back.

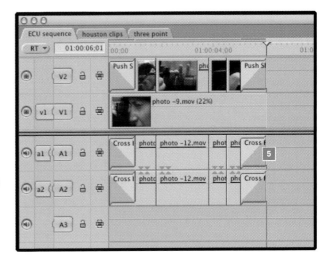

<TIP>
The default duration of an audio transition in Final Cut Pro is the same as a video transition: 1 second (30 frames). To change the duration of an audio transition, do one of the following:

- Double-click the Transition icon on the Timeline, and enter a new length in the Duration dialog box that opens.

- Drag the end of the Transition icon on the Timeline to make the transition longer or shorter.

4. **Click the tail of the last audio clip on Track A1 in the sequence.**
   You add a cross-fade transition to the last audio clip in the sequence.

5. **Choose Effects→Audio Transitions→Cross Fade (OdB).**
   The transition is added to the tail of the last audio clip in the sequence.

6. **Click the Play In to Out button in the Canvas to preview the audio transition.**
   The audio fades in nicely at the beginning and out at the end, adding a more polished feel to the sequence.

7. **Save the project.**
   In this tutorial, you added audio transition effects to the beginning and ending clips in the sequence. The audio transition effects you applied did not change any of the video in the sequence, nor did they change any of the other audio clips.

<NOTE>
Video files require much more complicated processing. This is why Final Cut Pro displays Unrendered in the Canvas instead of showing you your newly added video transitions.

Tutorial

» Editing and Tweaking Transitions Until You're Satisfied

As an editor, part of your job is being a perfectionist. You may never send your food back to the kitchen if you don't like the way it's prepared, but when it comes to the length of the shot and the timing of the transition, everything needs to work just right. Editing is a constant process of revision—when in doubt, cut it out. Even a decision that looked great a few minutes ago may not make sense the next time you look at it, so you recut. In this tutorial, you add a transition effect to the head and tail of the fit to fill clip in Track V1. Once you do this, it no longer makes sense to have the clips in Track V2 begin and end at their current locations, so you move them. Thanks to Final Cut Pro, it's just another day at the office.

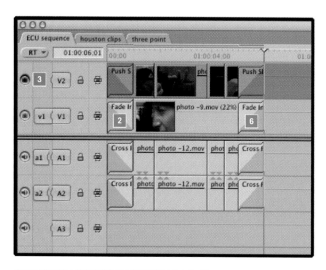

1. **Select the head of the clip on Track V1,** photo-9.mov.

2. **Choose Effects→Video Transitions→Dissolve→Fade In Fade Out Dissolve.**
   This transition fades the clip into view over the course of one second, the default duration of the transition.

3. **Set Track V2 to invisible by clicking the Visible icon.**
   Making the top layer video track invisible allows you to see and playback the video on Track V1.

4. **Preview the transition you just applied by using the arrow keys or by dragging the playhead to scroll through the clip in the Canvas.**

5. **Select the end of the clip on Track V1.**

6. **Choose Effects→Video Transitions→Dissolve→Fade In Fade Out Dissolve again to apply a Fade In Fade Out dissolve to the end of the clip.**
   Final Cut Pro adds a transition effect to the end of the clip, so it now fades in and out gracefully.

7. **Click the Visible icon next to Track V2 to make the track visible.**
   Once both tracks are visible again, you can preview them together.

8. **In the Canvas, preview both video tracks at the same time by scrolling through the sequence using the arrow keys or the playhead.**
   At the beginning, one clip fades in while the other moves across the screen. At the end, one clip fades out while the other moves off screen to the left.

9. **Double-click the Transition icon at the head of the first clip in Track V2.**
   The Transition Editor opens in the Viewer.

10. **Enter 15 in the Duration field, and press Return.**
    Final Cut Pro shortens the transition to 15 frames from the default of 30. Now that you've shortened the transition, you can move the clip.

11. **Select the Roll tool in the Tool palette.**

The cursor changes from an arrow to the Roll Tool icon, indicating you're about to make a roll edit. A roll edit changes the length of a shot without changing the length of the sequence. When you shorten the head of a clip with the Roll tool, Final Cut Pro automatically extends the tail of the clip to its left to fill in the gap. If you extend a clip with the Roll tool, Final Cut Pro trims the adjacent clip in the Timeline.

<TIP>
If the Roll tool is not visible, click and hold your mouse on the Ripple tool, and then click Roll tool when it appears.

12. **Select the head of the first clip on Track V2 with the Roll tool.**

13. **Type +30.**

A Roll Edit field appears on the Timeline containing the number you just typed. This instructs Final Cut Pro to perform a roll edit, moving the start of the clip 30 frames to the right.

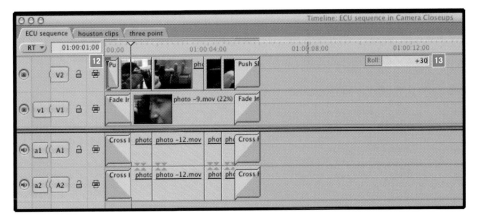

14. **Press Return.**

Final Cut Pro shortens the head of the clip by 30 frames, giving the video on Track V1 a full second to fade into view before the first clip on Track V2 comes into view.

15. **Click the Selection tool in the Tool palette.**

The cursor changes back to an arrow.

16. **Double-click the Transition icon at the end of the last clip on Track V2.**

The Transition Editor opens in the Viewer.

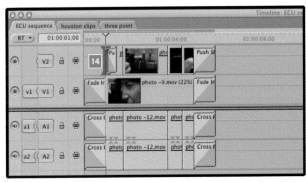

17. **Enter 15 in the Duration field, and press Return.**

Final Cut Pro shortens the second Push Slide to 15 frames. In step 14 you shortened the length of the clip in the Timeline. In this step, you shortened the length of the transition applied to the clip.

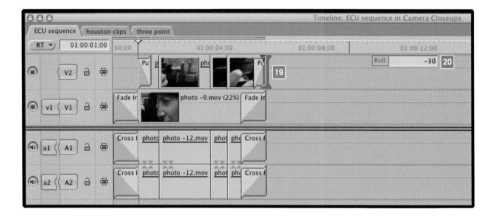

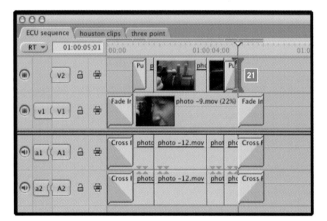

18. **Click the Roll tool in the Tool palette.**

19. **Select the tail of the last shot on Track V2.**

20. **Type -30 on the keyboard.**

21. **Press Return.**
    Final Cut Pro shortens the tail of the last clip by 30 frames.

22. **Choose Sequence→Render All→Both.**
    This renders everything in your sequence, allowing you to review your edits in real time.

<N O T E>
You may have noticed red bars at the top of the Timeline above the video transitions you added to the sequence. These bars indicate that the material needs to be rendered before you can watch it. Once you render the sequence, the red bars disappear.

23. **Click the Play In to Out button in the Canvas.**
    You can now review your edits in real time and enjoy the changes you made to the sequence.

24. **Save the project, and leave it open for the next tutorial.**
    In this tutorial, you edited the head of one clip and the tail of another using the Roll Edit tool. The roll edit shortened both clips but did not change the overall length of the sequence or require you to re-edit any other clips. You also adjusted and tweaked two transitions using the Transition Editor. Think Goldilocks—you're looking to make a transition that's not too long, not too short, but just right.

Tutorial
» Creating and Exporting Stills from Video Clips

Now that you have assembled a few sequences and started to refine them, you can get a feel for what your finished project will look like. As a filmmaker, once your project begins to take shape, it's time to start thinking about publicity. The first item of business—photos for your press kit. A good still image from your project makes a review of your work really stand out on the page. In the not-too-distant past, creating still images from a film or video project was no easy task. (In 1996, a friend paid $500 to produce a series of still images from his 16mm film project.) Now, by using Final Cut Pro, you can spend your money on something else.

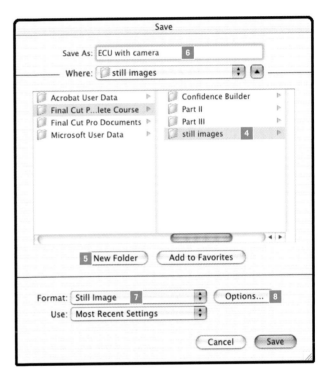

1. **Double-click the** photo -9.mov **clip icon in the Browser.**
   The clip opens in the Viewer.

2. **In the Viewer, bring the playhead back to the first frame in the clip.**
   When you export a still image, Final Cut Pro converts a frame of video to an image file. By default, the location of the playhead indicates which frame of video is exported.

3. **Choose File→Export→Using QuickTime Conversion.**
   The Save dialog box opens. This function saves the video you selected—in this case, a closeup of Sonia with her camera, in the file format of your choice.

<NOTE>
Exporting a still image is similar to exporting a QuickTime movie, which you did in the Confidence Builder. The difference lies in the kind of file you create.

4. **Navigate to the Final Cut Pro Complete Course folder that you created on your hard drive.**

5. **Click New Folder to create a new folder in the Final Cut Pro Complete Course folder. Name the new folder** still images.

6. **In the Save As field, enter the title** ECU with camera.

7. **Choose Still Image from the Format pull-down menu.**

8. **Click Options.**
   The Export Image Sequence Settings dialog box opens.

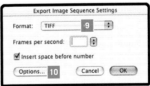

9. **Select TIFF from the Format pull-down menu.**
   Because you chose Still Image in Step 7, you can leave the Frames per second field blank—a still image is just a single image.

10. **Click Options.**
   The TIFF Options dialog box opens, where you can specify what type of TIFF file you want to export. A TIFF file is a graphic file that contains a great deal of information and, as a result, is often used by graphic designers. If you're going through the trouble of exporting a still image, make it a versatile file type that people can use.

<NOTE>
Final Cut Pro also allows you to export an image sequence that produces a numbered series of still images. Choosing Image Sequence from the Format pull-down menu in the Save dialog box exports a series of frames, each one as a separate image. You can use this series of images to create interesting effects in an animation program such as Macromedia Flash, or to export a batch of images for use in a print design project.

> **131**

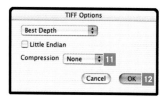

11. **From the Compression pull-down menu, choose None.**
An uncompressed file contains more information than a compressed file. Exporting an uncompressed image gives more options to the designer you work with.

12. **Click OK to close the TIFF Options dialog box, and click OK again to close the Export Image Sequence Settings dialog box.**
The settings you chose are applied.

13. **In the Save dialog box, click Save to export the still image.**
The Save dialog box closes. Final Cut Pro creates a subfolder called still images inside the Final Cut Pro Complete Course folder. The folder contains your recently exported image, ECU with camera.tif. In this tutorial, you exported a still image from a video clip in your project.

< N O T E >
You can use this export technique to export other still images from this project or from other projects you work on. The still image you exported in this tutorial uses a file format that designers and graphic artists can easily use to create print materials that promote your work. You can also work with the still image yourself in an image-editing program such as Photoshop or a layout program like Quark.

Discussion
Understanding Real Time, Rendering, and the Difference

Real time and rendering are both relatively straightforward concepts. *Real-time video* is something you can watch at full speed, broadcast quality, without having to wait. *Rendering* is the process of adding computer-generated content, such as transition effects, to audio and video clips so that you can ultimately watch them in real time and export them as finished pieces of video. Understanding what needs to be rendered, and learning how to navigate the time-consuming, hard drive-space-intensive rendering process makes your life considerably easier.

Remember that not everything needs to be rendered. Cuts only sequences (which contain no transitions or effects) don't need rendering before you play them back. Because cuts only editing simply places one video clip next to another, there are no transitions to worry about. Depending on the speed and power of your computer, you may not need to render titles or audio transitions. The more powerful your computer, the more you can accomplish with Final Cut Pro's real-time playback capabilities.

Complicated effects and transitions—for example, the Push Slides you added in this session—almost always need rendering. As you can already see, rendering isn't the end of the world; it just takes time. If your sequence needs an effect, add the effect. Render the video, and then decide if the transition works for you. Waiting for something to render is better than trying to live with an edit you don't like.

Use the following strategies to get the most out of your editing time in a world built on rendering:

» Put together a rough cut using as few render-intensive effects as possible. Your first cut is meant to give you an idea of what your footage looks like when it's assembled, and it doesn't need to mirror your finished project. Use the time you would have spent rendering to plow through the first draft of your project and get version 1.0 up and running.

» Render several items at once, preferably while you take a break. Rendering a complete project, even on a powerful system, can take a while. If you plan on going out for a bite to eat, start the rendering process on your way out the door so everything's ready to go when you come back.

» If you're really in a crunch and you just don't have the time, you can lower the Render Control settings of the sequence that you're working on. Things won't look good during playback because you've lowered the quality, but they'll render much faster so you can at least get a general idea of what your transitions and effects look like. When you're ready to commit, you can go back and render your final version at full quality.

To change the Render Control settings of a sequence, open the sequence in the Timeline and then choose Sequence→Settings to open the Sequence Settings dialog box. When it opens, click the Render Control tab.

The Frame Rate pull-down menu sets the playback rate for your sequence. You can reduce the playback rate by 50 percent or more, which allows your project to render much more quickly. Render files are generated one frame at a time, so reducing your frame rate by 50 percent means there are only half as many frames to render.

The Resolution pull-down menu reduces the image quality of rendered effects. The default frame size for NTSC digital video is 720 × 480 pixels. If you reduce the resolution by 50 percent, Final Cut Pro generates rendered effects at a resolution of 360 × 240. The effects play back at full size, but at a significantly reduced level of quality.

You can also deselect Filters, Frame Blending For Speed, and Motion Blur, but this means none of the items on this list are rendered. It saves you time but at the cost of possibly providing an incomplete preview of your work.

When you're ready to export at full quality, reopen the Sequence Settings dialog box and change the settings back to their defaults.

» Session Review

When you create an editing style that works well, your audience expects it to continue. This session addressed the need to create—and stay with—a visual style that works for your project. You used transition effects to bring video on-screen in ways that are more sophisticated than a straight cut, and you used the Transition Editor to fine-tune the transitions that you applied. You also used the Roll tool to edit the start and end of two clips you added transitions to, ensuring they started and ended exactly where you wanted them to. Performing a roll edit allowed you to change the length of the clips without damaging the transitions you applied, interfering with the surrounding clips, or changing the length of the sequence. In the final tutorial of the session, you exported a still image from a frame of video. This technique allows you to create professional-quality promotional material for print or the World Wide Web. Finally, this session examined the rendering process and provided a few strategies to keep rendering from slowing your work.

The following questions can help you review what the course covered in this session. The answer to each question is located in the tutorial or discussion that's noted in parentheses.

1. Why could it be a problem if all the edits in a sequence use straight cuts, except for one elaborate transition that uses a series of effects? (See Discussion: Straight Cuts or Snazzy Effects: Choosing a Visual Style and Sticking to It)

2. How do you determine the type of transition style you should use? (See Discussion: Straight Cuts or Snazzy Effects: Choosing a Visual Style and Sticking to It)

3. How do you unlink clips in the video and audio tracks so you can select either the video or audio only? (See Tutorial: Adding Transition Effects to Video)

4. What do you double-click to open the Transition Editor? (See Tutorial: Adding Transition Effects to Video)

5. What are two ways to preview a transition without rendering it? (See Tutorial: Adding Transition Effects to Video)

6. What are the ways to change the length of a video transition? (See Tutorial: Adding Transition Effects to Video)

7. What is the default length for a video and audio transition? (See Tutorial: Adding Transition Effects to Audio)

8. What are the ways to change the length of an audio transition? (See Tutorial: Adding Transition Effects to Audio)

9. How does the Roll Edit tool allow you to change the length of a clip without changing the length of the sequence? (See Tutorial: Editing and Tweaking Transitions Until You're Satisfied)

10. When you select the head or tail of a clip with the Roll Edit tool, and then type in a number of frames, what are you instructing Final Cut Pro to do? (See Tutorial: Editing and Tweaking Transitions Until You're Satisfied)

11. If you edit a clip that a transition has already been applied to, does Final Cut Pro automatically undo the edit? (See Tutorial: Editing and Tweaking Transitions Until You're Satisfied)

12. When you export a frame of video as a still image, how does Final Cut Pro choose the default frame of video to export? (See Tutorial: Creating and Exporting Stills from Video Clips)

13. Why don't you need to specify a frame rate when you use the Still Image setting? (See Tutorial: Creating and Exporting Stills from Video Clips)

14. What type of edits don't need rendering? (See Discussion: Understanding Real Time, Rendering, and the Difference)

15. What happens if you change the resolution in the Render Control setting for a sequence? (See Discussion: Understanding Real Time, Rendering, and the Difference)

Part IV:
Working with Audio

Session 6

Preparing Audio Files

Session Introduction

Video is an obviously visual medium, but without good audio, even the strongest project is incomplete. Good audio means more than mistake-free sound recordings and competent mixing; good audio adds to the power of your project by providing your audience with a richer, more satisfying experience. When you walk down the street, you don't just see things, you also hear what's going on around you. If you can bring the same level of aural and visual immersion to your film and video work (or purposefully exclude selected elements), you can involve your viewer in a way that completely draws him or her into your story.

Developing good audio requires both a technical understanding of the way sound functions in a digital environment and a conceptual understanding of the way your audience relates to the sounds you include. This session introduces the concept of sound design and explains the technical workings of digital audio and analog-to-digital conversion. Tutorials in this session show you how to prepare audio files, edit audio, and add layers of audio to a project.

TOOLS YOU'LL USE
Browser window, Timeline window, Viewer window, Stereo (a1a2) tab,
Source Control tab, Cross Fade (0dB), Sequence Settings dialog box,
Audible control, Zoom tool, Lock Track button, Cut function, Copy
function, Paste function

MATERIALS NEEDED
Session 5 project files

TIME REQUIRED
90 minutes

Discussion

Creating a Rich Sound Design

The idea of sound design is important. A well-crafted film or video project doesn't just use sound files that fall into place as the editor assembles a group of shots. An editor who is attentive to sound design deliberately places and structures layers of audio just as carefully and effectively as he or she edits the images that drive the production. Sound can reinforce what's happening on-screen. Sound can also augment your story by cueing the audience in to what's happening off-screen, and a sudden absence of sound or a change in the sound you use alerts your viewer to the significance of the sequence. A thoughtful use of sound adds texture to your project and raises the overall level of quality. Good audio rounds out a complete production.

Thin sound designs are sometimes described as "anemic." Try to imagine the opening of *Saturday Night Fever* without the Bee Gees. Something's missing. Even if your audience is not consciously aware of it, they know something isn't right if you don't completely realize the audio in your project. A good sound design adds to your audience's understanding of what they watch, and in many ways, it can shape their emotional response to the material. The most obvious example is scary music in a horror movie—it means get ready for something scary. Subtle uses of audio can be equally effective, if not more. A friend of mine was far more disturbed by the wet-thump sounds that accompanied the punches in the movie *Fight Club* than by the actual violence on-screen. And, the metallic zing of bullets whizzing by in the opening battle sequence of *Saving Private Ryan* added a terrifying immediacy to the chaos of D-Day.

Sound design can also be used to overtly shape the direction of the story. In *Blue,* director Krzysztof Kieslowski used a still (or static) shot of an empty country road and the sound of an off-screen auto accident to create an ominous opening scene that sets the tone for the remainder of the movie. In *What's Up Tiger Lily?,* Woody Allen took the voice tracks out of a Japanese spy movie and replaced them with his own dialog about the search for the ultimate egg salad recipe. In both these examples, sound eclipsed picture as the driving force in the production.

A good sound design can raise your project to an entirely new level of quality. At the same time, a weak sound design could keep your production from the success it deserves. Just as you would never leave an ugly shot in your sequence because you don't think anyone would notice, don't stop working on your audio until you're 100 percent satisfied.

Discussion
Understanding Digital Audio

The two keys to digital audio recording are sample rates and bit depth. Computers record digital audio by taking thousands of samples of the audio each second. Each sample is basically a snapshot of the sound, capturing the volume levels and sound frequencies for that very short section of audio. The computer then stores these samples as information. By assembling a group of samples and playing them back, a computer can reproduce a piece of audio exactly the same way each time. Because these samples are stored as digital information, they can also be transferred from one computer to another with no loss in quality.

Sample rates

The number of samples per second is called the *sample rate.* A higher sample rate means more audio information is available to the computer, which results in better audio quality. CD-quality audio uses 44,100 samples each second, which is abbreviated 44.1 kHz. The 44.1 kHz standard was set in the 1980s, so current recording equipment often uses much higher sample rates. NTSC DV cameras generally record at 48 kHz. As a result, Final Cut Pro allows you to work with audio at higher sample rates than a CD, providing better sound quality. Many people think of CD-quality sound as the benchmark for good audio, but these days, most recording studios work with audio at 48 kHz or even 96 kHz, and then *downsample* the audio (lower the sample rate) to put the music on a CD for distribution.

A higher sample rate results in a better audio recording because there's more information for the computer to process. This also means the sound file takes up more room on your computer's hard drive. Some people try to economize on drive space by using a lower sample rate, for example 22.050 kHz, which takes up half the space of a 44.1 kHz recording. The tradeoff is a loss in audio quality. Video files take up so much more room than the highest-quality audio files that, in comparison, you're already getting a bargain as far as storage space. My suggestion is to always record at the higher rate, and if you decide to use a lower sample rate in the future, you have the option of downsampling. If you start out with a reduced-quality sound recording, you can't improve it.

Bit depth

Bit depth refers to the amount of information in each sample. CD-quality audio uses 16-bit samples, so you often see references to 16/44.1 kHz audio. This means that each of the more than 44,000 samples per second contains 16 bits of information. NTSC DV cameras generally record at 16/48 kHz, which produces really good recordings. Some older recording technology, particularly early Internet-specific sound applications, used 8-bit audio that tended to produce distortion and add background noise. High-end recording studios that use 96 kHz recording equipment often record 24-bit audio, which provides substantially more information than most film productions need at this point.

Stereo versus mono

Stereo audio uses two channels to create two recordings—one for the left channel and one for the right. Professional sound recordists often use two different types of microphones and send one to the left channel and the other to the right to give the editor more options. One recording may sound better than the other, and the editor can choose which to include in the finished product. NTSC DV cameras generally record at 16/48 kHz stereo, and most of the time, this is all you need for a great sound recording. Some DV cameras, such as the Canon XL1, allow you to record two audio channels at 16 bits/48 kHz or four channels at 12 bits/32 kHz. 12-bit audio is significantly lower in quality than 16-bit audio, so unless you have a specific need for four distinct audio tracks recorded in the camera, I suggest using the option of two channels at 16/48 kHz. You can always add more audio tracks to your sequence in Final Cut Pro, but you can't go back and improve the quality of your original recording.

Waveforms

Sample rates and bit depth are the keys to recording; waveforms are the key to digital editing. *Waveforms* are a graphical display of the information contained in the samples of a sound file. The peaks represent the loudest points, and the flattest parts of the waveform represent the quiet parts. By moving through the waveform and adjusting or removing different sections, an editor can rework a sound file to take out mistakes, tighten up the content, and even improve or balance out problematic sound levels. As you become accustomed to editing using waveforms, you'll begin to see patterns and recognize sounds and words from their shapes in the waveform display.

Learning to work with waveforms gives an editor tremendous power. Using the audio-editing tools in Final Cut Pro, you can edit dialog so cleanly that no one will ever know you made a change. You can also use volume levels to subtly ease sounds in and out of a sequence or to blend different sounds together to create a deeply textured sound design.

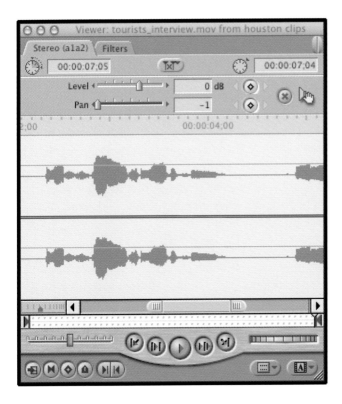

Audio editing works much the same way as video editing in Final Cut Pro. You can add insert edits to a sequence, overwrite existing material, or add transitions, fades, and filters. By combining different sounds on different tracks, you can create multilayered audio effects. You can also separate audio from video, which you do in this session, to combine audio from one clip with images and sound from another, giving you complete control over your sound design.

Because waveform editing allows you to work at the subframe level, you can make much more detailed changes with audio than you can with images. Because there are approximately 30 frames per second, picture editing in Final Cut Pro is frame-accurate to $\frac{1}{30}$ of a second. If you edit with waveforms in Final Cut Pro, you can make even more specific audio edits—down to $\frac{1}{100}$ of a frame, probably more control than you'll ever need.

Discussion

Using Analog Audio in a Digital Environment

Digital editing, especially audio, is closely tied to its analog roots. The terms *cut* and *paste* come from the not-too-distant past when film editors would cut a piece of magnetic film or ¼-inch audio tape and then splice it back together with adhesive tape to make an edit. (Think about that the next time you press ⌘+X and ⌘+V.) The times when the differences between analog and digital become most apparent are during editing (decisions are based on visual information in the waveform as well as the way a clip sounds when you play it back) and when you try to work with analog audio in a digital environment.

When you capture digital audio and video using a deck's FireWire connection, Final Cut Pro doesn't re-record the audio; it simply transfers it to your computer's hard drive as information. When you bring analog audio into your system, your computer needs to make a new, digital recording of the material before it can save the audio as a digital file. Audio levels are especially important in this process. When you record in analog audio, you have a fair amount of wiggle room before loud audio distorts. In digital audio, sounds that are too loud distort almost right away and quickly become unusable.

Digital audio ultimately results in recordings that are much easier to work with as an editor, but at the same time, digital audio is far less forgiving. Analog audio recordings are generally not as clean sounding. Because of sound produced in the mechanical recording and playback process, analog recordings contain tape hiss. Analog audio recordings are also not as durable: They wear out if you play them too many times. Still, a good analog recoding is fairly easy to achieve if you know what you're doing. Digital audio recording, on the other hand, can be a different story—especially if you're making a digital file from an analog recording. I went to a conference in 1994 where an engineer compared digital audio recording to walking off a cliff. Your results were either great recordings at the absolute high end of the quality spectrum, or they were completely unusable down at the bottom end of the scale. Consistently recording good-quality digital sound has gotten a lot easier over the last decade, but digital audio still doesn't yield positive results if you don't know what you're doing.

Digital audio records from a more narrow spectrum of sound than analog audio does. If you make an original recording using digital technology, the narrower spectrum isn't really noticeable. If you capture analog audio, however, it can become an issue. Because the analog recording already has a limited spectrum of recording information, and you record only part of that spectrum, the recording may not be exactly what you want. That's why people are sometimes disappointed with CDs that have been mastered from older analog recordings. When you make a digital file from an analog signal, you need a good analog-to-digital converter. Any Mac that ships with a microphone input or a sound-in jack comes with a factory-installed analog-to-digital converter, but the Final Cut Pro documentation recommends using an audio capture card to get the best performance. For information on compatible capture cards, take a look at the Final Cut Pro Web site at www.apple.com/finalcutpro.

Tutorial
» Preparing Audio Files to Replace Problem Sound

The most obvious use of editing is to fix mistakes. In an earlier session, you used basic edits to trim the problem pieces of video from some clips. In this session, you use audio from one clip to replace problem audio in another clip. The first step that you perform in this tutorial is to prepare the good audio. In the next tutorial, you use the good audio to overwrite the problem sound. In both cases, your goal is to replace the audio so smoothly that no one knows you made any changes.

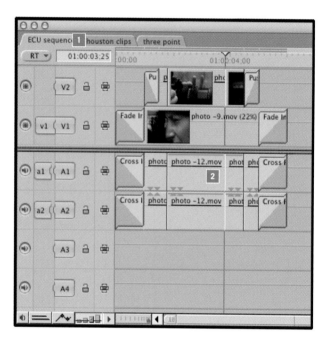

1. **Click the ECU sequence tab to make sure it's selected in the Timeline.**

2. **Bring the playhead to the head of the third audio clip in the sequence.**
   There's an audio issue here you need to fix.

3. **Click the Play button in the Canvas.**
   Notice how you can hear someone talking in the background of the last two shots? That sound needs to be removed. You can also hear the shutter on Sonia's camera click after the Push Slide transition has moved the video clip off the screen. In this session, you fix both problems at the same time.

< N O T E >

Dragging the playhead back and forth through a clip in the Viewer is called *scrubbing*, because as you move the playhead, you can hear the sound in each frame the playhead passes through. The term *scrubbing* comes from the days of analog production when editors would rock reels of audio tape back and forth to scrub a section of tape against the playhead of a deck, looking for a particular point in the sound. For this reason, the Timeline in the Viewer window is also called the Scrubber.

4. **Double-click** photo -11.mov **in the Browser.**

   The clip opens in the Viewer.

5. **Click the Stereo (a1a2) tab in the Viewer.**

   The Viewer changes to display the audio waveforms for the left and right stereo channels in the clip.

6. **Bring the playhead in the waveform to the frame just before the first peak (00:00:00;12).**

   The peak represents the shutter click. When you bring the playhead to this position, the shutter click becomes the first sound you hear when you click the Play button.

7. **Click the Play button in the Viewer.**

   The shutter clicks, and the film advances in the camera. The vocal sound appears at the head of this clip. Starting the audio later in the clip ensures the audience hears only the good part of the sound.

8. **Return the playhead to the frame just before the shutter click (00:00:00;12).**

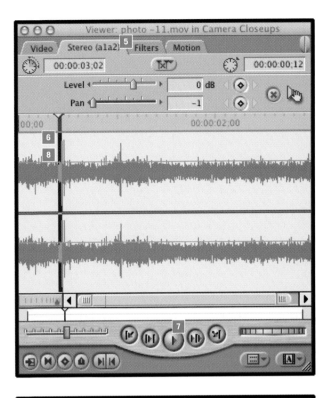

9. **Click the Mark In button to add an In point to the clip.**

   An In Point symbol appears in the Viewer and in the Scrubber. Adding an In point selects the shutter clicking as the start point instead of the voices.

10. **Save the project.**

    In this tutorial, you identified which part of an audio clip to use as a replacement for a sound clip in the current sequence. The audio is now fully prepped and ready to go.

Tutorial
» Separating Audio from Video

Now that you have identified which audio to add to the sequence, it's time to make the edit. In the previous tutorial, you set an In point on the Scrubber; in this tutorial, you set In and Out points in the ECU sequence.

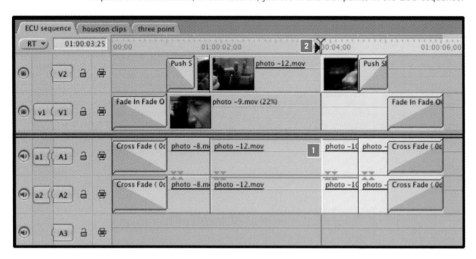

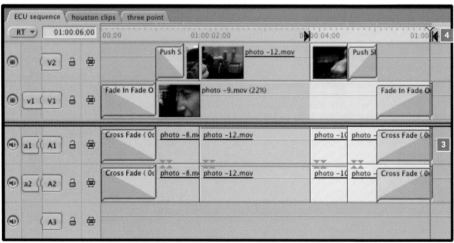

1. **Bring the playhead in the Timeline back to the first frame of the third audio clip in the sequence.**

2. **Click the Mark In button in the Canvas to set an In point in the Timeline.**
   An In Point symbol appears in the Timeline.

3. **Drag the playhead to the last frame in the sequence.**

4. **Click the Mark Out button in the Canvas.**
   You set In and Out points in the Timeline, and in the previous tutorial, you set an In point in the Scrubber. Remind you of anything? That's right—you're making a three-point edit. When you made a previous three-point edit, you set In and Out points in the clip, and an In point in the sequence. As a result, Final Cut Pro added the complete clip at the point you selected. In this case, you set the In point for the material in the clip and defined where the material begins and ends in the ECU sequence.

5. **Click Source Controls a1 and a2 to align them with Tracks A1 and A2.**

6. **Disconnect Source Control v1 to ensure you don't accidentally add video to the sequence.**

7. **Click the Overwrite Edit button in the Canvas.**
   Final Cut Pro adds the shutter click audio from the
   photo -11.mov clip to Tracks A1 and A2 in the ECU
   sequence, replacing the audio in the final two clips.

8. **Click the Play In to Out button in the Canvas.**
   The shutter click audio now plays as soon as the third clip
   comes on-screen and continues uninterrupted through the
   end of the last clip. Not only have you eliminated the
   unwanted background voices, but you also made the Push
   Slide transition appear more natural by extending the audio
   from the previous shot.

9. **Select the end of the last audio clips in the Timeline.**
   When you added new audio to the Timeline, you replaced
   the ending transition. No problem—you can just redo the
   transition.

10. **Select Effects→Audio Transitions→Cross Fade (0dB).**
    Final Cut Pro adds an even fade to the end of the new audio
    clips in the Timeline.

11. **Save the project.**
    You added a selection of audio to replace a problematic
    sound. Using a carefully chosen audio clip extended over two
    shots, you not only removed unwanted audio, but added conti-
    nuity to a transition that, without it, may have felt too sudden.

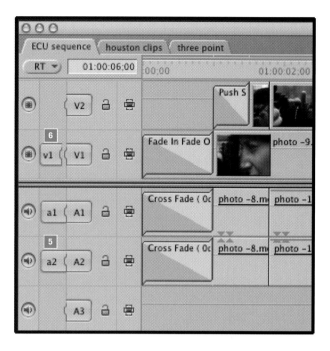

<NOTE>
You can also perform three-point edits by specifying the In and Out
points in a clip and adding an Out point to the sequence. The
material you selected in a clip would be added to the Timeline,
ending at the Out point you specified in the sequence.

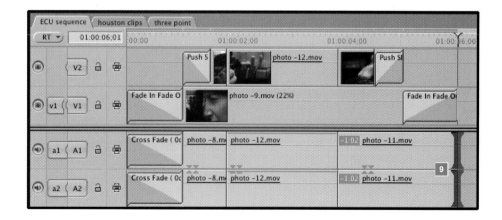

Tutorial

» Editing Audio: Dialog

In editing, as in life, a lot depends on timing. You get the good job because you're in the right place at the right time; you pause for a fraction of a second before delivering the punch line so the joke is that much funnier; and the edit works because you made the cut in just the right spot, especially when you're editing dialog. There are natural rhythms to human speech, and to function properly, your edits need to follow the same patterns. People don't consciously think about speech patterns when they listen to dialog, but everyone knows instinctively if the timing of a dialog edit is off, even slightly. In this tutorial, you shorten the pause in one of Sonia's interviews using the audio waveforms displayed in the Timeline. This tutorial shows you some tricks of the trade. The first trick is displaying audio waveforms in the Timeline so you can use the waveforms to edit.

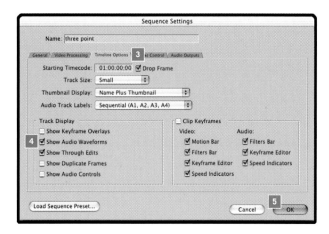

1. **Click the three point tab to open the sequence in the Timeline.**

2. **Choose Sequence→Settings.**
   The Sequence Settings dialog box opens.

3. **Click the Timeline Options tab.**
   The dialog box displays the current settings for the Timeline in the active sequence, in this case, three point.

4. **Select the Show Audio Waveforms check box.**
   Waveforms appear on each audio track in the Timeline. Displaying waveforms can slow the performance of a computer with less memory or a slower processor. However, when you edit dialog, looking at the waveform is indispensable.

<TIP>
You can toggle the Timeline's audio waveform display on and off by pressing ⌘+Option+W.

5. **Click OK to close the dialog box.**
   Each audio track in the Timeline now displays a waveform.

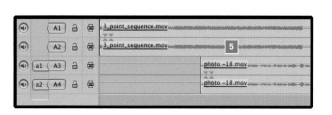

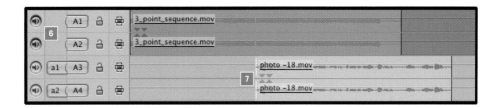

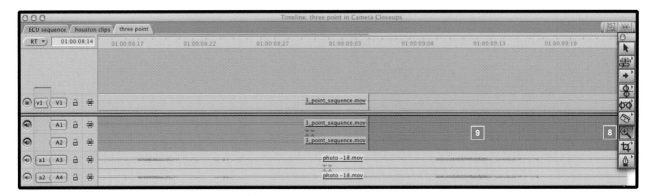

6. **Click the Audible controls for Tracks A1 and A2 in the Timeline.**

   Tracks A1 and A2 appear shaded. These controls function the same way as the Visible controls for the video tracks. A track is audible by default, so when you click the Audible control, the track becomes silent. Silencing these two tracks allows you to focus on the dialog in Tracks A3 and A4.

7. **Bring the playhead to the first frame of audio on Tracks A3 and A4, and click the Play button in the Canvas.**

   There are two long pauses in the sentence, "There's a real focus on the aesthetic." The first pause comes before the word "focus," and the second pause comes after the word "focus." If you look at the waveform, you can clearly see the second pause; it's the long, flat portion between 01:00:08;28 and 01:00:09;08. Tightening the pause before the word *on* helps the flow of the interview.

8. **Click the Zoom tool in the Tool palette.**

   You use the Zoom tool to select the area just before and after the first pause.

9. **Click the Timeline just to the left of the pause, hold down the mouse, and drag to the right to identify the area you want to magnify.**

   When you've selected the area you want to zoom in on, release the mouse. Final Cut Pro zooms in on the selected area, enlarging it to fill the Timeline window.

10. **Scrub the playhead back and forth through the end of the word** *focus,* **from about 01:00:08;23 to 01:00:08;26 in the Timeline.**

    When you edit audio, it's important not to cut off the end of a word. Words that contain an *s* at the end often extend farther in the Timeline than people expect.

<TIP>

To quickly zoom out, double-click the Timeline tool in the Tool palette. Final Cut Pro redraws the Timeline to accommodate the entire sequence again.

11. **Scrub the playhead back and forth through the beginning of the word** *on,* **from about 01:00:09;05 through 01:00:09;15.**

    If you listen carefully, you can hear the beginning of *on* at about 01:00:09;08, which is before the accompanying wave-form appears in the Timeline. The beginning of a word can be easy to miss, especially with words that start with vowel sounds, but if you clip off the start of the word, the clip doesn't sound right.

<NOTE>

Placing an edit as close as possible to the start of a new sound helps the edit by distracting the audience. If you cut the middle part of the pause, and kept the beginning and ending, the audience would be more likely to notice the edit. Placing the edit just before the start of a new sound, instead of a continuation of a current sound, shifts the audience's attention away from the audio edit and focuses the attention on a new sound.

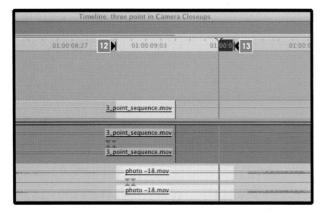

12. **Bring the playhead to 01:00:09;01, and click the Mark In button in the Canvas.**

    This frame is the first part of the pause you remove from the Timeline.

13. **Drag the playhead to 01:00:09;08, the beginning of the first sound in the word _on,_ and click the Mark Out button in the Canvas.**

    Final Cut Pro selects the pause in the Timeline after the word _focus_ and just before the word _on._

14. **Lock Track V1 and Tracks A1 and A2 to confine the edit to the dialog on Tracks A3 and A4.**

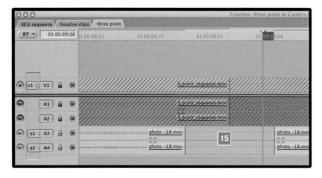

15. **Cut the material by pressing ⌘+X.**

    Final Cut Pro removes the pause from the sequence, leaving an empty space.

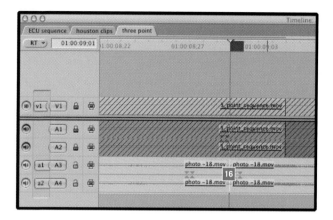

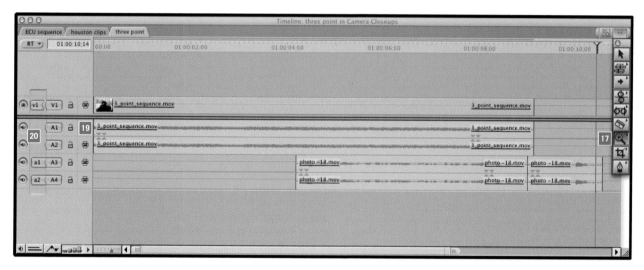

16. **With the playhead positioned in the gap in the audio, press Control+G to close the gap.**
    Final Cut Pro closes the gap by shifting the second set of audio clips to the left.

17. **Double-click the Zoom tool in the Tool palette to view the entire sequence in the Timeline.**

18. **Bring the playhead to the beginning of the audio on Tracks A3 and A4, and click the Play button in the Canvas.**
    The audio plays with a much shorter pause, and because you placed the edit in the right spot, the edit is not at all noticeable.

19. **Unlock Tracks A1, A2, and V1.**

20. **Set Tracks A1 and A2 to audible.**

21. **Save the project.**
    You just successfully edited your first dialog clip. Dialog audio edits can be performed so smoothly that the person who is interviewed may never know you changed his or her dialog. This technique can be especially helpful if you interview someone who has trouble getting to the point—you can just cut whatever is irrelevant.

    < T I P >
    The same technique can also be applied to remove extraneous sound, such as a doorbell ringing or a person coughing, that interrupts part of the interview.

Tutorial

» Editing Audio: Environmental Sound

Many times, a sound you want to snip from your soundtrack is located not in the dialog but in the environmental sound that occurred naturally during shooting. Environmental, or ambient sound, such as the noise from the traffic behind Sonia on Houston Street, is just as important to your project as dialog. In some ways, environmental sound is more important because it can be so obvious. Every shot has some type of sound associated with it. If your environmental sound is missing something it should have—for example, the sound of cars passing in the background—you need to add the sound. In this case, the environmental sound contains a brief unwanted element: An off-screen passerby hoots at our photographer. In this tutorial, you create a new, hoot-free ambience clip (also called an *ambience bed*) to use in place of the existing environmental sound.

1. **Click the houston clips tab to open it in the Timeline.**

2. **Click the Play button in the Canvas to watch the sequence.**
   The hoot comes at the end of the first clip.

3. **Double-click the** a_lot_of_tourists.mov **clip in the Browser to open the master clip in the Viewer.**
   In Session 3, you cut this clip into two subclips. In this tutorial, you use the entire clip to create a new ambience bed.

<NOTE>
Ambience beds use environmental sound to strengthen a sound design by selecting and controlling the background audio that appears with video in a sequence.

4. **In the Viewer, click the Stereo (a1a2) tab to display the clip's audio waveforms in the Viewer.**

   The hoot shows up in the waveform as a bulge that starts at about 00:00:02;09 and ends about 00:00:02;19, just before the current Out point in the Viewer.

5. **Choose Mark→Mark Clip to set new In and Out points in the first and last frames of the clip.**

   You can now place the entire clip in the Timeline and edit out the hoot. This provides a nice ambience bed with handles at the end for a subtle fade that you add later.

6. **Lock tracks V1, A1, and A2.**

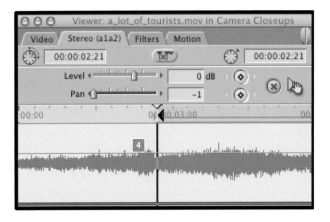

7. **Click the Audible control on Tracks A1 and A2 to make the first two audio tracks inaudible.**

8. **Click Source Control tab a1 and drag it to align with Destination Track A3.**

9. **Click Source Control tab a2 and drag it to align with Destination Track A4.**

   You are now working only with Tracks A3 and A4. The following edits you make won't affect other tracks, and when you play the sequence back, you won't hear audio on other tracks.

10. **Bring the playhead to the first frame in the sequence, and click the Overwrite Edit button.**

    Final Cut Pro adds the audio from the entire master clip to the Timeline, without changing any of the material on the other tracks.

11. **Press ⌘+Option+W to display audio waveforms in the Timeline.**

12. **Use the arrow keys to scroll slowly through the Timeline, and scrub through the beginning of the hoot.**

    This gives you a feel for the "hoot" sound and where it begins.

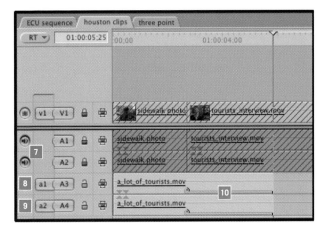

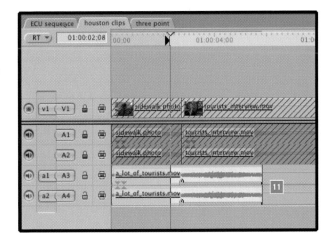

13. **Click the Mark In point button to add an In point to the Timeline at 01:00:02;08, just before the start of the hoot sound.**

14. **Drag the playhead to scrub to the right, past the end of the sound, and click the Mark Out point button to set a new Out point at 01:00:02;21.**

15. **Press ⌘+X to remove the hoot.**
    Because you locked the other three tracks in the sequence, only Tracks A3 and A4 are altered.

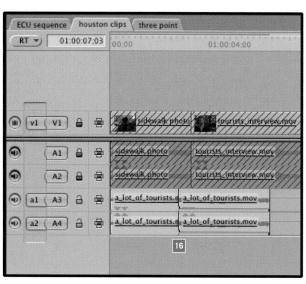

16. **Press Control+G to close the gap.**
    You now have a new ambience bed that contains no unwanted sound and extends into the next shot, leaving you with options for transitions you can add later.

17. **Bring the playhead back to the front of the sequence, and click the Play button in the Canvas.**
    You made a seamless audio edit that not only fixed a problem but also helped the transition from one shot to the next.

18. **Save the project.**
    In this tutorial, you edited ambient sound in the Timeline to create an ambience bed. In the following tutorial and the next session, you add this ambience bed to another part of the sequence and adjust the levels to ease the transition into and out of the interview.

Tutorial
» Adjusting Ambient Sound and Room Tone

When you added an ambience bed to the sequence, the end extended past the last frame of the accompanying video clip on the Timeline. The ambient sound of Houston Street now extends into the interview clip of Sonia in the studio. Ultimately, you don't want traffic noise during the interview. Instead, you want to blend the outgoing sound of the traffic into the incoming room tone behind Sonia's interview to provide a much smoother segue into and out of the interview than you would get with a straight audio cut. To create this audio segue, you need additional audio to fade out after the end of the first shot, which you added in the last tutorial, and additional audio to fade up before the visual cut to the last shot in the sequence, which you add now. In this tutorial, you also remove the original environmental sound from Tracks A1 and A2, giving yourself compete control over the audio that appears in your sequence.

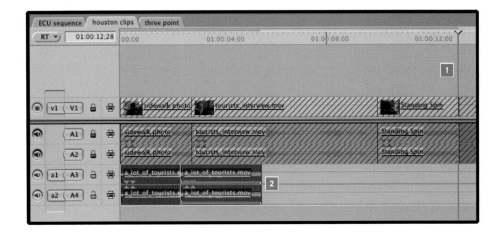

1. **Drag the playhead to the last frame in the houston clips sequence in the Timeline.**

2. **Choose the Selection tool from the Tool palette. Shift+click the clips you placed on Tracks A3 and A4 and edited in the last tutorial.**
   Final Cut Pro selects both clips. You can use this same ambience bed as a transition out of the interview. Because the audio in the second part of the edited ambience is the sound from the shot you see at the end of the sequence, it works seamlessly when you place it underneath Standing Spin. The first part of the clip provides a nice way to ease into the sound.

3. **Choose Edit➔Copy.**
   Final Cut Pro copies both parts of the edited ambience bed.

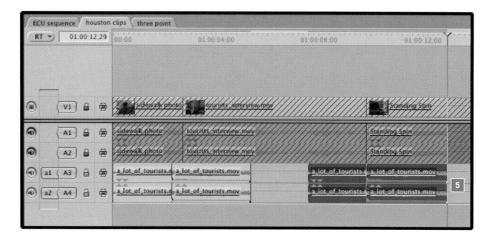

4. **Choose Edit→Paste.**

Final Cut Pro adds both parts of the ambience bed to the Timeline beginning at the playhead's current location.

<TIP>

The keyboard shortcuts for Copy and Paste are ⌘+C and ⌘+V, respectively.

5. **Drag the audio at the end of the Timeline to the left, until it snaps underneath the end of the sequence.**

6. **Click the Play In to Out button in the Canvas.**

You now have an edited ambience bed that overlaps the beginning and end of the interview clip, allowing you to create an elegant transition in the next session.

7. **Unlock Tracks A1 and A2.**

Because you added the ambience bed to Tracks A3 and A4, there's no reason to keep the original street sound on Tracks A1 and A2.

8. **Select the first audio clip on Tracks A1 and A2 (sidewalk photo), and press ⌘+X to delete it.**

9. **Select the last audio clip on Tracks A1 and A2 (Standing Spin) and press ⌘+X to delete it.**

Final Cut Pro removes the audio clips, and leaves a blank space in the Timeline. By removing the original natural sound from Tracks A1 and A2, you don't have to worry about the sounds competing or, for example, the hoot sneaking into your carefully crafted sound mix.

10. **Save the project.**

You now have an edited ambience bed at each end of the sequence.

» Session Review

This session examined the importance of sound design and the ways a thoughtful use of sound can raise a project to a new level of polish. The session provided a technical overview of the way digital audio works as well as some of the differences between digital and analog production that come to light when you work with analog audio in a digital environment. In the tutorials, you used a variety of techniques to manipulate sound files, both augmenting existing sound in the sequence and removing unwanted elements. You learned how to edit dialog tracks and environmental sound and how to arrange edited audio clips in a sequence.

Use the following questions to help review the material in this session. The answers can be found in the tutorial or discussion noted in parentheses.

1. How can sound add to the action on-screen or potentially change the direction of the story? (See Discussion: Creating a Rich Sound Design)

2. What is an audio sample? (See Discussion: Understanding Digital Audio)

3. What does the 44.1 mean in 16/44.1 kHz? (See Discussion: Understanding Digital Audio)

4. What does bit depth describe? (See Discussion: Understanding Digital Audio)

5. What does the 16 mean in 16/44.1 kHz? (See Discussion: Understanding Digital Audio)

6. Is CD-quality audio the best technical quality possible? (See Discussion: Understanding Digital Audio)

7. How can using a waveform help you to edit audio? (See Discussion: Digital Audio)

9. What are two ways you can scrub through the audio in a clip to find the beginning and end of a sound? (See Tutorial: Preparing Audio Files to Replace Problem Sound)

10. How can three-point edits help you replace problem audio in a sequence? (See Tutorial: Separating Audio from Video)

11. When you edit an audio track, should the head of the incoming audio clip contain silence or sound, and why? (See Tutorial: Editing Audio: Dialog)

12. How can you easily duplicate an edited ambience bed, or another clip, in a sequence? (See Tutorial: Editing Audio: Environmental Sound)

13. When you add an edited ambience track to a sequence, why is it a good idea to remove the original natural sound that accompanies a video clip? (See Tutorial: Editing Audio: Environmental Sound)

Editing Audio Clips

Tutorial: **Adjusting the Volume of an Entire Clip**

Discussion: **Keyframes, Timelines, and the Ability to Precisely Control Your Project**

Tutorial: **Setting Different Volume Levels Within a Clip**

Tutorial: **Working with Audio Effects**

Tutorial: **Using the Audio Mixer to Set the Levels of an Entire Clip at Once**

Tutorial: **Using the Audio Mixer to Create Complex Volume Control Effects**

Discussion: **Knowing When to Add Sound and When to Let Your Film "Breathe"**

Tutorial: **Fine-Tuning the Audio Tracks at the Subframe Level**

Tutorial: **Using the Vocal DeEsser Audio Filter**

Discussion: **Why Film Must Sound Better than Real Life**

Session Introduction

Now that you've edited dialog and ambient sound, and rearranged audio clips in the Timeline, it's time to fine-tune some clips. Final Cut Pro offers you the ability to precisely control every aspect of the audio in your program. The audio in the Timeline may sound good now, but the adjustments discussed in this session can make it sound even better. In the following tutorials, you learn how to adjust the volume settings of an entire clip, how to set different audio levels within a clip, and how to mix audio tracks. (*Mixing* means adjusting the levels of an audio clip relative to the levels of the clips around it.) You also learn how to adjust clips to focus the audience's attention on different elements in your audio. Not all sound is equally important to your project—part of your job as an editor is to ensure the most significant audio in your sound design is also the most prominent.

TOOLS YOU'LL USE
Timeline window, Canvas window, Viewer window, Selection tool, Zoom tool, Viewer Audio tab, Level slider, Clip overlay, Record Audio Keyframes button, Audio Mixer, Audio faders, Audio meters, Effects tab, Vocal DeEsser filter

MATERIALS NEEDED
The Session 6 houston clips sequence and the Session 6 three point sequence

TIME REQUIRED
90 minutes

Tutorial

» Adjusting the Volume of an Entire Clip

In the houston clips sequence you worked on in Session 6, the sound level of the interview was too low. The street sound overpowered the interview so listeners in the audience could not understand what Sonia was saying. To fix this, you need to raise the volume of the entire interview and adjust the volume of the ambience bed to blend smoothly into the interview sound without overpowering it.

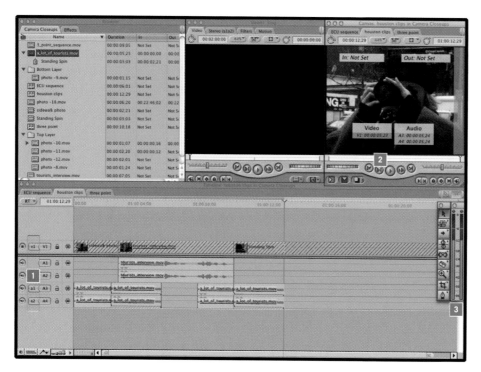

1. **If Tracks A1 and A2 are set to inaudible, click their Audible controls so you can hear the audio on all four sound tracks.**

2. **Click the Play In to Out button in the Canvas.**

   Trying to understand the first few words of dialog can frustrate your audience and may annoy you too. The relative volume levels of the interview and the street sound are too similar. The first step in the process is to slightly raise the volume of the interview clip in the Timeline.

3. **Choose Window→Audio Meters to bring the audio meters back on-screen.**

   The audio meters measure the volume of the sound in your project. If a sound gets too loud, it distorts and becomes unusable. Your goal is to make the sound loud enough that you can hear it clearly, but not so loud that it becomes a problem.

4. **Double-click the audio clips for the**
   `tourists_interview.mov` **clip in the Timeline.**
   The waveform of the portion of the clip in the Timeline opens in the Viewer.

5. **Click the Play In to Out button in the Viewer.**
   As the audio plays, watch the peak levels in the audio meters. The levels in the audio meters increase at the loudest parts of the sound, called the *peaks,* and then decrease during the quieter sections. When you work with digital audio, your goal is to prevent the peaks from rising into the red portion of the meter, or worse yet, from rising to the top of the meter. When audio gets too loud, part of the sound is cut off, or *clipped.* Clipped audio is a mistake you want to avoid at all costs because it sounds terrible.

6. **Drag the Level slider slowly to the right.**
   When the number in the dB field changes from 0 to 1, stop dragging. You just increased the volume level of the entire clip by 1 decibel, or 1dB.

7. **Click the Play In to Out button in the Viewer.**
   The levels at the loudest point in the clip peak just below the red area in the audio meters. A really aggressive editor may push the levels up a little farther, but this level is safe.

8. **Save the project.**
   Raising the level of a clip in the Viewer evenly increases the volume of the entire clip. Leave the project open. In the next tutorial, you add keyframes to a clip to set different levels at different points.

Red area of the meter. Levels in the meter are good, peaking only at the yellow. If levels were any higher, there could be problems.

Discussion

Keyframes, Timelines, and the Ability to Precisely Control Your Project

Transitions and effects in Final Cut Pro rely on two things: keyframes and timelines. The Timeline controls where each shot begins and ends, and where each shot appears in your sequence. Keyframes are special frames that you place in a timeline to control an effect or a transition.

The term *keyframe* comes from animation. A senior animation artist, who had more experience and was paid more money, would draw the important (or key) frames. A junior animator would then take over and draw the frames in between. A keyframe is a frame where a change in the action takes place. One keyframe might be Wyle E. Coyote pausing in midair as he realizes he has just run past the edge of the cliff; the next might be when he starts to fall. The frames between each keyframe (called *in-between frames*) are also important. Without them, you have an incomplete cartoon, but the keyframes set the creative direction and drive the story.

In Final Cut Pro, you use keyframes to set the parameters of an effect, especially if the effect changes over time. For example, if you were applying an audio effect to a clip and wanted the effect to become more noticeable toward the end you would add keyframes at the beginning and end of the clip and set different effect parameters at each keyframe. Final Cut Pro then adjusts each frame of the shot, evenly creating a more noticeable effect as the clip plays in your sequence.

In the following tutorial you use keyframes to set different volume levels at different points in an audio clip. This gives you precise control of the volume levels in your project, and enables you to create intricate volume control effects. In later sessions you use keyframes to make objects fade into and out of view on-screen, and to control the speed of a clip. Keyframes allow you to determine the exact behavior of each clip in your sequence, and to make specific changes at particular points in a clip to achieve the exact effects you want, exactly where you want them.

Tutorial
» Setting Different Volume Levels Within a Clip

Raising the volume of the interview clip is a successful first step. However, the levels in the sequence still need work. The street audio is too loud, and it ends abruptly. The ambience bed you created in Session 6 should come in at a slightly lower volume level and then gradually fade out just as the interview begins. In this tutorial, you set the levels for the ambience beds at the beginning and end of the sequence to create a much nicer transition from the shot of the photographer on the street to the interview of the photographer in her studio.

1. **Shift+click both clips in the first ambience bed to select them at the same time.**

2. **Choose Modify→Levels.**
   The Gain Adjust dialog box opens.

3. **Drag the slider in the Gain Adjust dialog box to the left until the dB field reads –3.**
   Leave the Make Changes drop-down menu set to Relative. This means that the change is made relative to the clips' present level—the clips are made 3dB quieter.

4. **Click OK to close the Gain Adjust dialog box.**

5. **Play the sequence in the Canvas.**
   The first two clips on Tracks A3 and A4 play back at notice-ably quieter levels than the last two, which you have not yet adjusted. Now it's time to fade the audio out just before the interview starts.

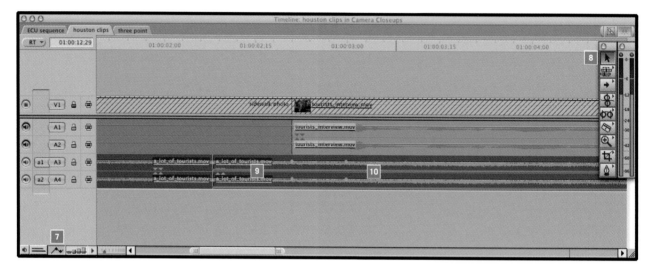

6. **Use the Zoom tool to zoom in on the area where the ambience bed and the interview sound overlap.**
   Don't be bashful about zooming in. If you go too far, you can always zoom back out and try again.

7. **Click the Clip Overlay button at the bottom of the Timeline.**
   An overlay appears in the Timeline similar to the overlay that is displayed on top of the waveform in the Viewer.

8. **Click the Selection tool in the Tool palette.**

9. **Option+click the overlay of the ambience bed, directly under the first frame of the interview clip.**
   Final Cut Pro adds a keyframe to the clip at the point that you just clicked. A keyframe represents a frame in the clip where a change takes place. It doesn't matter if you click on A3 or A4. Because the tracks are linked, any keyframe applied to one is applied to the other

10. **Option+click the overlay again to add a second keyframe slightly to the right of the one you added in the last step.**
   The audio of this second keyframe is the one that you lower in volume, creating a fade in between the first and the last keyframe.

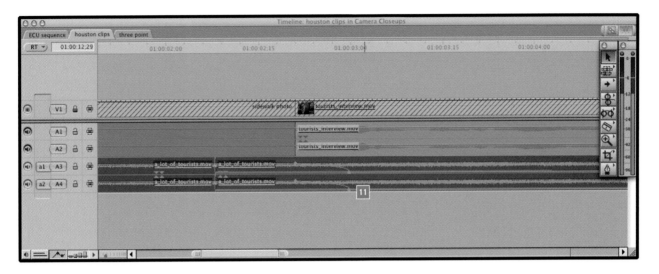

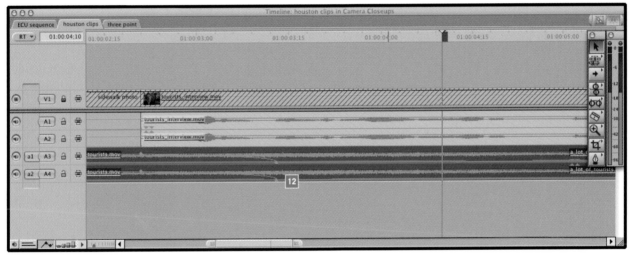

11. **Click the second keyframe in Track A3 and drag it to the bottom of the track.**

    This silences the track from the second keyframe on. The volume level at the first keyframe—and before—remains unchanged. In between the keyframes, the level fades out evenly. The ambience bed fades under the interview, so you can clearly hear what Sonia is saying. The fade is still a little more abrupt than it could be, but don't worry. The best thing about keyframes is that they're easy to rearrange.

12. **Click the second keyframe and drag it to the right to the approximate end of the silence in the Timeline (just before Sonia says the word *individuality*).**

13. **Play the sequence in the Canvas again.**

    Moving the second keyframe extended the fade, easing the audio out gradually as the interview begins.

14. **Save the project.**

    In this tutorial, you changed the volume levels of two entire clips in the Timeline and then added keyframes to create a custom fade out. You also moved one of the keyframes to extend the fade, creating a much nicer transition from the image of the photographer on the street to the interview of the photographer in her studio.

<TIP>

To create a more complex fade, you can place additional keyframes in the Timeline between the two you just added. This enables you to make the change in audio levels faster in some parts and slower in others.

Tutorial
» Working with Audio Effects

The beginning ambience bed is now ready to go. You lowered the audio level by 3dB in both clips, and you faded out the sound as the interview started. The second half still needs work, however. In this tutorial, you refine the second ambience bed using Final Cut Pro's audio effects, and you reshape the content so that it doesn't sound like you're using the same audio twice in one short sequence.

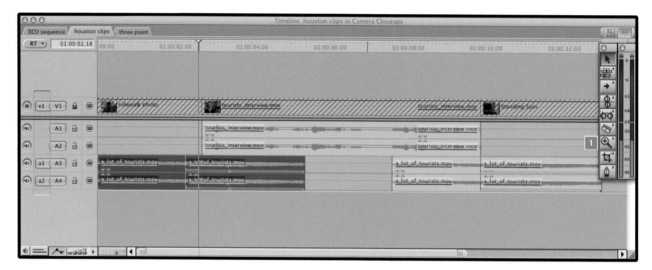

1. **Double-click the Zoom tool to zoom out so that the entire houston clips sequence is visible in the Timeline.**

   You want the second ambience bed to function almost exactly the same as the first: It should fade in gradually as the speech ends and transition smoothly into the next shot. At the same time, your audience should not recognize the sound as a reprise of the same two clips you used in the last ambience bed. That's where your creativity and skill as a sound designer come into play. The change that you make is subtle, but subtlety is what good audio is all about.

2. **Click the Ripple tool in the Tool palette, and use it to select the tail of the first** `a_lot_of_toursists.mov` **clip in the second ambience bed.**

   If the Ripple tool is not visible in the Tool palette, click and hold on the Roll tool until the fly-out menu showing the Ripple tool becomes available.

3. **Drag the tail of the clip 15 frames to the left.**

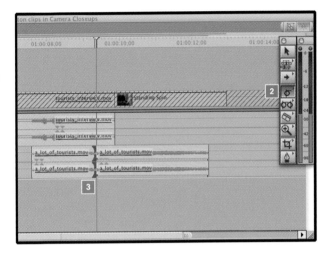

4. **Select the head of the second** `a_lot_of_toursists.mov` **clip with the Ripple tool, and drag the head of the clip 15 frames to the right.**

   You have now shortened the ambience bed by a total of 1 second by removing 15 frames (or one-half second) from each clip. The length of the cross fade you apply is 1 second and blends material before and after the start and end of each clip to create a seamless transition. If you applied the cross fade without shortening the clips, the hoot that you worked so hard to edit out would have snuck back in.

5. **Click the Selection tool, and use it to shift+click both clips in the second ambience bed.**

6. **Choose Modify→Audio→Gain −3dB.**

   This lowers the volume level of the second ambience bed to the same volume level as the first ambience bed.

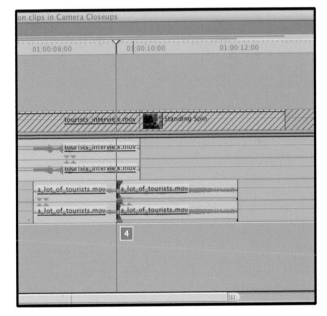

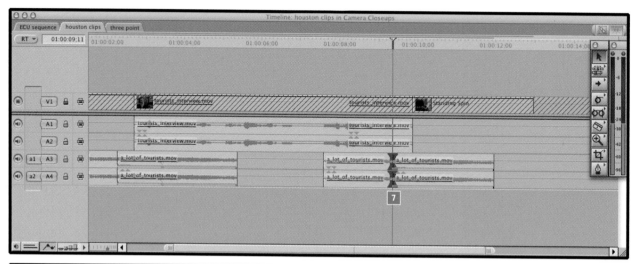

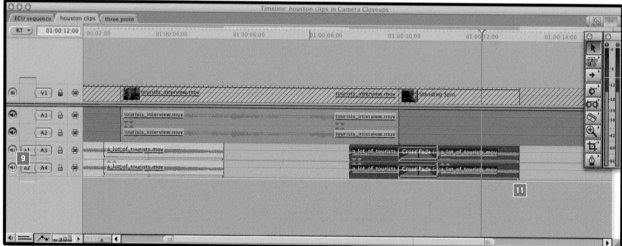

7. **Click the Selection tool in the Tool palette, and use it to select the edit between the two clips.**

8. **Choose Effects→Audio Transitions→Cross Fade (+3dB).**
   Final Cut Pro adds a cross fade to the transition between the two clips. A cross fade blends two clips together seamlessly by combining audio in the Timeline with additional unused audio from each clip. In this case, Final Cut Pro extends each clip by a half-second to create a 1-second overlap in which the outgoing clip fades out and the incoming clip fades in.

9. **Click the Audible controls for Tracks A1 and A2 so the tracks are silent.**

10. **Click the Play In to Out button in the Canvas to listen to both ambience beds.**
    Even though you use the same two clips in each ambience bed, the two ambience beds no longer sound alike, and that's what you want.

11. **Shift+click both clips in the second ambience bed, and drag them to the right until they snap into place and align with the tail of the shot that's on Track V1.**
    All that's left is to fade the ambience bed up from silence at the end of the interview clip.

12. **Click the head of the second ambience bed to select it.**

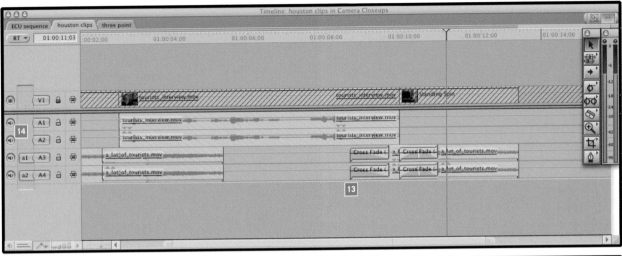

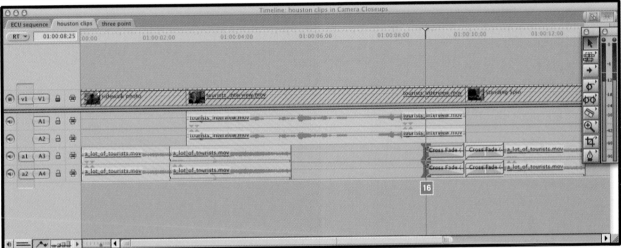

13. **Choose Effects→Audio Transitions→Cross Fade (0dB).**

    Final Cut Pro adds a fade to the head of the clip. Because there's no clip in the Timeline immediately before the frame that you selected, Final Cut Pro fades the audio up from 0 instead of blending it with other sound.

14. **Click the Audible controls for Tracks A1 and A2 so you can hear the interview sound.**

15. **Play the sequence in the Canvas.**

    The second ambience bed fades in nicely, but starts too soon.

16. **Using the Selection tool, click the head of the second ambience bed.**

    The cursor changes to the Roll Tool icon.

17. **Click and drag the head of the clip seven frames to the right.**

    The ambience bed now starts a quarter of a second later, without harming the fade.

18. **Play the sequence in the Canvas.**

    The second ambience bed fades in just as Sonia finishes answering the question and starts to laugh. The audio not only works aesthetically (it sounds great), but it also provides a natural transition from the end of one shot to the beginning of another.

19. **Save the project.**

    In this tutorial, you edited two clips and added a cross fade to create a second ambience bed. The new ambience bed serves the same function as the first, easing the transition into and out of the interview clip, and it sounds different enough so your audience won't think you're recycling material. You also moved the modified clips so the audio fades in just as the interview ends, and continues through the last frame of the final video clip in the sequence. This placement gives the sequence a polished feel and is an excellent example of effective sound design.

Tutorial

» Using the Audio Mixer to Set the Levels of an Entire Clip at Once

One of the great new features of Final Cut Pro 4 is the Audio Mixer. The mixer enables you to dynamically set—and change—the volume levels of the tracks in your sequence as they play in real time. This means you can raise or lower the level of a clip as you listen to it and immediately hear the changes in your mix. In the past, you would have to make the change and then play the sequence back to hear how it sounded. Sometimes—dare I even mention it—editors would have to stop working on their sound all together and wait for the sequence to render. The Audio Mixer in Final Cut Pro 4 makes good sound design significantly more accessible, because you can now mix your entire program, start to finish, in one application. Like they said each week in the opening sequence of *The Six Million Dollar Man,* "We have the technology."

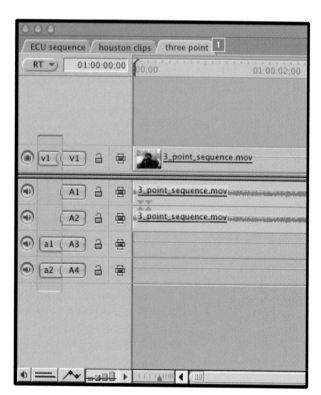

1. **Click the three point tab in the Timeline to bring the three point sequence to the foreground.**

2. **Choose Tools→Audio Mixer.**
   The Audio Mixer opens in the Tool Bench, on top of the Viewer, which is still open underneath.

3. **Choose View→Loop Playback.**
   Once you click the Play button, this sets the material in the Timeline to play back repeatedly until you click the Stop button. Because you haven't set any In or Out points in the Timeline, Final Cut Pro plays the entire three point sequence repeatedly until you click the Stop button. Looped playback is exceptionally helpful when you work with real-time audio. You can make changes to a specific section of your project and refine your mix at length without having to stop and click the Play button each time the sequence ends.

<NOTE>
The term *loop* comes from analog audio when editors would splice the end of a piece of tape to the beginning, and let the tape play over and over.

<TIP>
You can toggle looped playback on and off by pressing Control+L.

<TIP>
Looped playback can be exceptionally annoying to anyone else in the room. Experience has shown that hearing the same audio clip all afternoon is always far more tolerable for the editor than for the editor's colleagues or neighbors. This may be a good time to use headphones.

4. **Play the sequence in the Canvas.**

   The three point sequence plays in a loop. The audio meters for each track display the volume level of the sound at the play-head's current location. Just as in the last sequence you worked on, the natural sound on Tracks A1 and A2 competes with the interview sound on Tracks A3 and A4 because the levels are too close. The first step is to raise the volume of the interview clips.

5. **While the interview audio is playing, raise the faders for Tracks A3 and A4 until the number field below each track displays 4.5.**

   Because the tracks are a stereo pair, when you adjust one of the faders, the other follows. As soon as you make the change, you can hear Final Cut Pro adjust the playback level. Because you edited the audio earlier to shorten a pause, there are now two clips on Tracks A3 and A4, so be sure to change the level for both clips.

<TIP>

You can only change the level of a clip when the playhead is inside that particular clip. If the playhead moves out of the clip before you're finished, don't worry; just try again when the audio loops back.

<TIP>

To reset the changes you made to a track using the Audio Mixer, hold down Control, click the track's fader, and select Reset.

6. **While the interview audio is still playing, lower the level of the natural sound on Tracks A1 and A2 slightly so that their numeric displays read −1.6.**

   Final Cut Pro lowers the natural sound by 1.6dB.

7. **Stop the playback.**

<TIP>

Pressing the spacebar is the shortcut to toggle between Play and Stop.

8. **Save the project.**

   In this tutorial, you used the Audio Mixer to change the sound levels in your sequence in real time. Because the sequence contains no keyframes, any changes you make to the sound levels apply to the entire clip. In the next tutorial, you set different audio levels within the clips as they play back.

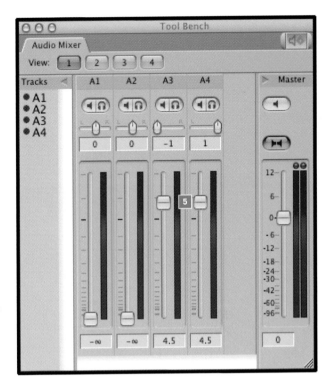

The Audio Mixer, Faders, and Meters

The Audio Mixer contains one fader and one audio meter for each of the tracks in your sequence. In this case, the sequence contains four tracks, so the corresponding four faders and four audio meters appear next to one another in the middle part of the window. This part of the window is called the Track Strips pane. The faders mimic the function of the controls on a physical audio mixing board: When you push them up, the sound on the track they control becomes louder; when you pull them down, the sound becomes quieter. The audio meters work just like the audio meter that you work with in the Timeline. At the bottom of each fader/meter combination, a number field displays the amount by which you have raised or lowered the audio level.

The Audio Mixer also contains a master fader and audio meter, which appear in the right side of the window. These master controls determine the output levels of the combined sounds for your entire project. You don't need to adjust the master controls for this project, but you should look at the master levels to make sure that none of your sound clips get too loud.

Tutorial

» Using the Audio Mixer to Create Complex Volume Control Effects

Setting the Audio Mixer to record audio keyframes enables you to set different levels within a clip and create complicated volume control effects. Final Cut Pro records the changes that you make using the Audio Mixer's faders and adds keyframes to the Timeline. You can revise the changes by adjusting the faders again, or you can manipulate the keyframes directly in the Timeline.

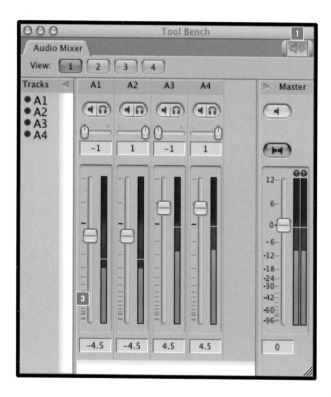

1. **Click the Record Audio Keyframes button in the upper-right corner of the Audio Mixer window.**
   Final Cut Pro now records any changes that you make using the faders and adds appropriate keyframes to the Timeline. Final Cut Pro begins recording each time you hold down the mouse and stops recording when you release it.

2. **Play the sequence.**
   Your goal is to fade the natural sound of the street under the interview audio. Because images of the street remain on-screen, the associated natural sound should not disappear entirely; it should just be low enough that the audience can easily focus on the interview sound.

3. **As soon as the interview sound starts to play, gently lower the faders for the natural sound on Tracks A1 and A2 to –4.5.**
   Try to fade the audio down during the first third of the interview. Once you have lowered the faders to –4.5, leave them in place until the natural sound ends.

4. **Release the mouse, and allow the audio to continue playing.**
   Final Cut Pro automates your recorded fader movements and lowers the faders from –1.5 to –4.5 with each loop of the sequence.

5. **Stop the sequence.**

<TIP>
The real-time mixing controls in Final Cut Pro are nondestructive. If you're not satisfied with a change, just press ⌘+Z and start again.

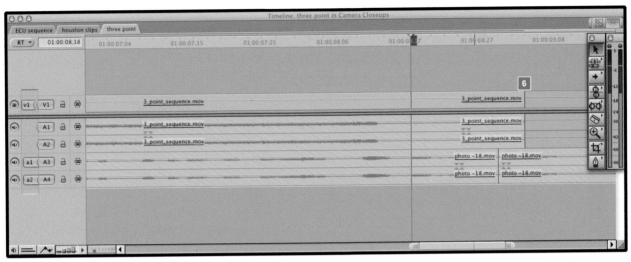

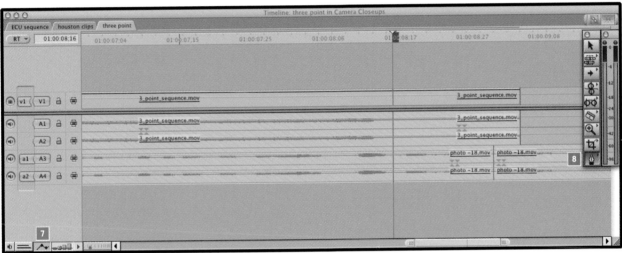

6. **Click the Zoom tool, and use it to select the end of the natural sound in the sequence.**

   If you listen carefully, there's a slight bit of unidentifiable conversation in the background. The audience won't be able to understand what people are saying, but the sound could still divert attention away from the interview. Lowering the volume of this section of audio ensures it doesn't become an issue.

7. **Click the Clip Overlay button in the Timeline.**

   A clip overlay becomes visible on each track. The clip overlay is a thin pink line running horizontally through the center of each audio track, and a thin black line at the top of the video track.

8. **Click the Pen tool at the bottom of the Tool palette.**

   The Pen tool allows you to add keyframes to a clip overlay.

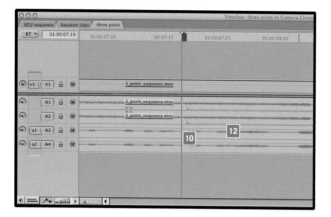

9. **Using the Pen tool, click the Track A1 clip overlay just before the conversation starts (at about 01:00:07;19).**

   Final Cut Pro adds a keyframe where you just clicked. Because the track is part of a stereo pair, Final Cut Pro also adds a keyframe in the same location on Track A2.

10. **Add an additional keyframe a few frames to the right.**

    When you lower the audio level for the remainder of the track in the next step, the change only affects audio to the right of the second keyframe. The area to the left of the first keyframe, including the adjustments you made with the mixer, does not change.

11. **Click the Selection tool in the Tool palette.**

12. **Using the Selection tool, click the clip overlay to the right of the second keyframe and drag the overlay down to the bottom of the track.**

    This silences the end of the clip.

13. **Play the sequence in the Canvas.**

    You successfully removed the conversation at the end of the natural sound clip. In doing so, however, you created an ambience gap at the end of the clip. It's time to fix it.

    < T I P >

    You can also add a keyframe by Option+clicking a clip overlay with the Selection tool.

14. **Double-click the Zoom tool so you can see the entire sequence at once.**

    A reliable way to fix an ambience gap is to place additional ambient sound on a separate track and fade it in. To do this, you need two more tracks.

15. **Choose Sequence→Insert Tracks.**

    The Insert Tracks window opens.

16. **Enter 2 in the Audio Tracks field, and then click OK.**

    Final Cut Pro adds two audio tracks to the sequence.

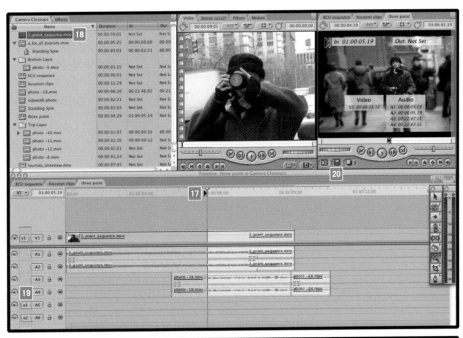

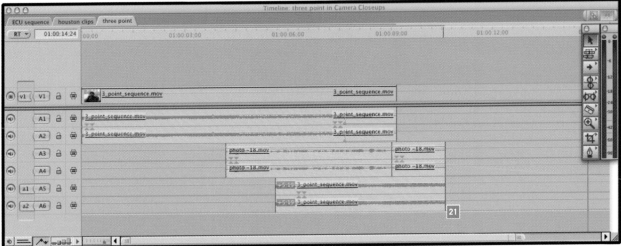

17. **Add an In point to the sequence at 01:00:05;19.**
    The natural sound on Tracks A1 and A2 fades out after
    01:00:07;19. Placing additional natural sound on Tracks A5
    and A6 two seconds earlier gives you time to fade the new
    sound in and cover the gap.

18. **Double-click** 3_point_sequence.mov **in the Browser.**
    The clip opens in the Viewer, replacing the Audio Mixer. The
    mixer is still open; it's just hidden momentarily.

19. **Align Source Controls a1 and a2 with Destination Tracks A5 and A6.**
    This enables you to perform an overwrite edit, adding audio
    from the clip in the Viewer to the two new audio tracks in the
    Timeline. Be sure the video Source control is not connected to
    Track V1.

20. **Click the Overwrite Edit button in the Canvas.**
    Final Cut Pro adds audio to the last two tracks.

21. **Select the Arrow tool from the Tool palette, and drag the tail of the
    audio on Tracks A5 and A6 to the left until the audio ends at the same
    point on the Timeline as the interview dialog on Tracks A3 and A4.**

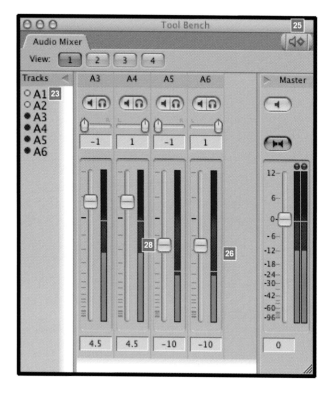

<TIP>
You can resize the Tool Bench window to create a larger display with room for more track strips.

<NOTE>
It may take a few attempts to get the fade just the way you like it. You may decide that it is easier to reposition the keyframes in the Timeline using the Selection tool. Both methods (the Audio Mixer and the Timeline) achieve the same result.

22. **Choose Window→Tool Bench to bring the Audio Mixer out from behind the Viewer.**
    The Audio Mixer now displays faders and audio meters for all your tracks. Depending on your screen resolution, one or more of the tracks may not be visible in the Audio Mixer.

23. **Click the circles next to Tracks A1 and A2 on the left side of the Audio Mixer to hide the track strips for the first two audio tracks.**
    The tracks still play back. (The Audible controls have not been disabled; the tracks are not displayed in the Audio Mixer to save space.)

24. **Play the sequence in the Canvas.**
    As the sequence plays, the new audio you added comes in at full volume, which is the default setting.

25. **Click the Record Audio Keyframes button again to stop recording audio keyframes.**

26. **Lower the volume of the clips on Tracks A5 and A6 to about –10.**
    Because the mixer is not recording keyframes, Final Cut Pro lowers the audio level for the entire clip at once. Now that the clip no longer comes in at full volume, you can fade it in unobtrusively.

27. **Click the Record Audio Keyframes button.**
    In the next step, you use the faders to raise the level gradually, so recording keyframes is important.

28. **When the audio on Tracks A5 and A6 starts to play, slide the fader for one of the tracks up to –4.5.**
    Earlier, you set the natural sound on Tracks A1 and A2 to the same level. By carefully fading the natural sound you just added up to the same level as the existing natural sound in the sequence, the audio blends together seamlessly. If you fade the sound on Tracks A5 and A6 up to –4.5 before the sound on Tracks A1 and A2 fades out, your audience won't know where one clip ends and the other begins.

29. **Stop the playback.**

30. **Save the project.**
    In this tutorial, you used the Audio Mixer and keyframes in the Timeline to create a complicated volume control effect. You seamlessly blended natural sound underneath interview material, and you edited the natural sound to remove any potential distractions. Adding two new tracks of ambient sound to the sequence enabled you to mix supplemental audio under the interview and to subtly fill in a gap in your background sound. The volume control effects you added to the sequence in this tutorial are so complex that your audience will most likely never realize you made any changes to the sound.

Discussion
Knowing When to Add Sound and When to Let Your Film "Breathe"

Sound breaks down into two broad categories: foreground sound and background sound. Foreground sound, such as dialog or narration, draws the audience's full attention. Background sound, such as environmental sound or music that doesn't dominate the sequence, adds to the material on-screen without drawing attention to itself.

Video almost always needs some type of sound to accompany it, because if all the sound in your sequence suddenly drops out, it looks like a mistake. The ambience beds you created and reshaped in the last few tutorials are good examples of background sound—they add to your audience's viewing experience without becoming the focus of the show. The key to a successful sound mix is knowing what type of sound a sequence needs and understanding when to use foreground sound and when not to.

In the 1931 film *M,* police are unable to apprehend a child murderer, so the city's other criminals work together to stop him because he's bad for business. The film, directed by Fritz Lang, holds up today as a brilliantly stylish and exciting thriller—except for some parts of the climactic chase scenes that appear without any audio. The film was completed shortly after the introduction of sound in motion pictures, and sound design was still in its infancy. When the mob of criminals scours the city for Peter Lorre, the killer, there are times when the film goes completely silent—no footsteps, no traffic sounds or distant conversations, nothing other than the image on the screen. If the film were redone today, you can imagine what it would sound like. Filmmakers use audio to set the emotional tone just as effectively as they use images.

At the same time, some sound designers overdo it and add way too much audio. Have you ever seen a show with tons of foreground sound crammed into every available second of video? At the first pause in the action, the editor adds some narration. When there isn't enough excitement on-screen, the editor adds a song. This is a recipe for an overcrowded sound mix. The viewers never get a chance to slow down and absorb what they've taken in, so often they mentally tune out, or worse, walk away with a headache.

Stepping back and letting a sequence play with no foreground audio is sometimes referred to as letting the film "breathe." There are times when the action on-screen and its accompanying ambient sound should be enough to carry the film on its own. Adding some breathing room to your film can also help you build up to a big climactic moment. Once your audience gets used to a subtle use of natural sound and ambience, any foreground audio you add becomes especially notice-able. A graphic designer once pointed out to me that if everything on the page is bold, then nothing is really bold anymore. The same is true in sound design: If everything is a big explosion of audio, then nothing in the film stands out. A rich sound design makes effective use of silences as well as crescendos.

Tutorial

» Fine-Tuning the Audio Tracks at the Subframe Level

Occasionally when you make a precise edit, you may find that a pop or some other unwanted sound has appeared as a result of the cut. You may also find that a recording contains an exceptionally brief unwanted sound surrounded by material you want to use. In both cases, subframe audio adjustments can remedy the situation. Because Final Cut Pro is a video-editing program, each edit is based on a particular frame. Subframe audio operations enable you to zoom in and perform edits on sections of audio that are even smaller than one frame, meaning you can edit even more precisely than $\frac{1}{30}$ of a second.

1. **Bring the playhead to about 01:00:09;01 in the Timeline, the point where you shortened the pause in the interview clip on Tracks A3 and A4.**

   There's a very slight tick in the tail of the outgoing clip that you remove in this tutorial.

2. **Double-click the first instance of the interview clip in the Timeline (the clip on tracks A3 and A4 to the left of the playhead's current location).**

   The clip's waveform opens in the Viewer. The playhead in the Viewer is at the same location in the clip as the playhead in the Timeline. Notice how the waveform is not flat at the Out point of the clip? That small plateau in the waveform represents a barely noticeable tick in the audio. Silencing the tick removes an imperfection that people may not consciously notice but that nonetheless detracts from the quality of the audio in the sequence.

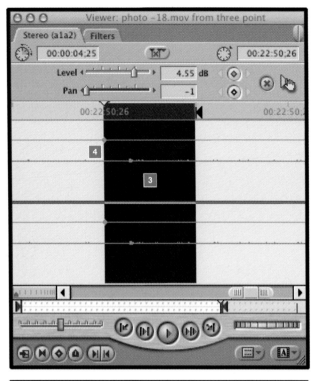

3. **Zoom in as far as possible on the playhead's current location in the Viewer by using the Zoom tool or by pressing ⌘++ multiple times.**
   Part of the waveform appears highlighted. That highlighted area represents a single frame of video, approximately ⅓₀ of a second in length.

4. **Add a keyframe at the playhead's current location.**
   Final Cut Pro adds a keyframe at the left edge of the shaded area. The slightly raised area in the waveform inside the shaded area represents the tick at the tail of the first clip. To surround the area with keyframes so that you can silence it, you need to move the playhead in increments smaller than one frame.

5. **Hold down Shift, and drag the shaded area to the right, positioning the left edge of the shaded area just before the start of the tick.**

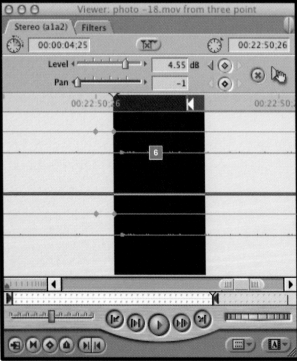

6. **Add another keyframe.**
   Now that you have two keyframes, you can silence the tick without changing the audio level for the rest of the clip.

7. **Drag the clip overlay after the second keyframe to the bottom of the track.**

   The audio to the right of the second keyframe is now silenced. The audio to the left of the first keyframe remains unchanged, meaning the interview audio continues to play back at full volume.

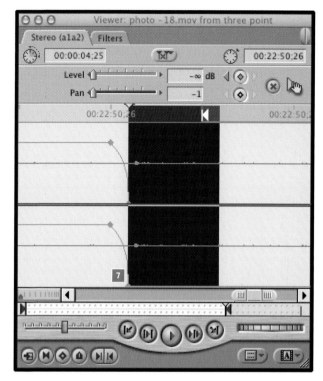

8. **Add two more keyframes immediately before the end of the clip.**

9. **Raise the last keyframe to 4dB so the audio matches the level of the rest of the clip.**

   You have now lowered and raised the audio levels inside the space of one frame.

10. **Play the sequence.**

    The interview transitions from one clip to another, tick-free.

11. **Save the project.**

    By editing at the subframe level, you removed a problem without damaging the material around it. Frame-accurate was once the standard for precision editing. In this tutorial, you performed edits that were subframe-accurate. You now have complete control over the sounds you include in the sequence and the sounds you take out.

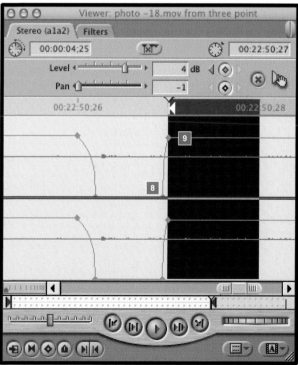

Tutorial
» Using the Vocal DeEsser Audio Filter

Final Cut Pro comes with a full suite of audio filters designed to help you solve problems and create effective sequences. One helpful filter is the Vocal DeEsser, which is so named because it reduces overly pronounced *s* sounds in audio clips. Did you ever notice that when snakes talk in cartoons, they overemphasize *s* sounds in words so that it seems as if they're hissing? Some people do the same thing—generally to a much lesser degree—and some microphones add to the problem by accentuating high frequencies. The Vocal DeEsser filter reduces the frequencies that cause overaccentuated *s* sounds, but it does not eliminate them. If it did, you would have no *s* sounds in your clip.

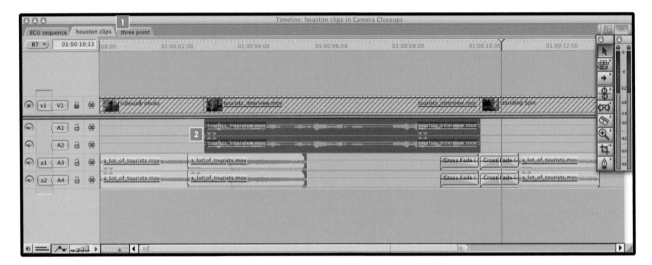

1. **Click the houston clips tab in the Timeline to bring the sequence to the front.**

2. **Select the interview clip on Tracks A1 and A2.**

3. **Play the sequence in the Canvas.**
   The interview clip contains a few prominent *s* sounds—including style, some, and tourists. The Vocal DeEsser filter takes the edge off these sounds and makes them less noticeable.

4. **Double-click one of the audio tracks for the interview clip to open it in the Viewer.**

5. **Click the Filters tab in the Viewer.**
   The Filters tab opens and displays any filters that are applied to the clip. Because you have not applied any yet, no filters appear in the list.

6. **Choose Effects→Audio Filters→Final Cut Pro→Vocal DeEsser.**
   The Vocal DeEsser is listed in the Viewer's Effects tab, along with sliders for different parameters. Depending on the severity of the sounds you want to adjust, you can increase the Ratio and Emphasis sliders.

7. **In the Vocal DeEsser filter, set the Ratio slider to 4.51 and the Emphasis slider to 10.**

< T I P >
You can also adjust the parameters of a filter by entering numeric values directly into the parameter fields, instead of using the sliders.

8. **Play the sequence in the Canvas.**
   The *s* sounds are now greatly reduced.

< N O T E >
If you bring the Ratio and Emphasis sliders to their highest settings, the *s* sounds are almost completely removed, as if Sonia left the *s* sounds out of her interview.

< T I P >
You can easily reset any Final Cut Pro effect to its factory default by clicking the Reset button (it looks like a red X).

< T I P >
You can temporarily turn off an effect by deselecting its check box the Effects tab. You may do this to compare the clip with the effect, to the clip without the effect. When you re-click the check box, the effect will once again apply to the clip, using your most recent settings.

9. **Save the project.**
   In this tutorial, you added an audio effect to a clip in the sequence, reducing an overemphasized *s* sound, which is also referred to as *sibilant*. Final Cut Pro also has a similar effect, called a Vocal DePopper filter, that removes overemphasized *p* sounds.

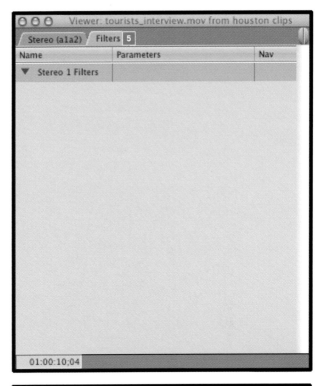

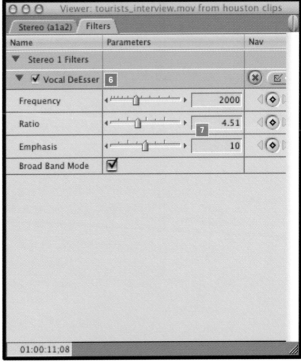

Discussion

Why Film Must Sound Better than Real Life

When you go to the movies, you don't pay $10 a ticket to listen to mistakes, and let's face it, neither does your audience. Part of the reason people like to watch movies (including good documentaries) is because the world on-screen looks and sounds better than the world we live in. This enables cinematographers and sound recordists to make a living.

In daily life, the human brain does a remarkable job of filtering out bad audio. You can have a conversation with someone at work without being distracted by the sound of the air conditioner or the hum from an overhead lighting fixture. Your brain understands that these are everyday background sounds and separates them from the foreground audio of the conversation. If your brain couldn't perform this function and separate noise from speech, you wouldn't be able to make sense of anything. Your world would just be audio pandemonium.

People respond to recorded audio all together differently. Think of the audio you worked on in this session. Before you adjusted the levels to distinguish the foreground audio from the background audio, you couldn't understand the dialog clearly. When an audience watches a film or video, the combined audio tracks form one sound. People don't listen to the interview on Track A1 and tune out the street ambience on Track A4—they listen to the mix that you created. If that mix contains the sound of an air conditioner and the hum of an electric light, and these sounds are competing with dialog for your audience's attention, people who are watching your project may have a hard time understanding what people on the screen are saying. Problems in your mix stand out and so do mistakes in content.

The news director of the radio station I worked for told me about a time he visited his mother while she was watching the *Today Show*. There was a substitute host who stumbled as he spoke. The news director's mother looked at the host and asked, "What's wrong with this guy?" She was a tough audience. Everybody knows that people stumble as they speak, but the news director's mother was used to the regular host of the *Today Show* who spoke without mistakes. Even though making mistakes is more common, and in daily life less noticeable than perfect speech, a mistake on TV stands out because it's an exception. Hollywood movies and network TV shows spend countless dollars on audio production to make sure each sound is perfect. So much attention is paid to audio production that people are even hired to theatrically create new sound for audio that may be missing, and other people are paid to lay the new and improved sound back onto the picture.

Every line of speech, every footstep, and the background ambience of every room are carefully scrutinized and, if necessary, re-created.

Into this environment steps your project. People in our culture watch TV and movies nonstop from their early childhood onward, and they quickly grow accustomed to perfect audio. When an audience watches your work, people expect the sound to be equally perfect. If not, mistakes really stand out. Whether consciously or not, audiences notice good sound design. Paying careful attention to audio is a good way to give your audience what it wants.

» Session Review

This session addressed the finer points of audio editing. You used a variety of tools to change the audio level of an entire clip and used keyframes to set multiple levels within a single clip. You also used Final Cut Pro's new Audio Mixer to dynamically change audio levels in real time. By using each of these techniques, you created a complex volume control effect to remove unwanted background conversation from your sequence and replaced it with unobtrusive ambience. This section of the course also addressed the subject of when you should add sound to your work and when you should just let things be. Last but not least, you worked at the subframe level to remove a tick in the audio, and you applied the Vocal DeEsser audio filter to deemphasize a harsh *s* sound in the interview. As I mentioned in the final discussion, film must sound better than real life. This session showed you how to make sure your sound works exactly the way it should.

The following questions are provided to help you review the information in this session. Answers for each question are found in the tutorial noted in parentheses.

1. What are three ways to adjust the audio level of an entire clip in the Viewer? (See Tutorial: Adjusting the Volume of an Entire Clip)

2. When audio "clips," what happens? (See Tutorial: Adjusting the Volume of an Entire Clip)

3. How can you add keyframes to the Timeline using the Selection tool? (See Tutorial: Setting Different Volume Levels Within a Clip)

4. How does adding keyframes change your ability to alter the volume levels within a clip? (See Tutorial: Setting Different Volume Levels Within a Clip)

5. How does a cross fade use handles to blend two clips together? (See Tutorial: Working with Audio Effects)

6. What are two ways that you can change the level of a sound using the Modify menu? (See Tutorial: Setting Different Volume Levels Within a Clip, and Tutorial: Working with Audio Effects)

7. What is the purpose of the faders in the Audio Mixer? (See Tutorial: Using the Audio Mixer to Set the Levels of an Entire Clip at Once)

8. How does looped audio help an editor mix in real time? (See Tutorial: Using the Audio Mixer to Set the Levels of an Entire Clip at Once)

9. When you click the Record Audio Keyframes button, what happens? (See Tutorial: Using the Audio Mixer to Create Complex Volume Control Effects)

10. Why would it benefit you to use keyframes in the Timeline in conjunction with the Audio Mixer? (See Tutorial: Using the Audio Mixer to Create Complex Volume Control Effects)

11. Other than pressing ⌘+Z, how can you reset changes that you made to a clip using the Audio Mixer? (See Tutorial: Using the Audio Mixer to Set the Levels of an Entire Clip at Once)

12. How can you set more than one keyframe inside one frame of audio? (See Tutorial: Fine-Tuning the Audio Tracks at the Subframe Level)

13. How does the Vocal DeEsser audio filter reduce problematic *s* sounds in a sequence? (See Tutorial: Using the Vocal DeEsser Audio Filter)

14. Why would it be a problem if the Vocal DeEsser filter removed all the *s* sounds from a clip? (See Tutorial: Using the Vocal DeEsser Audio Filter)

Part V:
Creating and Animating Titles

Working with Titles

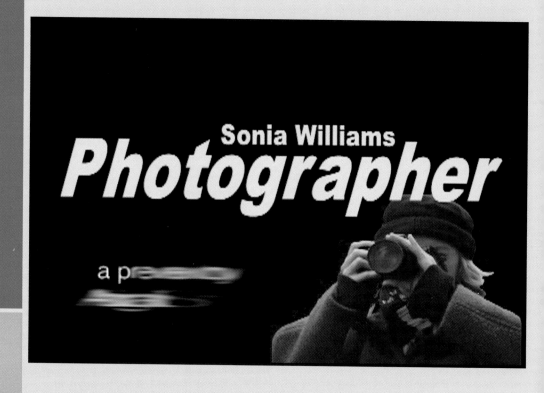

Session Introduction

A title is something that no film or video can live without. At its most basic level, the title tells your audience the name of your project. A good title also serves a number of other functions, primarily, helping to establish an identity for your project. Who doesn't remember the title sequence from *Star Wars*? A good title tells people what a film is about, and the presentation of your title can also set an engaging visual tone. In this session, you learn the ins and outs of title creation, and you use a variety of tools as you build the main title sequence for the *Sonia Williams: Photographer* project. In the following tutorials, you use elements created in other programs and learn how to work with them in Final Cut Pro.

TOOLS YOU'LL USE
Timeline window, Canvas window, Wireframe mode, Source controls, Destination Track controls, Choose a File dialog box, Insert Tracks dialog box, LiveType Fonts tab, LiveType Effects tab, LiveType preview window

MATERIALS NEEDED
Session 8 folder on the FCP Complete Course CD,
title_text.png, transparent_sonia.psd

TIME REQUIRED
90 minutes

Discussion

Maintaining Your Visual Style

There's no single way to make a good title. As the editor, you set the visual tone of your project, and the title is no exception. Final Cut Pro ships with a broad array of title tools, giving you a tremendous amount of latitude in controlling the look and feel of the title graphics. Final Cut Pro also works well with Adobe Photoshop, enabling you to integrate edited Photoshop images into your sequences and combine them with your title graphics.

With all the options available to you, the trick is to not only come up with cool graphics and titles but also to work the titles into the visual style of your project. If you use the same visual style for the main title, the ending credits, and any intertitles or lower-third IDs, your project looks really well put together.

In the movie *Boomerang,* a friend's father tells Eddie Murphy the key to fashion success is "to coordinate." To emphasize the point, he notes that the mushroom print on his belt exactly matches the mushroom print lining of his jacket. I'm not suggesting you go that far. You don't need to use the same font, the same size, or even the same color for each title. As long as the titles fit together visually, and the audience can easily identify a common visual style, you're all set.

As you work to establish a consistent style for your title graphics, keep in mind that the style of your titles should match the content of your program. For example, a project about medieval England may not be the best place for space-age animated text. This doesn't mean that your titles should be predictable, and it certainly doesn't mean that your titles should be boring. The title-creation capabilities of Final Cut Pro bring some powerful tools to your repertoire. Put them to good use.

Tutorial

» Building the Main Title: Images

In the Confidence Builder, you used Final Cut Pro's title generator to create animated text for your company logo. In this tutorial, you bring in two highly styled images: one that was created in a vector graphics creation program called Macromedia Fireworks and another that was created in Adobe Photoshop, the industry-standard photo-editing program. Together, these images make up the main title. Using these images together demonstrates how well Final Cut Pro handles complex images that were created in other programs and shows that you know how to create a professional title.

1. **Choose File➔New➔Sequence.**
   Final Cut Pro adds a new sequence to the Browser.

2. **Name the sequence** main title**.**
   The name of the sequence appears highlighted in the Browser, so any text you type becomes the title once you press Return.

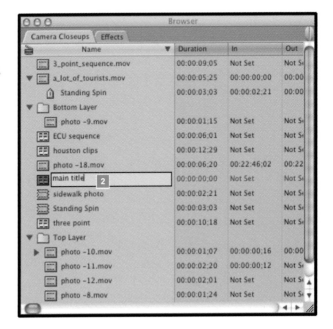

3. **Double-click the main title sequence in the Browser to open it in the Timeline.**
   A blank sequence opens. Now you're ready to import the graphics.

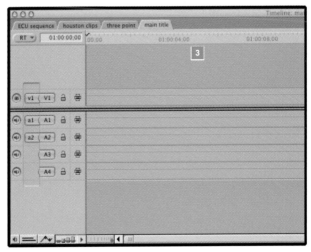

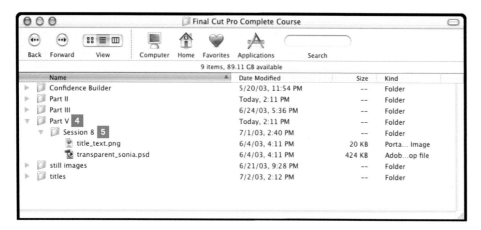

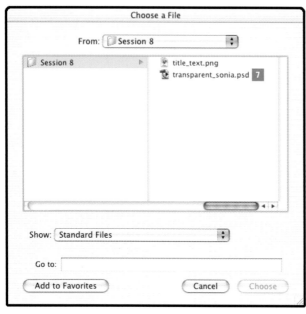

4. **Navigate to the Final Cut Pro Complete Course folder on your hard drive, and create a new subfolder named Part V.**

5. **Insert the FCP Complete Course CD into your computer, and drag the Session 8 folder from Part V into the new folder that you created on your hard drive.**

6. **Go back to Final Cut Pro, and choose File→Import→Files.**
   The Choose a File dialog box opens.

7. **In the Choose a File dialog box, navigate to the Session 8 folder that you just dragged to your hard drive and select** `title_text.png` **and** `transparent_sonia.psd`**. Click the Choose button in the dialog box to finish importing the images.**
   The `title_text.png` file contains the text of the main title graphic, and `transparent_sonia.psd` is a photo of the photographer on a transparent background. Editing images in another program extends the title-creation abilities of Final Cut Pro. When you import the images into Final Cut Pro, the application creates video clips for each image, which you soon combine with other elements to create a very slick title.

8. **Create a new bin in the Browser named title, and place the files** title_text.png **and** transparent_sonia.psd **in the title bin.**

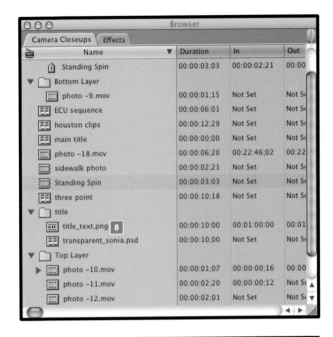

9. **Add an In point in the Timeline at 01:00:00:19.**

10. **Open the title bin, drag** transparent_sonia.psd **onto Track V1, and align the head of the clip with the playhead.**
The first image in the sequence—and thus the preview—is this image of the photographer with her camera. Waiting almost a second to introduce the first image of the preview makes its appearance especially dramatic.

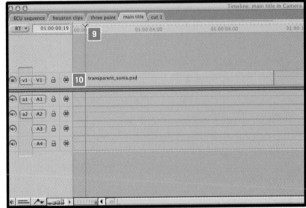

11. **Choose Sequence→Insert Tracks to open the Insert Tracks dialog box.**

12. **Enter 1 in the Video Tracks field, leave After Last Track selected, and click OK.**
Final Cut Pro adds an additional video track above the current video track in the Timeline.

<TIP>
You can also add a new video track by control-clicking the gray area above your top track and selecting Add Track.

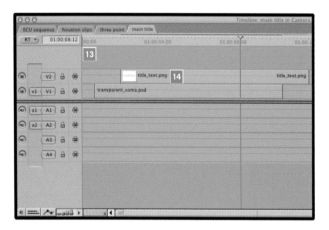

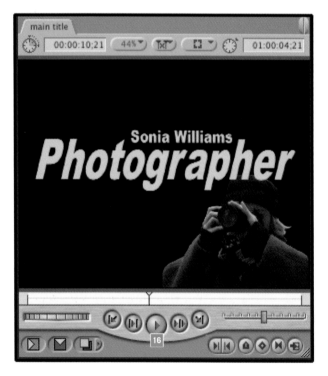

13. **Add an additional In point at 01:00:02;01.**

14. **Drag** `title_text.png` **onto Track V2 so that the head of the clip aligns with the playhead.**

    The Timeline now contains two video clips that display simultaneously. Both images were created using transparent backgrounds. Because the default background in Final Cut Pro is black, the photographer (the bottom-layer image) appears against a black background. Because the image on the top track (the text) also uses a transparent background, you can see both images at the same time. Depending on your system, you may need to render the sequence before you can play it back.

    < N O T E >
    The red line above the clip on Track V2 indicates that you need to render the sequence before you can play it.

15. **Choose Sequence→Render→Video.**

    Final Cut Pro generates a composite image of the two clips that you can now play back as full-speed, broadcast-quality video.

16. **Play the sequence in the Canvas.**

    One clip appears, followed closely by the other. The text may appear with slightly jagged edges in the Canvas, but don't worry, the edges really are smooth. Final Cut Pro sometimes draws text at a slightly lower level of quality during playback so as not to overload the computer. To see what the file looks like when it's finished, export the file as a QuickTime movie, as you did in the Confidence Builder.

17. **Save the project.**

    In this tutorial, you imported two complex graphics created in other programs and added them to the Timeline. Leave the project open for the next tutorial where you add sound to make the opening of your movie even more dynamic.

Tutorial
» Building the Main Title: Sound Effects

A good title sequence consists of more than just a shot or two of video. Combining styled text with carefully edited images and well-chosen sound produces a much more effective result. In this tutorial, you add audio effects to the title sequence to make it really sharp. Your opening sequence sets the tone for the entire project—if you can hook your audience now and engage them immediately, they're much more likely to pay attention to the rest of your work.

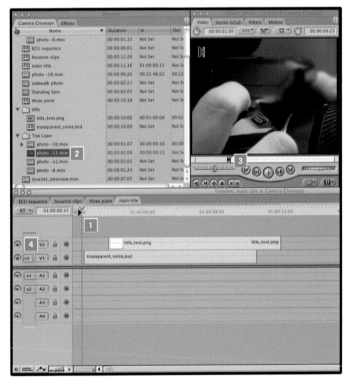

1. **Mark an In point in the sequence at 01:00:00;15.**

   In the final version of the preview, both images are accompanied by the sound of film advancing in the photographer's camera. Adding the sound a fraction of a second before the first frame of the image enables the viewer's brain to process one element before the next appears. Placing both the sound and the image in the Timeline in the same spot may be a little much for the viewer to digest.

2. **Double-click** photo -11.mov **to open the clip in the Viewer.**

3. **Add an In point in the Viewer at 00:00:00;23.**

   A great camera sound begins in this frame.

4. **Disconnect Source Control v1 from Destination Track V1.**

   In the next step you perform an overwrite edit. Disconnecting Source Control v1 prevents you from accidentally adding any video to the sequence.

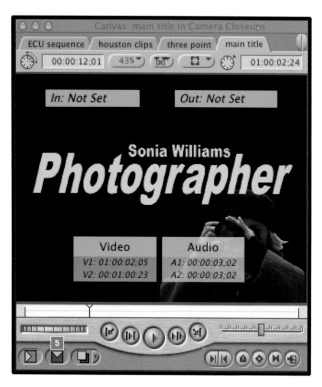

5. **Click the Overwrite Edit button.**

   Final Cut Pro adds the sound to Tracks A1 and A2, just before the first clip appears.

6. **Add an In point to the sequence at 01:00:01;27, just before `title_text.png` appears.**

7. **Align Source Controls a1 and a2 with Tracks A3 and A4.**

8. **Click the Overwrite Edit button.**

   Final Cut Pro adds the camera sound from `photo -11.mov` to Tracks A3 and A4 just before the second image appears on-screen.

9. **Click the Play In to Out button in the Canvas to play the sequence.**

   Both images appear on-screen accompanied by a camera sound, which is entirely appropriate for a movie about a photographer and demonstrates significant attention to detail.

10. **Save the project.**

    In this tutorial, you constructed a richly textured sequence of images and sounds that work together to pique the audience's interest in the preview they're about to watch. Adding sound effects to precise locations in the Timeline focuses the audience's attention on the images that appear in time with each sound. Giving people in the audience more than what they expect is a great way to win them over.

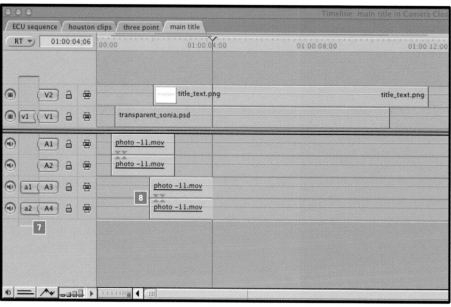

Tutorial

» Using LiveType: Creating Text

Final Cut Pro 4 ships with a new title-creation program called LiveType. LiveType lets you easily go beyond the basics of creating a static title, providing you with the ability to turn your titles into stylish motion graphics. In the Confidence Builder, you used Final Cut Pro's title tool to create an animated logo. In this tutorial, you use LiveType to create a dynamic credit for yourself in the opening sequence of the *Sonia Williams: Photographer* preview.

1. **Open the LiveType application.**

   LiveType is designed specifically for use with Final Cut Pro. When LiveType opens, you're presented with a new, blank project.

2. **Click the Fonts tab in the Media Browser.**

   LiveType displays a list of fonts that you can choose from.

3. **Select Arial from the Family menu.**

   LiveType displays a sample of the font that you choose at the top of the Media Browser window. LiveType also displays a sample sentence written in the selected font at the bottom of the window.

<NOTE>

The list of fonts on the Fonts tab displays choices that are available from your computer's list of system fonts. You can apply an almost unlimited array of styles and effects to fully customize these fonts as you like.

Title-safe boundary

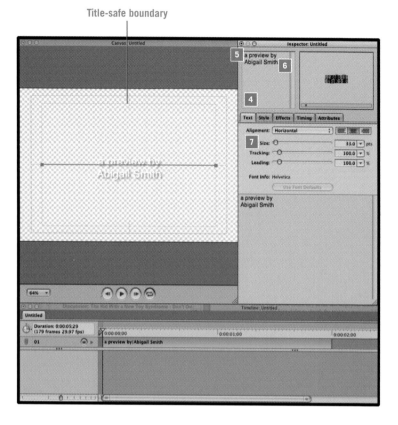

4. **Click in the text box at the upper-left corner of the Inspector window.**

5. **Type** a preview by**, and press Return.**

    The text that you type in this box appears in the LiveType Canvas in the font that you chose in Step 3. Pressing Return starts any additional text on a new line, making it easier to fit on the screen. Your text also appears on a track in the LiveType Timeline, which functions much like the Timeline in Final Cut Pro.

6. **Type your name.**

    Give credit where credit is due, and take your place in the limelight. Because you pressed Return in the previous step, your name appears on a second line of text.

7. **Drag the Size slider to the left to shrink the text to a manageable size.**

    The text in the example is set to 33 points (pts). You can use a larger or smaller size, just be sure your text fits the title-safe area of the Canvas—anything beyond those borders may be cut off. This text ultimately goes in the lower-left corner of your preview, but don't worry about the placement for now— you adjust that in Final Cut Pro.

< N O T E >

The viewable area in the LiveType Canvas window, as well as in Final Cut Pro's Canvas and Viewer windows, is larger than what audiences see on their television monitors. As a result, the images you see in LiveType and Final Cut Pro are slightly different than what displays on a video monitor. Title safe refers to a smaller area of the screen in which you can safely position your titles, without having the edges cut off. The title-safe area, and making your work title safe is explained in depth in session 9.

< N O T E >

You can also adjust the size of the text in Final Cut Pro, so you can decide to change it later if the size you set now isn't perfect.

8. **Choose File→Save to save the project.**

   The Save as dialog box opens.

9. **Create a subfolder named titles in the Final Cut Pro Complete Course folder on your hard drive.**

   You create a new subfolder on your computer's hard drive—
   "titles" does not refer to the bin you created in the Browser.

10. **Name the project** a_preview_by.

11. **Click Save to close the dialog box and save your project.**

    You selected a font and used it to create a basic title in
    LiveType. In the following tutorials, you animate this title and
    add it to the opening sequence of the preview.

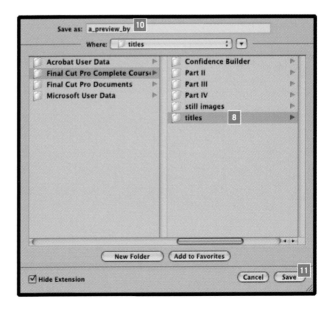

When and How Often to Use Lower-Third IDs

A *lower-third ID* is text used to identify a person on-screen. When
you watch an interview and identifying text appears below the
speaker (for example, Jodi Miller, Art Director), that text is an
example of a lower-third ID. The idea is to use a short line of text
to provide the audience with information that helps to explain a
person's presence in your show.

The same people often appear on-screen in more than one
sequence, and when they do, you don't need to add a new lower-
third ID each time. Veteran documentary filmmaker Bill Jersey
developed the "20-minute rule"—he gives a person a lower-third
ID in their first appearance and doesn't give the person another
unless they've been off-screen for at least 20 minutes.

A lower-third ID, or *lower-third* for short, doesn't need to appear at
the bottom of the screen. As you develop the visual style of your
project, you may decide to creatively place your lower-thirds in
the upper-right or upper-left corner of the screen, or somewhere
else that fits the needs of your production. Ideally, if you use
lower-thirds, you can incorporate them into your design in a way
that adds to the audience's understanding of your story without
focusing attention away from the content of your work. Just as you
work to create a sound design so carefully manipulated that the
audience thinks your sound is naturally perfect, a good lower-third
works its way onto the screen so naturally that people take it for
granted.

Tutorial

» Using LiveType: Adding Effects

At the start of the preceding tutorial, I made LiveType sound pretty cool. At this point, you may be asking what the hype is all about, because so far, the title that you created is just some basic text. The power of LiveType comes from its ability to animate titles, and the extent to which you can customize the titles you create. In this tutorial, you add effects to produce a dynamic end product.

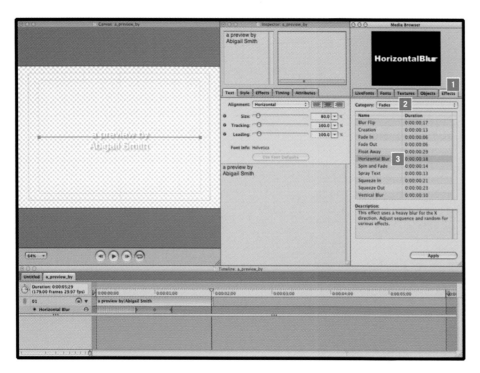

1. **Click the Effects tab in the Media Browser.**

2. **Choose Fades from the Category drop-down menu.**
   A list of preconfigured fade effects that can add to the text in your project appears.

3. **Double-click Horizontal Blur to apply the Horizontal Blur effect to your text.**
   A new track labeled Horizontal Blur appears in the Timeline underneath your text. LiveType applies each of the preconfig-ured effects to its own track in the Timeline.

4. **Choose File→Render Preview→Normal.**
   LiveType generates a preview of the effect. When the preview is ready for you to watch, it opens in a new window.

5. **Click the Play button in the preview window.**
   Your text fades into view and into focus. Now all you need is a fade out, and you're ready for the big time.

6. **Close the preview window by clicking the button in the upper left corner of the window.**

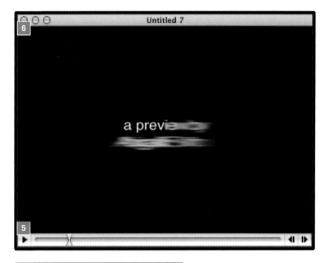

7. **Click Fade Out in the list on the Effects tab in the Media Browser.**

8. **Click Apply to add the effect to your text.**
   LiveType adds a third track that contains the Fade Out effect to the Timeline.

9. **Choose File→Render Preview→Normal to render another preview so you can see how the fade looks in combination with the Horizontal Blur effect.**
   Everything looks cool, but one effect blends into the next so quickly that it's hard to read the text. This demonstrates the essential challenge of title design—things have to look good *and* be readable.

10. **Click the tail of the Horizontal Blur track, and slide it back to about 0:00:01;00.**
    This shortens the first effect to 1 second.

11. **Click the head of the Fade Out effect, and slide it to the right to approximately 0:00:01;15.**
    This shortens the fade out, and more importantly, leaves the text on-screen for a full half-second between the end of the first effect and the start of the second effect. This makes it much easier for your audience to read the text.

12. **Render a preview of the title.**
    Both effects still look good, and your credit is now fully legible.

13. **Save the project.**
    Adding two preconfigured effects changed this credit from a static element to a dynamic, visually appealing part of your opening sequence. Adjusting the length of each effect enabled you to tailor the effects' parameters to fit the needs of your sequence.

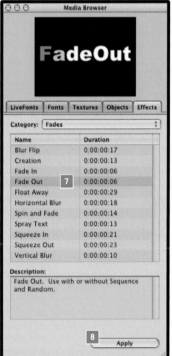

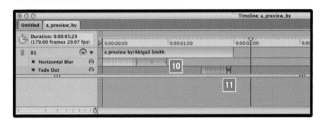

Tutorial

» Using LiveType: Rendering and Adding the Title to Your Project

Your title is now ready to go. All you need to do is export the title, bring it into Final Cut Pro, and add the title to your Timeline. When LiveType generates a render preview, it creates a file that you can watch to see what your title looks like, but the preview isn't something that you can bring into Final Cut Pro. In this tutorial, you export a file that is compatible with the rest of the video in your Final Cut Pro project.

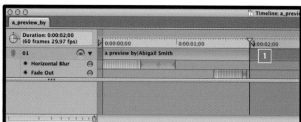

1. **Move the playhead to the last frame in the sequence, 2 seconds into the Timeline, and add an Out point.**
   By default, LiveType adds an In point at the beginning of the Timeline.

2. **Choose File→Render Movie.**
   The Save dialog box opens.

3. **In the Save dialog box, name the file** a_preview_by.mov. **Save the file in the titles folder with the LiveType project file.**
   Be sure that the Render Only Between In/Out Points check box is selected at the bottom of the Save dialog box, so LiveType only renders the area that you selected in the Timeline instead of the blank space that follows.

4. **Click the Create new movie file button to render the movie.**
   When LiveType has rendered the movie, the movie automatically opens full size in a new window.

5. **Play the completed movie in its new window.**
   Pretty cool, isn't it?

6. **Save the project, and quit LiveType.**

7. **Return to Final Cut Pro.**

8. **Choose File→Import→Files.**
   The Choose a File dialog box opens.

9. **Navigate to the titles folder you created, and double-click a_preview_by.mov to import the file.**
   The file appears in the Browser window.

10. **Insert a new video track after the last track.**
    This is where you place the new title.

11. **Align Source Control v1 with the new video track, V3.**

12. **Disconnect Source Controls a1 and a2 so you don't change the audio in the sequence.**

13. **Drag the a_preview_by.mov clip from the Browser to Track V3 so it starts about 4 seconds into the sequence.**

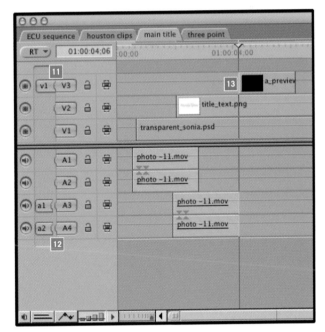

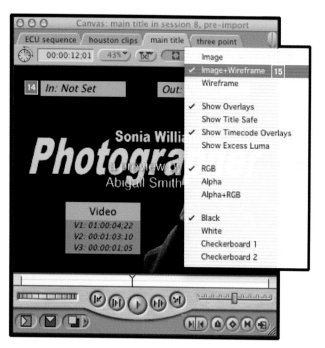

14. **Use the arrow keys on the keyboard to scroll through the sequence and preview the clip you just added.**

    Because the Timeline now contains material on all three video tracks, Final Cut Pro must render the sequence before you can play it back. As you scroll through, it becomes obvious that the new title appears in the wrong spot, smack dab in the middle of the main title. No problem—you just need to adjust the center point of the clip.

15. **Click the View button at the top of the Canvas, and choose Image+Wireframe from the pop-up menu that appears.**

    A wireframe is an outline of an object. In the next step, you use a wireframe to adjust the center point of the title you just added to the sequence.

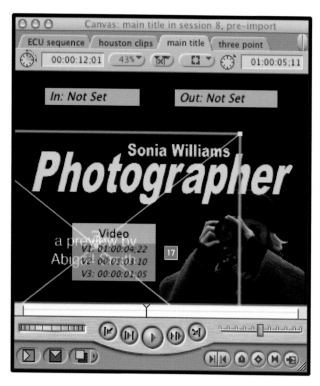

16. **Click the a_preview_by.mov clip in the Timeline.**

    The clip's wireframe appears in the Canvas.

17. **Click inside the Canvas, and drag the clip toward the lower-left corner so that it resembles the figure.**

    Don't bring the clip too far down or too far over. If you do, you can drag it off screen and cut off the edges.

18. **Scroll through the clip using the playhead or the arrow keys.**

    Now that you've adjusted the clip's position, the text fades into view and disappears without interfering with the other elements in the title.

19. **Choose Sequence→Render All→Video.**

    Final Cut Pro renders the new title into your opening title sequence.

20. **Click the Play In to Out button in the Canvas to play the sequence.**

    Your new title fades elegantly into and out of view. Nice work!

21. **Save the project.**

    In this tutorial, you exported a finished title animation from LiveType and imported it into Final Cut Pro. Your newly created animation works well with the rest of your title sequence, making your project look very professional.

» Session Review

One of the programs you use in this session is LiveType, a new text-animation program that ships with Final Cut Pro 4. LiveType helps you to create professional-quality animated titles and easily incorporate them into your Final Cut Pro projects. Working with elements created in additional programs, such as LiveType and Photoshop, enables you to expand the capabilities of Final Cut Pro and create a title design specifically tailored to your project. Adding sound to the project, as you did in this session, brings an extra layer of detail and thoroughness to your work.

The following questions can help you review what you learned in this session. The answer to each question is located in the tutorial or discussion noted in parentheses.

1. Why did you need to render the main title sequence you created in the first tutorial? (See Tutorial: Building the Main Title: Images)

2. Why don't the edges of the text you imported look smooth, even after you render the sequence? (See Tutorial: Building the Main Title: Images)

3. Will the edges of the text you imported look jagged when you export the finished product? (See Tutorial: Building the Main Title: Images)

4. Why is it important to add a sound effect a fraction of a second before the first frame of the accompanying image? (See Tutorial: Building the Main Title: Sound Effects)

5. According to documentary filmmaker Bill Jersey, if the same person appears on-screen repeatedly, how often should he or she be identified with a lower-third ID? (See Discussion: When and How Often to Use Lower-Third IDs)

6. How do you control the size of text in LiveType? (See Tutorial: Using LiveType: CreatingText)

7. Does rendering a preview in LiveType generate a file compatible with your Final Cut Pro project? (See Tutorial: Using LiveType: Adding Effects)

8. How can you easily apply an effect from the list on the Effects tab to your text in LiveType? (See Tutorial: Using LiveType: Adding Effects)

9. How can you change the length of an effect in LiveType? (See Tutorial: Using LiveType: Adding Effects)

10. Once your LiveType file is ready, how do you render a version compatible with your Final Cut Pro project? (See Tutorial: Using LiveType: Rendering and Adding the Title to Your Project)

11. How do you add a LiveType animation to a sequence in Final Cut Pro? (See Tutorial: Using LiveType: Rendering and Adding the Title to Your Project)

12. If an element appears on-screen in a location you're not happy with, how can you adjust it? (See Tutorial: Using LiveType: Rendering and Adding the Title to Your Project)

Session 9

Creating Animated Credits

Session Introduction

Credits are the place where you get to acknowledge everyone who helped take your film from an idea to reality. How many friends spent hours listening to you describe each specific detail of the story, every last frame of tape, or that great new transition you added? Inviting them to watch their names in the credits at the premiere of your show is a great way to reward their patience.

For professionals who work on your project, credits are even more important. The members of professional film crews develop *reels,* or collections of their work, to use as resume tapes. The end credits serve as proof that someone really did the lighting, the makeup, or the cinematography that his or her resume says he or she she did.

Credits are also a place where ego becomes especially noticeable. I worked on a documentary that was coproduced by two competitive people, and as assistant editor, it was my job to build the credits. One producer was certain the other's name appeared on-screen for more time. Fortunately, I had anticipated the problem and was able to show that both appeared in the Timeline for exactly 5 seconds. In the meantime, I made my own name 2 points larger than everyone else's. The producers never noticed—they were too busy worrying about each other—but it made me very happy.

TOOLS YOU'LL USE
Browser window, Viewer window, Canvas window, Wireframe mode,
Scrolling Text generator, Crawling Text generator, Overwrite Edit
button, Title Safe boundary, Action Safe boundary

MATERIALS NEEDED
Session 8 project files

TIME REQUIRED
90 minutes

Tutorial

» Making Sure Your Work Is Title Safe

No matter how much time and care you put into your credits, they're worth nothing if the audience has trouble reading them. The borders of a television screen show a smaller part of the image than does the Canvas in Final Cut Pro. This means your credits, or titles, may look great in Final Cut Pro but lousy when you output them to tape. Professional video equipment is created to show the entire image so you can see even the slightest imperfections. This process of showing more than a TV monitor is called *underscanning*. To help you tell the difference between what you see in professional equipment and what your audience sees on their home TV sets, Final Cut Pro provides Action Safe and Title Safe boundaries, which you use in this tutorial to ensure your work appears the way you want it to on your audience's television screen.

Title safe (inside line)

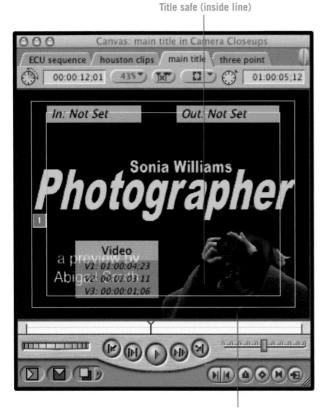

Action safe (outside line)

1. **Click the View button in the Canvas, and then click Show Title Safe from the menu that appears.**

   Two rectangular boundaries appear in the Canvas. The larger is the Action Safe boundary, which is 5 percent smaller than the video frame. This is an estimate of what's visible on a television screen. The smaller boundary is the Title Safe boundary, which is 10 percent smaller than a frame of video. Some TV monitors may show slightly more or less of the frame, so the Action Safe boundary is an approximation—some of the image that's inside this boundary may still be cut off. The Title Safe boundary is a more conservative boundary, so you can feel confident that images inside this area will appear on a TV monitor. Sizing all of your titles to fit the Title Safe area helps to ensure that all credits remain readable and don't get cut off.

   < N O T E >

   When you export a project as a QuickTime multimedia file, the entire video frame is visible. If your means of distribution is a multimedia format, such as a CD or a Web-based streaming video file, you can position the elements in your project so that they fill the entire frame and are not limited to the Title Safe or Action Safe areas.

2. **Drag the playhead to a point in the Timeline where all three video clips appear in the Canvas.**

   This enables you to see what is title safe and what isn't. The word *Photographer* clearly extends past the Title Safe boundary, so you need to shrink it.

3. **Click the** `title_text.png` **clip in the Timeline.**

   Because Image+Wireframe is still selected in the View menu, a wireframe of the image appears in the Canvas. (You used a wireframe to reposition the LiveType title in the preceding session.)

4. **Position the cursor at the upper-right corner of the wireframe in the Canvas.**

   The cursor changes from an arrow to a cross hair.

5. **Hold down the mouse, and drag the cursor to the left.**

   This resizes the image of the title text to a smaller scale. Notice that the aspect ratio doesn't change—that is, the relative height and width stay the same—the image just gets smaller.

6. **Drag the cursor until the bottom of the *P* and the top of the *r* in *Photographer* both fit inside the Title Safe boundary.**

7. **Release the mouse.**

   You successfully scaled down the image to fit the Title Safe area. At this point, the still image of Sonia Williams remains well outside of the Action Safe area, which is done on purpose. You want to make sure the still image extends past the Action Safe boundary so that it fills that portion of the screen. Because you resized the text, it's a good idea to also slightly shrink the still image to maintain the proportion of text to image. If you shrink the still image too much, however, black may appear at the edges, which you don't want.

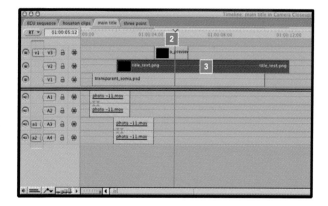

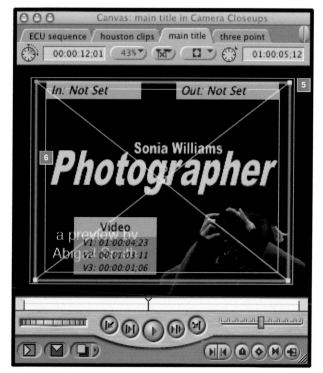

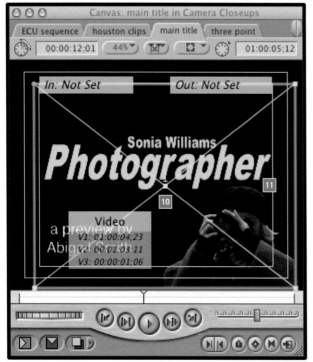

8. **Click the** `transparent_sonia.psd` **clip in the Timeline.**
   The clip's wireframe appears in the Canvas.

9. **Drag the upper-right corner of the wireframe to scale down the clip until it fits inside the Action Safe area.**

10. **Click the center point of the wireframe, and drag the scaled-down still image until the edges are clearly outside of the Action Safe boundary.**
    This ensures the image fills the lower-right corner of the audience's screen.

11. **Drag the still image a little farther down to ensure the top of the photographer's hat doesn't crowd the bottom of the text.**

12. **Render the sequence.**
    Because you resized two clips of video, you now need to reren-der the sequence before you can play it back.

13. **Click the Play In to Out button in the Canvas.**
    The text now fits safely on-screen along with the resized still image.

14. **Save the project.**
    In this tutorial, you changed the size of two clips to fit the Title Safe and Action Safe boundaries in the Canvas. This ensures your work appears the way you want it to on your audience's television screen.

Tutorial
» Creating a Scrolling Title

Regardless of whether you're someone who stays in his or her seat to watch all the end credits of a film, you've probably noticed that most credits scroll up from the bottom of the screen and then out through the top. The story ends, the screen goes to black, and the credits roll. In this tutorial, you create a scrolling credit sequence for *Sonia Williams: Photographer*.

1. **Click the Video Generator button in the Viewer, and choose Text→Scrolling Text from the menus that appear.**
   The Scrolling Text generator appears in the Viewer.

   <TIP>
   You can also click the Effects tab in the Browser window, open the Video Generators bin, and select Scrolling Text from the Text bin.

2. **Click the Controls tab in the Viewer.**
   The controls for the Scrolling Text generator become visible.

3. **Click in the Text window—where it currently says Sample Text— and type in the credits for this project as shown in the figure.**
   Press Return after each line, and add an extra return between each entry as shown in the figure. Insert your name on the line after Editor—give credit where credit is due.

4. **Choose Arial Narrow from the Font drop-down menu.**

5. **Drag the Size slider to 60.**

   <TIP>
   You can also type **60** in the Size window.

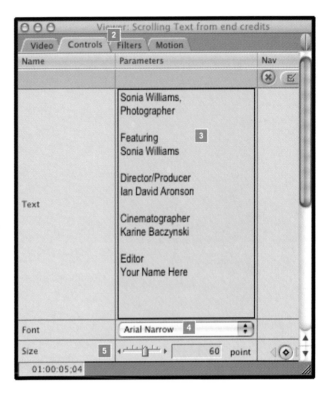

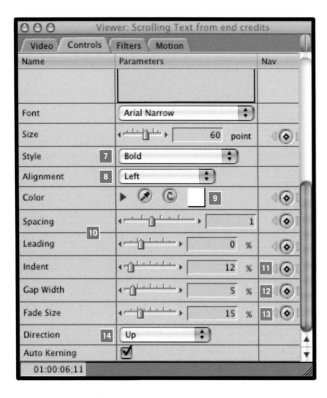

<TIP>
You can also type **12** directly in the Indent field.

6. **Click the scroll bar, and scroll down in the Viewer to display the bottom half of the Scrolling Text Controls tab.**

7. **Choose Bold from the Style drop-down menu.**

8. **Choose Left from the Alignment drop-down menu.**

9. **Leave the Color option set to white.**

10. **Leave the Spacing and Leading sliders at their default settings.**
    The Spacing slider adjusts the space between each letter, and the Leading slider adjusts the space between each line of text.

11. **Drag the Indent slider to 12%.**
    The Indent field is only enabled when you use a left- or right-aligned title. Because the part of the frame closest to the edge is not title safe, you need to set an indent to make sure nothing is cut off. Setting the Indent at 12% adds a nice buffer.

12. **Leave the Gap Width slider at 5%.**
    Because you use a left-aligned title, the gap width is irrelevant. The Gap Width setting only functions with a center-aligned title.

13. **Set the Fade Size slider to 15%.**
    The Fade Size setting narrows the area in which your text displays on-screen at full opacity and creates areas at the top and bottom of the screen where your text fades in and out. With the Fade Size set to 15%, the scrolling title fades into view as it passes through the bottom 15 percent of the screen and fades out of view as it passes through the top 15 percent.

14. **Leave the Direction drop-down menu set to Up.**
    This scrolls your title up from the bottom and out through the top of the screen. If you wanted to be truly original, you could scroll your text in from the top. I've never seen a film that scrolled its credits down from the top, but it might be a nice surprise and would definitely be memorable.

Creating Easy to Read Motion Text

Larger text is easier to read as it scrolls or crawls across the screen. Because credits generally move by fairly quickly you need to make them as easy to read as possible. Remember to keep everything in the title-safe boundaries.

Wider text is easier to read on a computer or video screen, and it's easier to animate smoothly. Choose bold from the Style drop down menu.

White text against a black background is the easiest to read. If you truly feel inspired, you can click the color sample to select a new color, or you can use the Select Color Eyedropper tool to select a color from a video clip currently displayed in the Canvas. This text may look really cool, but it may be much more difficult for people to read.

Final Cut Pro generates 10-second video clips from the scrolling or crawling text you create. The speed at which your scrolling or crawling text moves across the screen is determined by the amount of space the clip occupies in the Timeline. A shorter crawling or scrolling clip moves by much more quickly than a longer clip of the same material. Also, a clip that moves too fast is harder to render effectively on-screen—it doesn't look as good. So, not only is a faster clip harder for your audience to read, but also it doesn't move smoothly. Problems with crawling text are much more noticeable than problems with scrolling text. Once you take the time and effort to make the perfect text clip, give it enough time in your sequence so you can be sure it looks the way you want.

15. **Click the Video tab in the Viewer, then Click the View button and select Show Title Safe from the menu that appears.**

16. **Use the arrow keys to scroll through the credits you just created.** You created a scrolling title for your end credits. The credits fade in at the bottom of the Title Safe area and fade out as they roll up to the top. You can also preview your credits by clicking the Play In to Out button in the Viewer, but they play back without the Title Safe overlays, so you can't judge how well they fit in the Title Safe area.

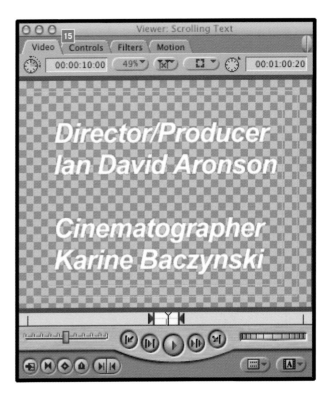

Creating Two-Column Text

The Gap Width setting is very helpful if you'd like to create two-column credits. Film projects often use credits which list the names of the crew in one column and each crew member's job in the other. Two-column credits save space, and are used extensively because they fit more information on each line.

When you create center-aligned text, Gap Width enables you to define the amount of space between two items that you place on the same line and separate with an asterisk. For example, if you have a center-aligned credit and want Art Director and Jodi Miller to appear on the same line separated by a space, you would type Art Director*Jodi Miller, and it would appear as Art Director Jodi Miller on-screen. The first illustration shows a two column credit in the Control Tab of the Viewer. The second illustration shows the same two-column credit as a video clip.

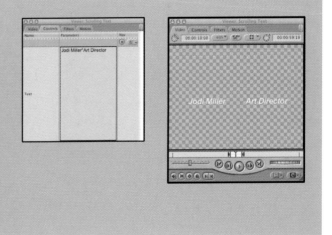

Tutorial
» Adding Scrolling Credits to the Timeline

Now that you've created some end credits, it's time to add them to your project. In this tutorial, you create a new sequence and add the scrolling credit.

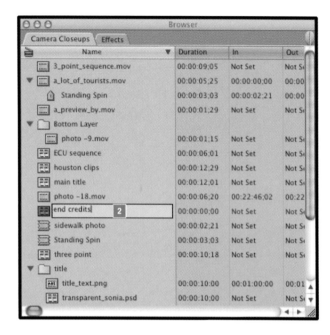

1. **Choose File→New→Sequence.**
   A new sequence appears in the Browser window.

2. **Name the sequence** end credits.

3. **Double-click the end credits sequence to open it in the Timeline.**

4. **Click in the Viewer, and drag the credits onto the beginning of Track V1.**
   When you generate scrolling text, Final Cut Pro creates a 10-second video clip, which is what you just added to the Timeline. This clip expands or contracts to fill the space that you give it in the Timeline, meaning that if you shorten the clip, the text moves by more quickly. If you stretch out the clip, the text moves by more slowly. For now, leave the text at its default length. A 5-second scrolling text credit would pass by at twice the speed of this 10-second credit—give the audience time to read the credits that you've gone through so much work to make.

5. **Render the sequence.**
   When you add the clip to the Timeline, a red line appears above the clip, indicating you need to render before you can play back the clip. Rendering credits may take a while, because generating 10 seconds of moving text can heavily tax your computer's processor.

6. **Click the Play In to Out button in the Canvas.**
   The text scrolls through the screen.

7. **Save the project.**
   In this tutorial, you created a new sequence and added the scrolling credits. As the course continues, you create additional credits to add to the sequence, along with an additional image that you turn into a multilayered video composite.

Tutorial
» Creating Crawling Text

Just as you can create scrolling titles, you can also use Final Cut Pro to create crawling text that moves along the bottom of the screen. Crawling text, or *crawls,* have become increasingly popular in the last few years. Crawls were once reserved for stock quotes on financial news shows but are now commonly used by television stations to update viewers on important stories without interrupting the regularly scheduled programming. I also noticed recently that the Telle Tubbies use a crawl for their end credits, but this is highly unusual. Creating a crawl is similar to creating a scroll, but you have fewer options. For example, in creating a crawl, you don't have choices for alignment, indent, or fade size. Crawls can also be difficult to read and can distract your viewers from action on other parts of the screen. Use crawls sparingly, and keep them short.

1. **Click the Video Generator button in the Viewer, and choose Text→Crawl from the pop-up menu that appears.**
   The Crawling Text generator opens in the Viewer.

<TIP>
You can also click the Effects tab in the Browser window, open the Video Generators bin, and select Crawl from the Text bin.

2. **Click the Controls tab in the Viewer.**
   The controls for the Crawl Text generator become visible.

3. **Click in the text window, and type** To all my friends and family, thank you.

4. **Choose Arial Narrow from the Font drop-down menu.**

5. **Drag the Size slider to 50.**

<TIP>
You can also type **50** directly in the Size field.

<NOTE>
These settings are made for the design of this particular project. As you work with Final Cut Pro, experiment with each setting to see what works best for the credits you're making.

6. **Choose Bold from the Style drop-down menu.**

7. **Leave color set to white.**

8. **Leave the Spacing slider set at 1.**
   Spacing determines the space between each letter.

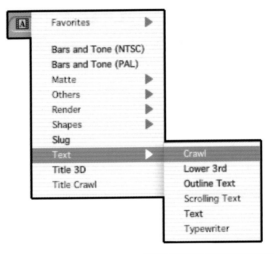

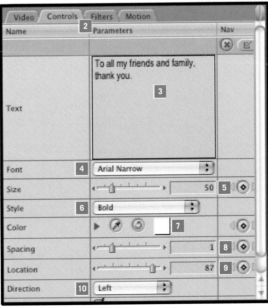

9. **Drag the Location slider to 87.**

   The Location slider determines where your crawl appears in the frame's *y* (or vertical) axis. A Location setting of 0 places your crawl at the top of the screen—so high up that only the very bottom of each letter would be visible. A setting of 100 aligns the baseline of your text with the bottom of the screen. This brings your text outside both the Title Safe and Action Safe areas of the screen and could easily make your crawl invisible.

   < T I P >

   You can also type **87** directly in the Location field.

10. **Leave the Direction drop-down menu set at Left.**

    This means that your text comes into view on the right side of the screen and crawls toward the left. Because your audience reads lines of text from left to right, this is just about the only way your text makes sense—unless you're writing in Hebrew or Chinese.

11. **Click the Video tab in the Viewer.**

    Final Cut Pro creates a 10-second video clip of the crawl, which is now visible in the Viewer.

12. **Use the arrow keys to scroll through the crawl.**

    The text crawls by from right to left and is title safe. Even the lowest points of the *y*s stay within the Title Safe boundary. In this tutorial, you created crawling text to complement the scroll you added to the Timeline in the previous tutorial. In the following tutorial, you add the crawl to the Timeline.

Tutorial
» Adding Crawling Text to the Timeline

When you generate crawling text, Final Cut Pro creates a new video clip, just as it does when you create scrolling text. In this tutorial, you add the crawl to the Timeline as a three-point edit.

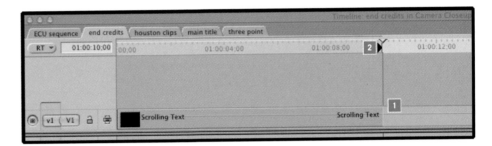

1. **Bring the playhead to the end of the scrolling text clip on Track V1.**
   In the next few steps, you add the crawl so it enters the screen just after the last line of the scroll moves off-screen.

2. **Mark an In point at the playhead's current location.**
   You now have three points selected: an In point in the Timeline, an In point in the Viewer, and an Out point in the Viewer. When you create crawling or scrolling text, Final Cut Pro creates a 10 second video clip and automatically adds In and Out points in the Viewer.

3. **Click the Overwrite Edit button in the Canvas.**
   Final Cut Pro adds the crawl to the Timeline. The red line above the clip means you need to render the portion of the sequence you just added.

4. **Render the sequence.**

5. **Click the Play In to Out button in the Canvas.**
   Your scroll moves smoothly across the screen, immediately followed by the crawl.

6. **Save the project.**
   In this tutorial, you added a crawl, which now appears in your sequence along with the scrolling credits. Nice work!

Discussion

The "Kid with a New Toy" Syndrome— Don't Overdo It

I attended a panel discussion on youth-created media at which a teenage film-maker said, "If you have a good story and basic technology, at the end of the day, you still have a good story." Obviously, I love the title- and effects-creation ability of Final Cut Pro just as much as anyone else does or I wouldn't be writing this book, but at the end of the day, this teenager is right: Your story is what people remember.

One of the best opening credit sequences I've seen appears in *The Price of Milk,* a comic love story from New Zealand. In a stroke of low-tech genius, the filmmakers sewed the credits into a quilt, and let light fall on different areas to acknowledge the work of different people.

Film buffs love the opening sequence of *Citizen Kane,* not because Orson Welles used a series of dissolves that were technically advanced but because the dissolves are so subtle people hardly notice them. This opening sequence holds up more than 60 years after it was made, while more overt uses of special effects quickly become dated. I recently watched part of the original *Terminator* on cable TV and was amazed at how something that looked so good when I was in the ninth grade could look so old-fashioned now. (I'm referring specifically to the sequence in which the terminator repairs itself in a hotel room.)

I like to ask students if they've ever seen a Web site that looks like it was made by someone who just learned Adobe Photoshop and wanted to use all the effects at the same time. People always know what I'm talking about, and sometimes they start laughing just thinking about a particularly overdone site. I don't bring this up here to imply that people will laugh at you for using too many effects in your titles or credits, but you shouldn't let anything overshadow the story that drives your project. The greatest opening sequence I can think of is *Delicatessen,* which relies on surprise and ambiguity far more than technology—I won't ruin the surprise by telling you more about it; just think of me when you see it.

» Session Review

In this session, you learned how to perfect the work that you did in Session 8 by using Final Cut Pro's Title Safe and Action Safe boundaries. These two guides help to ensure your work appears the way you want it to when your audience watches it on a variety of monitors. You also created detailed scrolling credits and crawling text, carefully adjusting each before placing both in the Timeline. You now have complete control over the appearance of your end credits, from the space between each line of text to their placement on the screen, as well as the speed at which they scroll or crawl across the screen.

The following questions are provided to help you review the information in this session. Answers for each question are found in the tutorial noted in parentheses.

1. What is the difference between the Title Safe and the Action Safe boundaries? (See Tutorial: Making Sure Your Work Is Title Safe)

2. When you export a finished project as a multimedia file, it displays differently than a finished project you export as a VHS tape. Why is this true? (See Tutorial: Making Sure Your Work Is Title Safe)

3. How can you easily resize a clip? (See Tutorial: Making Sure Your Work Is Title Safe)

4. When you resize a clip or reposition a clip, do you always need to render the sequence? (See Tutorial: Making Sure Your Work Is Title Safe)

5. What's the difference between spacing and leading? (See Tutorial: Creating a Scrolling Title)

6. What does the Gap Width setting control? (See Sidebar: Creating Two-Column Credits)

7. How do you determine where scrolling text fades into and out of view? (See Tutorial: Creating a Scrolling Title)

8. What is the default length of a scrolling text clip generated by Final Cut Pro? (See Tutorial: Adding Scrolling Credits to the Timeline)

9. How can you change the speed of crawling text? (See Tutorial: Adding Scrolling Credits to the Timeline)

10. How do you adjust where crawling text appears on-screen? (See Tutorial: Creating Crawling Text)

11. Which direction of crawling text is easier to read—left to right or right to left—and why? (See Tutorial: Creating Crawling Text)

12. Which is easier for Final Cut Pro to animate smoothly—a fast-moving crawl or a slow-moving crawl—and why? (See Tutorial: Adding Crawling Text to the Timeline)

Featuring
Sonia Williams

Director/Producer
Ian David Aronson

Cinematograph
Karine Baczi

Part VI:
Adding Transparency and Video Effects

Using Transparency, Compositing, and Video Effects

Session Introduction

In Session 8, you built the main title sequence for *Sonia Williams: Photographer* using three layers of video: one for the title text, one for your credit as an editor, and another for the still image of Sonia. When you rendered the title sequence, Final Cut Pro created a composite of all three layers so each element is visible at the same time. Final Cut Pro enables you to use different forms of transparency to combine several video elements, such as multiple video clips, animated text, and edited images, into one seamless video presentation. You control the way each element appears on-screen and the way the different elements interact. Just as you learned to control, manipulate, and mix audio in Part IV of this book, in this session, you learn to control and manipulate the visual elements of your project. Final Cut Pro provides you with powerful digital video effects capabilities, and the following tutorials and discussions show you how to make use of them.

TOOLS YOU'LL USE
Timeline window, Viewer window, Canvas window, Motion controls (Crop, Opacity, Center), Wireframe mode, Clip Overlay button, Source control, Destination control

MATERIALS NEEDED
Session 9 project files and `pip_fullscreen.mov` and `pip_window.mov`, located in the Session 10 folder.

TIME REQUIRED
90 minutes

Discussion

Understanding Layers, Alpha Channels, Cropping, and Opacity

Each video track in your sequence is a layer of video. By adding tracks and combining layers of moving and still images, you can create fantastically detailed and complex visual compositions. Just as you layer audio tracks to augment your sound design or replace problem audio, you can layer and composite video tracks to bring your audience something truly worth paying attention to. The key to compositing video is understanding the parameters of a video clip and knowing how you can control each one. The following sequences in *Sonia Williams: Photographer* rely on composited layers of video:

» Opening title sequence

» Closing credits

» ECU sequence

» Picture-in-picture sequence

Each of these sequences exploits a different characteristic of digital video to achieve a specific video effect. In the following tutorials, you learn to work with each of the parameters described here.

Alpha channels

In the opening title sequence, each of the three elements is visible at the same time because they all appear on transparent backgrounds. One image contains an edited still image of the photographer on a transparent background, another contains the text against a transparent background, and the last contains your animated credit, also against a transparent background. Because the background of each element is transparent, you can stack them one on top of another and still see all three at the same time. The technology that enables you to create a transparent background is called an *alpha channel.*

A computer creates images using three colors: red, green, and blue. By combining these colors at different intensities, a computer creates the millions of colors you see on your screen. Each color is stored on its own channel, for a total of three channels. An alpha channel is a fourth channel that a computer imaging program, such as Adobe Photoshop or Macromedia Fireworks, or a video-editing program, such as Final Cut Pro, uses to define transparent areas in an image. In your animated editing credit, a_preview_by.mov, everything except the animated text is defined as transparent, so you can see through the background of the clip to the video tracks below.

The edited still image of the photographer also uses an alpha channel, enabling you to place the photographer's picture in front of your scrolling credits later in this session so that the credits appear behind her and then roll into view. Both the opening title sequence and the closing credits function in essentially the same way: A transparent background enables you to see more than one layer of video at the same time.

Cropping and scaling

Other sequences, such as the picture-in-picture sequence and the ECU sequence, require you to scale and crop the clips so that you can see one behind another. In Session 9, you scaled down images on two tracks of video to make them title safe. You use essentially the same process in this session to create a picture-in-picture effect—you scale down the clip on the top layer of video so that you can see the larger image behind it at the same time. You can also crop an image so that instead of displaying a smaller version of the entire frame, you only display a selected area. Later in this session, you crop the images on the top and bottom layers of the ECU sequence to parts of both tracks at the same time.

Opacity

The final parameter of image control is opacity. An image set to 100 percent opacity becomes fully opaque, meaning you can't see through the image to anything that may appear behind it. Setting the opacity for the same image to 0 percent would make it completely transparent, which means it would be invisible. An opacity somewhere in between—for example, 50 percent—makes the image translucent so you can see it clearly and still view any images behind it.

You can use keyframes to set different opacity values for different parts of the same clip, making the image fade in or out as it plays. This effect can provide a much smoother transition than popping a scaled or cropped image onto the screen at its fullest opacity. In this session, you keyframe the opacity of clips in both the ECU sequence and the picture-in-picture sequence, creating highly polished visual effects.

<NOTE>
The word keyframe can be used as either a verb or a noun. When used as a verb, it means to add and adjust keyframes to achieve a desired effect.

Understanding and controlling the parameters of clips in a sequence gives you complete control over the way your work appears on-screen and the way your audience experiences it. Few things in our society have the power of a moving image. Final Cut Pro provides you with complete control over each image in your project.

Tutorial
» Completing the End Credits

To complete the end credits sequence, you need to add the still image of Sonia Williams to Track V2 so that the credits scroll behind it. Using thematically similar material at the beginning and end of a project is called *bookending* and can be a really nice way to wrap things up.

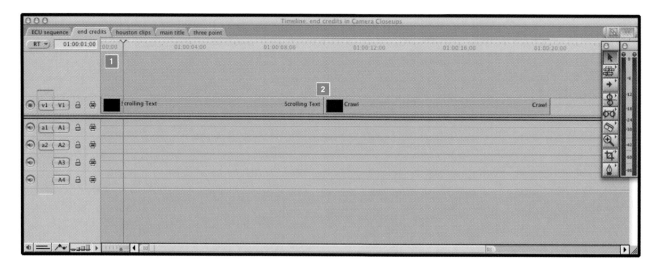

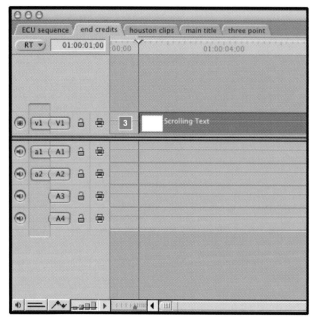

1. **Bring the playhead to 01:00:01;00.**

   The credits appear a full second after the image starts to fade in, so the first thing you need to do is clear some space in the Timeline.

2. **Shift+click the Scrolling Text clip and the Crawl clip in the Timeline so that they're both selected.**

   <TIP>

   Because these are the only two clips in the Timeline, you can also press ⌘+A, which is the keyboard shortcut for Edit→Select All.

3. **Drag the clips to the right until the first clip snaps into place at the playhead.**

   Now you're ready to insert the still image on a new video track.

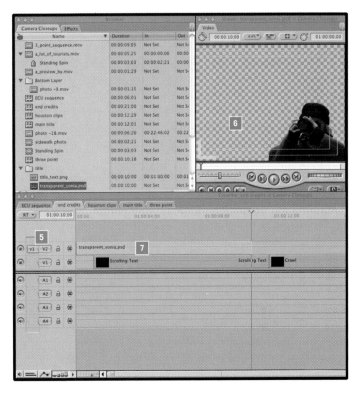

4. **Choose Sequence→Insert Tracks, and add one video track after the last track.**
   A new track appears in the Timeline.

5. **Align Source Control v1 with Destination Track V2.**

6. **Drag** transparent_sonia.psd **from the Browser window into the Viewer.**
   The same image you used in the opening sequence now appears in the Viewer so that you can add it to the Timeline.

7. **Bring the playhead back to the start of the sequence, and click the Overwrite Edit button.**
   Final Cut Pro adds the still image to Track V2.

8. **Use the arrow keys or drag the playhead to scroll through the sequence.**
   Because the edited still image on Track V2 appears against a transparent background, the scrolling credits are clearly visible behind it. Now you're ready to fade the still in from black.

<NOTE>
The still image extends beyond the Title Safe and Action Safe boundaries, but enough of the image remains on-screen that it's not a problem.

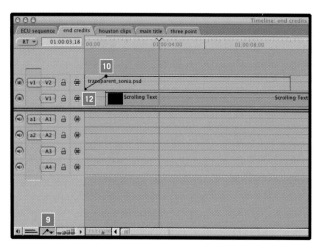

9. **Click the Clip Overlay button at the bottom of the Timeline window.**
The display changes to show the overlays for each video clip in the Timeline. In Part IV of this book, you used clip overlays to adjust audio levels; here you use clip overlays to set opacity.

10. **Option+click the overlay of** transparent_sonia.psd **to add a keyframe at 01:00:01;00.**

11. **Option+click the overlay again to add another keyframe earlier in the Timeline.**

12. **Drag the keyframe that you just added to the bottom of the track, as far to the left as you can.**
The opacity in the first frame of the clip is now set to 0, and the opacity at the second keyframe is set to 100.

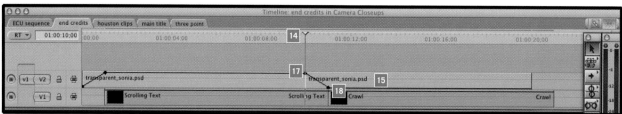

13. **Scroll through the clip by using the arrow keys or by dragging the playhead.**
The still image of the photographer now fades fully into view just before the text begins to scroll.

14. **Bring the playhead to the end of the** transparent_sonia.psd **clip.**

15. **Click the Overwrite Edit button to add the** transparent_sonia.psd **clip to the Timeline again.**
Final Cut Pro adds a second transparent_sonia.psd clip, allowing the image to remain on-screen twice as long. You don't use the full length of the second clip; instead you change the Opacity controls to fade the image out between the scrolling and crawling text.

16. **Option+click the** transparent_sonia.psd **clip overlay to add a new keyframe at the point where the first clip on Track V1 ends and the second clip on Track V1 begins.**

17. **Option+click the overlay to add a new keyframe slightly earlier in the Timeline, and then slide the newest keyframe to the point where the two** transparent_sonia.psd **clips meet on Track V2.**
The two keyframes that you just added are now about 1 second apart.

18. **Click the keyframe that is farthest to the right, and drag it to the bottom of the track.**
The opacity of the still image fades from 100 to 0 after the credit scroll ends and just before the crawling text enters the screen.

19. **Render the sequence.**
Final Cut Pro composites the edited still image with the text that scrolls behind it. This is a complicated animation that may take your computer a fair amount of time, but it looks really sharp.

20. **Click the Play In to Out button in the Canvas to play the sequence.**
The still image fades in evenly and the credits roll behind it, and once the credits roll out through the top of the screen, the still image fades away to make room for the crawling text.

21. **Save the project.**
In this tutorial, you added an edited still image to the end credit sequence. By keyframing the opacity, you gently eased the still image into and out of view. The image's alpha channel enabled you to place the image in front of the text.

Tutorial
» Scaling a Clip to Create a Picture-in-Picture Sequence

The picture-in-picture sequence, which shows two different angles of our photographer at work, uses the same layering and opacity techniques as the end credits you completed in the previous tutorial. The picture-in-picture sequence also uses a scaled video clip on the top layer and adds a drop shadow and a time effect. In the following tutorial, you control the placement, size, and speed of a video clip that you composite onto the base layer.

1. **Create a new subfolder in the Final Cut Pro Complete Course directory on your hard drive and name it** Part VI.

2. **Drag the Session 10 folder from the CD into the Part VI subfolder you just created.**

3. **Choose File→Import→Files to open the Choose a File dialog box. Navigate to the Session 10 folder, and select** pip_fullscreen.mov **and** pip_window.mov. **Click Choose to import the files.**
Both clips appear in the Browser window. The clip named "pip_fullscreen" is the bottom video layer, which fills the entire screen. The clip named "pip_window" (as you may have guessed) is the layer you scale into a picture-in-picture window.

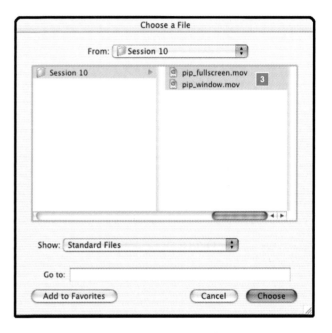

4. **Move the playhead to the beginning of the end credits sequence.**

5. **Double-click** pip_fullscreen.mov **to open the clip in the Viewer.**

6. **Align Source Control v1 with Destination Track V1 in the Timeline.**
pip_fullscreen.mov is the last clip in the preview before the end credits. Rather than building an entirely new sequence for the picture-in-picture effect, you can add the clip directly to the start of the existing end credits sequence and save yourself a step.

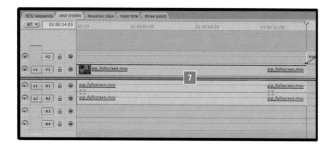

7. **Click the Insert Edit button in the Canvas.**

   Final Cut Pro adds video to Track V1 and audio to Tracks A1 and A2. Because you used an Insert Edit, the material already in the Timeline was not changed.

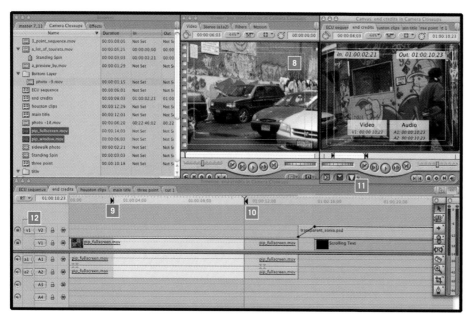

8. **Double-click `pip_window.mov` to open the clip in the Viewer.**

9. **Bring the playhead to 01:00:02;21, and mark an In point.**

   This is where the top-layer video clip starts to fade in.

10. **Move the playhead to 01:00:10;23, and add an Out point to the Timeline.**

    The space between the In point and Out point is 8 seconds and 2 frames; the video clip is 2 seconds shorter. To make the clip fit, you need to use a fit to fill edit.

   <NOTE>

   The two video clips were both shot with the same camera, which means that you're not working with two angles of the same action but rather with two different takes. Changing the speed with a fit to fill edit helps to match the action in the top-layer clip with the action in the base layer. Making the clips look like different angles of the same shot enables you to hone your skills as an editor—and perhaps even show off a little bit.

11. **Click and hold the Replace Edit button in the Canvas, drag over to the Fit to Fill Edit button, and release the mouse.**

    The Fit to Fill edit button looks like a green envelope, you can find it on the fly-out menu that opens when you hold down the Replace Edit button. When you select it, the Fit to Fill edit button takes the place of the Replace Edit button in the Canvas. Selecting the Fit to Fill Edit button in this step does not perform an edit, it just enables you to perform a fit to fill edit later in this tutorial.

12. **Align Source Control v1 with Destination Track V2, and disconnect both audio source controls.**

    This allows you to add video to Track V2 without adding any audio to the sequence.

13. **Click the Fit to Fill Edit button.**

    Final Cut Pro adds the `pip_window.mov` to the Timeline and slows it to fit the space you defined in Steps 8 and 9. The next step is to scale down the clip on Track V2 so that both clips appear on-screen at the same time.

14. **Place the playhead inside the** `pip_window.mov` **clip in the Timeline.**

    The clip displays in the Canvas.

15. **Click inside the Canvas to display the clip's wireframe.**

16. **Drag a corner of the wireframe in toward the center, and scale the clip down until it's small enough to display without blocking the clip underneath.**

17. **Click the center of the clip on Track V2, and reposition the clip toward the lower-right corner of the frame.**

Keep the clip inside the Title Safe boundary, and leave some extra space so that the clip is not flush against the edge.

18. **Double click `pip_window.mov` in the Timeline to open the clip in the Viewer, and click the Motion Tab in the Viewer window.**

The Motion controls for the clip on Track V2 become visible.

19. **Select the Drop Shadow check box to add a drop shadow to the clip.**

A slight shadow appears along the right side and the bottom of the clip, visually differentiating it from the video beneath.

20. **Save the project.**

In this tutorial, you added a carefully crafted picture-in-picture effect that combined two layers of video and included a scale effect, a fit to fill motion control effect, and even a drop shadow. Next, you use the Opacity controls to ease the top-layer clip into and out of view.

Tutorial
» Adjusting the Picture-in-Picture Opacity

You can set opacity keyframes using the Viewer window as well as by clicking a clip overlay. In this tutorial, you use the controls in the Viewer window to make a smoother transition into and out of the picture-in-picture effect.

1. **Place the playhead two frames before the end of the pip_window.mov clip on Track V2.**

2. **In the Viewer, click the small triangle next to the word *Opacity*.**
   The Opacity controls become visible.

3. **Click the circle with a small diamond in it (at the right of the Opacity field) to add an Opacity keyframe.**
   Final Cut Pro adds a keyframe to the clip.

< T I P >
You can also achieve the same function by Option+clicking the clip overlay.

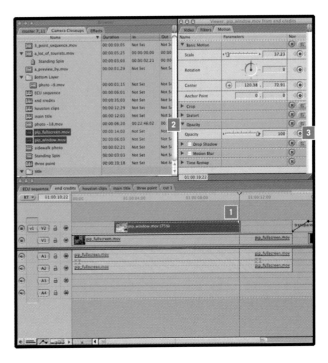

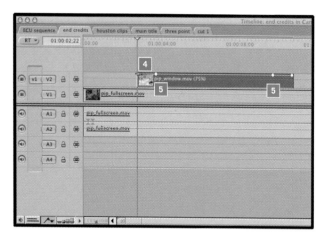

4. **Add another Opacity keyframe one frame after the start of the clip.**

5. **Place two more keyframes in the clip, one about 1 second from the head and the other about 1 second from the tail.**
   Now that you have four keyframes in the clip, you can change the opacity to fade the clip in and out.

<NOTE>

The button you used to add opacity keyframes to the clip contains arrows on either side. Clicking these arrows enables you to easily move from one keyframe to the next.

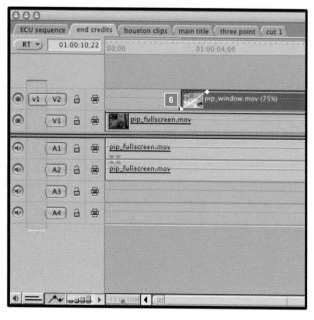

6. **Move the playhead to the first keyframe, and type 0 in the Opacity field in the Viewer.**
   When you press Return, Final Cut Pro makes the head of the clip invisible but leaves the opacity at 100 in the remaining three keyframes.

7. **Move the playhead to the last keyframe (01:00:10;21 in the Timeline).**

8. **In the Viewer, drag the Opacity slider to 0.**
   This lowers the opacity in the last keyframe without changing the opacity of the clip at the middle two keyframes. You've now set the clip to fade in and out.

9. **Render the sequence.**
   Notice that Final Cut Pro renders this part of the sequence much more quickly than it rendered the work you did in the last tutorial. This is because the work you did here does not contain text.

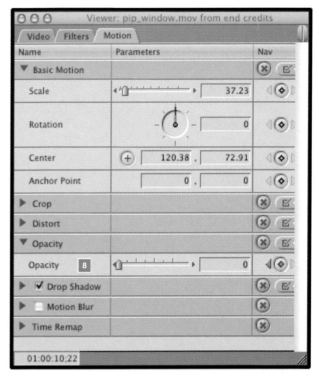

10. **Click the Play In to Out button in the Canavs.**
    The top layer of video fades in nicely. The action in the smaller frame matches the action in the base layer. The timing works well, too—the picture-in-picture effect fades out just as Sonia walks out of the frame followed by a group of tourists.

11. **Save the project.**
    Fading the clip in and out refines the sequence and reflects an understanding of Final Cut Pro's effect controls and an attention to detail. Easing the clip in and out, rather than bringing it in fully visible, is a small change that has a big impact on the overall quality of your work.

Tutorial

» Cropping the ECU Sequence to Create a Split Screen

In addition to scaling a video clip, you can also crop a video clip. Unlike scaling, where you proportionally reduce the size of an entire image, *cropping* displays a selected portion of the image at full size—the rest is hidden. Cropping enables you to change the composition of a shot and can be especially useful when you want to fit two clips on-screen together. In this tutorial, you use the Crop controls to resize each shot in Track V2 to enable video from Track V1 to show through.

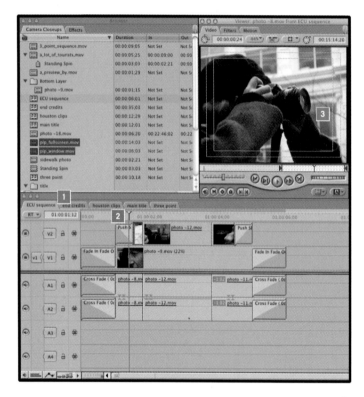

1. **Click the ECU sequence tab to open the sequence in the Timeline.**
   You spent a considerable amount of time building and refining the sequence, but you can only see part of your work because the top layer obscures the video underneath. It's time to crop.

2. **Position the playhead inside the first clip on Track V2.**

3. **Double-click the clip to display it in the Viewer.**

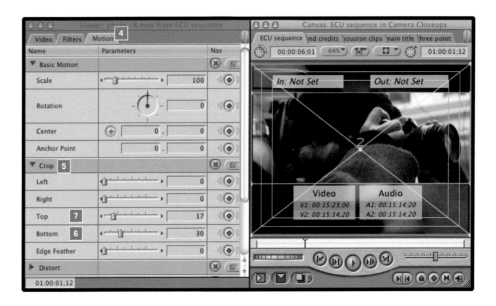

4. **Click the Motion tab in the Viewer.**

   Final Cut Pro displays the parameter controls for the clip you selected.

5. **Click the triangle next to the word *Crop* to display the Crop controls.**

   These controls allow you to specify how much of the image you want to hide, or crop out.

<NOTE>

When you crop a clip, part of the image is hidden, not removed. This means that if you change your mind later, you can go back and display the full image or redo the crop to display a different part.

<TIP>

You can also crop an image using the Crop tool in the Tool palette. However, the numeric Crop controls that you use in this tutorial are more precise.

6. **Drag the Bottom slider to 30.**

   Final Cut Pro hides the bottom portion of the image so the shot ends just below the photographer's collar.

<TIP>

You can also type a value directly into any of the crop fields (Top, Bottom, and so on).

7. **Drag the Top slider to 17 so the image starts at about the middle of her hat.**

   You can now see the video on Track V1 behind the smaller clip on Track V2. The next step is to align the top of the clip on Track V2 to the top of the screen.

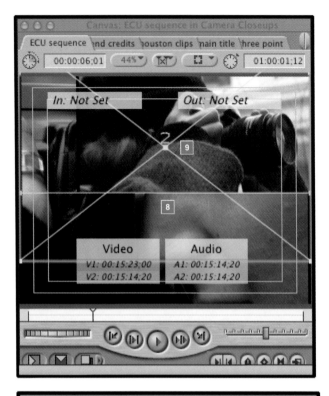

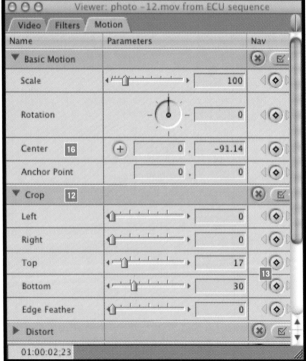

8. **Click the center point of the clip's wireframe in the Canvas.**

9. **Drag the clip to the top of the screen.**

<TIP>
If you press Shift as you drag vertically, Final Cut Pro constrains the motion so that you don't accidentally drag the clip to the left or right.

10. **Drag the playhead to scroll through the clip.**
    Cropping did not harm the Push Slide transition you added earlier; Final Cut Pro simply slides in the smaller clip. One crop is complete; there are three more to go.

11. **Double-click** photo -12.mov, **the next clip in the sequence, to open it in the Viewer.**

12. **Click the Motion tab and the Crop triangle to display the Crop controls.**
    An easy way to crop this image to exactly the same dimensions as the last one is to type a value directly in the Top and Bottom fields.

13. **Type** 17 **in the Top field, and type** 30 **in the Bottom field.**
    It's important that the bottom of each clip lines up, or else they appear uneven when you play the sequence. Because you just cropped this image to the same size as the last clip, you can align their center points to the same location.

14. **Double-click the first clip on Track V2 to open it in the Viewer again, and then click the Motion tab.**
    Note the numbers in the Center fields. These are the coordinates of the clip's center point on Final Cut Pro's x and y axes, respectively. In this example, the center coordinates are 0, –91.14.

15. **Double-click the** photo -12.mov **clip in the Timeline to reopen the clip in the Viewer, and then click the Motion tab.**

16. **Enter** 0 **and** –91.14 **in the Center fields, and press Return.**
    Because the first two clips are the same size, you can align their center coordinates to the same location.

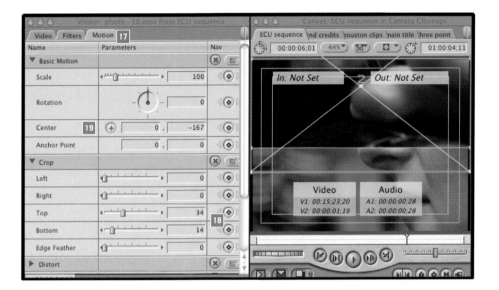

17. **Double-click** photo -10.mov, **and then click the Motion tab in the Viewer.**

    This clip requires a slightly different crop because it is composed differently than the previous clips.

18. **Enter** 34 **in the Top field and** 14 **in the Bottom field.**

19. **Set the Center coordinates to** 0 **and** –167.

    This aligns the clip so its bottom edge lines up evenly with the bottom edges of the other clips. Because this clip has been cropped differently, it requires different center-point coordinates.

20. **Use the arrow keys to scroll through the sequence.**

    Each of the first three clips now fits at the top of the frame, allowing the video on Track V1 to show through. Three clips down, one to go.

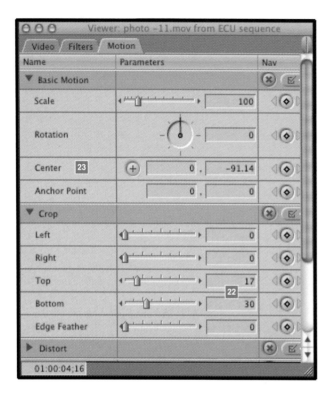

21. **Click the final clip in the sequence, photo -11.mov, to open it in the Viewer, and then click the Motion tab.**
    If you double-click the transition that you applied to the clip earlier, the Transition controls open. Instead, click the head of the clip before the transition starts.

22. **Enter 17 in the Top field and 30 in the Bottom field.**
    The composition of this clip enables you to use the same cropping dimensions you used in the first two shots.

23. **Set the Center coordinates to 0 and –91.14.**

24. **Render the sequence.**
    Because you changed the size of the clips, you need to render the sequence before you can play it back.

25. **Click the Play In to Out button in the Canvas.**
    You successfully cropped each of the clips in the sequence, resizing each one and aligning them all to the top of the screen.

26. **Save the project.**
    In this tutorial, you used the Crop controls to resize each shot on Track V2 by hiding parts of the frame. Because you resized the clips, video from Track V1 now shows through. In the next tutorial, you complete the sequence by adjusting the video on Track V1. You reposition the clip on Track V1 to show through at the bottom of the frame and add a Flop effect so the photographer faces the same direction in each shot.

Tutorial

» Combining Crop, Scale, and Flop Effects to Finish the ECU Sequence

The ECU sequence is composed of five shots: four on Track V2 and a fifth on Track V1. The photographer faces to the right of the frame in all clips except one. In the clip on Track V1, which you slowed to extend through the entire sequence, the photographer faces to the left of the frame. In this tutorial, you apply an effect that points the image on Track V1 in another direction without disturbing any of the transitions or crops you already added. You also reposition the clip to make the best possible use of the visible area that you created in the bottom half of the frame when you cropped the clips on Track V2.

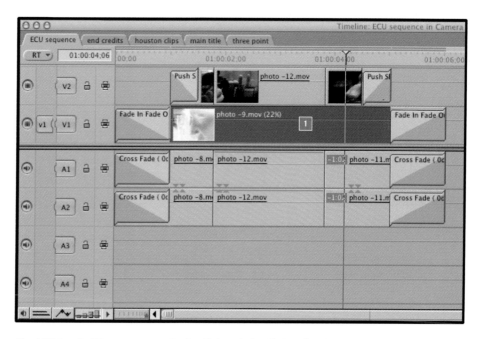

1. **Click the** photo -9.mov **clip on Track V1 to select it.**

2. **Choose Effects→Video Filters→Perspective→Flop.**
   Final Cut Pro "flops" the clip so that instead of looking to the left of the frame, the photographer now faces to the right. This effect works the same way as the Flip Horizontal command in Adobe Photoshop.

3. **Scroll through the clip by using the arrow keys or by dragging the playhead.**
   The photographer clearly faces the same direction in each shot, but only the lower part of her face is visible for most of the sequence, which looks odd.

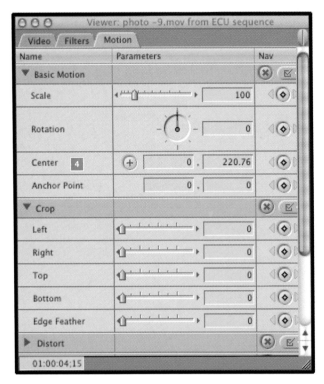

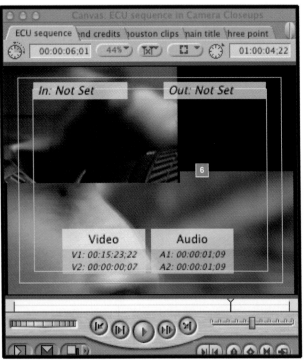

4. **Set the Center coordinates to** 0,220.76.

This positions the clip so that the photographer's eye is always visible in the bottom half of the frame. She looks up as she lowers the camera, so her eyes are at a higher point in the end of the sequence than in the beginning. Setting the Center coordinates to 0, 220.76 keeps her eyes at a good height throughout the shot.

5. **Scroll through the clip by using the arrow keys or by dragging the playhead.**

The video on Track V2 overlaps the shot on the bottom layer. If you look closely, you can see that the bottom of the clips that slide in and out on Track V2 are slightly lower than the top of the clip on Track V1. As a perfectionist editor, this is annoying and must be remedied. Your audience may not consciously sense that the two clips don't line up properly, but they will see that something doesn't quite look the way it should.

6. **Drag the playhead in the Timeline to location where the clip on Track V2 has been pushed partly out of the frame.**

In the following steps, you crop the clip on Track V1 to line up with the bottom of the clips on Track V2. Viewing a frame where the top shot has been moved to the left makes it easier to see the overlap, because you can see both the bottom of Track V2 and the top of Track V1.

7. **Double-click the** photo -9.mov **clip to open it in the Viewer, and then click the Motion tab.**

8. **Click the triangle next to the word** *Crop,* **enter 5 in the Top field, and press Return.**

   This lowers the top of the clip on Track V1 just enough so that it lines up evenly with the bottom of the shots on Track V2.

9. **Scroll through the clip by using the arrow keys or by dragging the playhead.**

   Notice that the top and bottom layers align cleanly. This is especially visible when the clips on Track V2 slide into and out of the frame.

10. **Render the sequence.**

11. **Click the Play In to Out button in the Canvas.**

    The photographer looks in the same direction in all the clips, and each shot lines up cleanly with the next.

12. **Save the project.**

    In this tutorial, you refined the ECU sequence to ensure each clip lines up with the others, that the photographer faces the same direction in each shot, and that the main part of the photographer's face appears in the Action Safe area of the frame.

» Session Review

In this session, you made extensive use of Final Cut Pro's parameter controls to shape each shot in the ECU sequence. You cropped and positioned the clips on both the top and bottom layers to create an impressive split-screen effect where two tracks of video play back at the same time. You also combined a scale effect, a motion control effect, and an opacity effect to create a picture-in-picture sequence in which a small frame of video fades in and out as it plays over a larger frame. Last but not least, you produced a slick end credits sequence in which your credits scroll behind a still image of the photographer on a transparent background. Parameter controls are the key to mastering the appearance of video in Final Cut Pro, and in this session, you changed a variety of parameters to achieve some professional effects.

The following questions are provided to help you review the information in this session. Answers for each question are found in the tutorial noted in parentheses.

1. Which channel of an image defines transparency? (See Discussion: Understanding Layers, Alpha Channels, Cropping, and Opacity)

2. What is the difference between scaling and cropping a frame of video? (See Discussion: Understanding Layers, Alpha Channels, Cropping, and Opacity)

3. How can you adjust the opacity of a clip using the Timeline? (See Tutorial: Completing the End Credits)

4. How can you set different opacity levels within the same clip? (See Tutorial: Completing the End Credits)

5. What is the keyboard shortcut that you use to select all clips in the Timeline? (See Tutorial: Completing the End Credits)

6. How can you resize a clip in the Canvas? (See Tutorial: Scaling a Clip to Create a Picture-in-Picture Sequence)

7. What do you click to add a drop shadow to the top layer of a video clip? (See Tutorial: Scaling a Clip to Create a Picture-in-Picture Sequence)

8. How do you change the opacity of a clip using the Viewer window? (See Tutorial: Adjusting the Picture-in-Picture Opacity)

9. When you crop an image in Final Cut Pro, are the cropped parts of the image permanently removed? (See Tutorial: Cropping the ECU Sequence to Create a Split Screen)

10. Instead of dragging the center point to a new position in the Canvas, how else can you set the Center coordinates of a clip? (See Tutorial: Cropping the ECU Sequence to Create a Split Screen)

11. What video effect can you apply to a clip so that a person on-screen faces the opposite direction? (See Tutorial: Combining Crop, Scale, and Flop Effects to Finish the ECU Sequence)

Using Advanced Compositing Effects and Color Correction

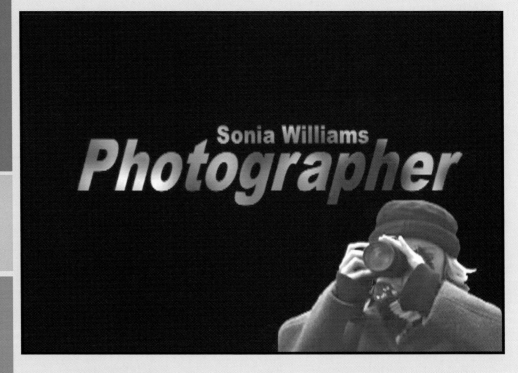

Sonia Williams
Photographer

Session Introduction

In this session, you add the finishing touches to your opening and closing sequences of the *Sonia Williams: Photographer* project. You use a special compositing technique, called a Travel Matte, to display a video clip in the shape of the main title text, and then you combine the matte with a cube spin transition. This session also addresses the importance of color correction, which enables you to make sure the colors in your video look the way they should and conform to broadcast standards. In the final tutorial of this session, you apply a filter to two sequences to make the color levels broadcast-safe.

TOOLS YOU'LL USE
Timeline window, Browser window, Viewer window, Source controls, Destination controls, Overwrite Edit button, Composite mode, Opacity control, Scale control, Cube Spin transition, Range Check overlay, Broadcast Safe filter

MATERIALS NEEDED
Session 10 project files, Session 11 media files located in the Session 11 folder.

TIME REQUIRED
90 minutes

Tutorial
» Compositing a Travel Matte

A *matte* is a device that lets you show part of one image through another. Think of the way a matte functions when you mount a printed photograph in a frame—the matte creates a border around the photo, and the image is visible through the open space in the center. Mattes work essentially the same way in Final Cut Pro. A *travel matte* is a combination of three elements: a foreground image, a background image, and the matte. The alpha channel in the matte enables the foreground image to show through the matte clip and appear on top of the background image. In this tutorial, you use a travel matte to play a video clip through the text of the main title.

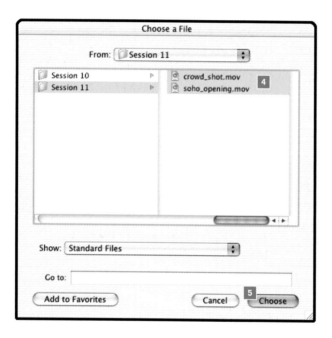

1. Locate the Session 11 folder in Part VI of the FCP Complete Course CD.

2. Copy the Session 11 folder to the Part VI subfolder of the Final Cut Pro Complete Course folder on your hard drive.

3. Choose File→Import→Files to open the Choose a File dialog box.

4. Navigate to the Session 11 folder that you just copied to your hard drive. Shift+click `crowd_shot.mov` and `soho_opening.mov` to select both clips.

5. Click the Choose button.
   Final Cut Pro imports the clips, and both appear in the Browser.

6. **Click the main title tab to display the sequence in the Timeline.**
   The `crowd_shot.mov` clip is an abstract shot of people walking down Broadway in the afternoon. In the following steps, you add the clip to the Timeline so that it displays through the `title_text.png` clip, which is currently on Track V2.

7. **Double-click the `crowd_shot.mov` clip in the Browser to open the clip in the Viewer.**

8. **Position the playhead one frame past the tail of your editing credit on Track V3, and add an In point to the sequence.**

9. **Position the playhead at the last frame of the sequence, 01:00:12;01, and add an Out point.**

10. **Make sure that Source Control v1 is aligned with Destination Track V3.**

11. **Click the Overwrite Edit button.**
    Final Cut Pro adds the clip to the sequence just after your editing credit. Because you just added the clip to the highest-level video track, the clip obscures the title text. The way to make the text layer visible and to create the Travel Matte effect is to change the clip's Composite mode.

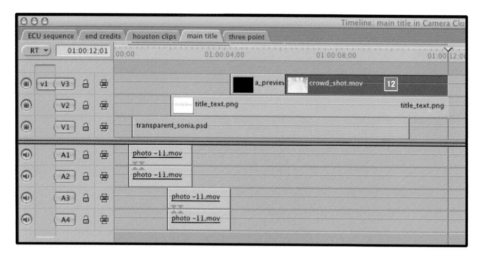

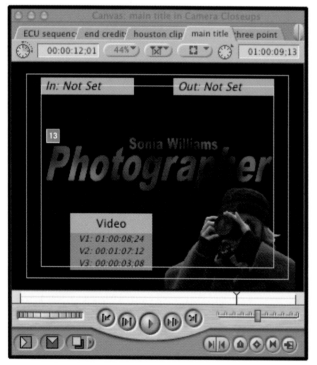

12. **Select the** `crowd_shot.mov` **clip in the Timeline.**

13. **Choose Modify→Composite Mode→Travel Matte – Alpha.**
    Final Cut Pro changes the Composite mode to create a travel
    matte using the alpha channel of the `title_text.png` clip.
    The title text, which was previously one solid color, now dis-
    plays the video of the crowd shot. As people walk through the
    frame, the video shows through the outline of the text. The
    transparent area of the `title_text.png` clip stays transpar-
    ent, so the photographer's still image remains in the lower-
    right corner of the frame.

14. **Render the sequence.**

15. **Click the Play In to Out button in the Canvas.**
    The sequence plays just as it did before, except now the title
    text changes to become an animated clip, displaying shapes of
    abstract video through its outline.

16. **Save the project.**
    In this tutorial, you added a new clip to the sequence and
    changed the Composite mode to create a travel matte. The
    new clip became the foreground image, and the title text
    became the matte. The matte's alpha channel determines
    what parts of the foreground image are visible. The sequence's
    black background remains on-screen as does your editing
    credit and the still image of the photographer.

Tutorial

» Fine-tuning the Travel Matte and Adding a Cube Spin Transition

The Travel Matte effect you created in the previous tutorial starts as soon as your preview credit disappears. In this tutorial, you create a smoother transition for the Travel Matte effect and you transition into a new clip to complete the opening sequence.

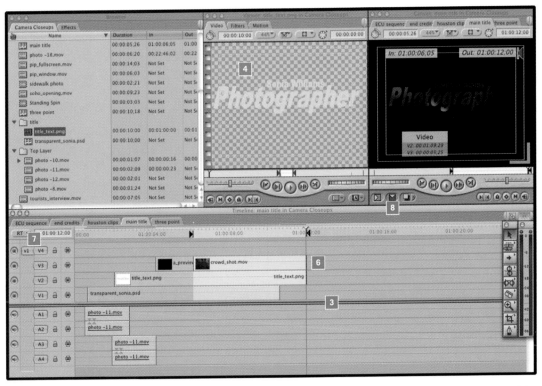

1. Choose Sequence→Insert Tracks to open the Insert Tracks dialog box.

2. Insert one video track after the last track.
   Final Cut Pro adds a fourth video track to the sequence.

3. Drag the border that separates the video tracks from the audio tracks in the Timeline so that all four video tracks are fully visible.

4. Double-click the title_text.png clip in the Browser to open the clip in the Viewer.
   Rather than fading the travel matte in and out to create a smooth transition, in this tutorial, you add a second title_text.png clip to the Timeline and gradually fade it out to reveal the travel matte. Because the crowd shot and the title text on Track V2 are composited together, you can't fade one without making the other disappear as well.

5. Position the playhead at the first frame of the crowd_shot.mov clip in the Timeline, and add an In point.

6. Position the playhead at the last frame of the crowd_shot.mov clip in the Timeline, and add an Out point in the Canvas.

7. Align Source Control v1 with Destination Track V4.

8. Click the Overwrite Edit button.
   Final Cut Pro adds a title text clip to the Timeline, obscuring the matte. To complete the effect, you need to scale the top clip to make it the same size as the clip on Track V2, and keyframe the opacity.

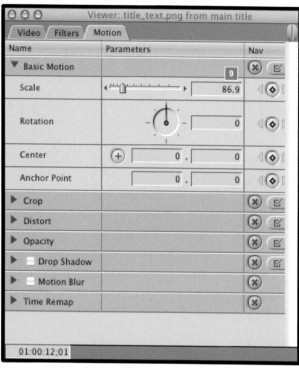

9. **Double-click the clip on Track V2 so that it appears in the Viewer, and then click the Motion tab.**

   The scale field displays the size of the title_tex.png clip in the Timeline as a percentage of the original clip. For example, the clip in the demonstration has been scaled to 86.9 percent of its original size. Applying the scale setting of the clip on Track V2 of your project to the clip on Track V4 of your project makes both clips the same size.

10. **Double-click the clip on Track V4. In the Scale field, enter a setting equal to the scale setting of the clip on Track V2.**

    When you press Return, the top-layer clip scales to the size of the travel matte.

11. **Position the Playhead in the first frame of the clip on Track V4.**

12. **Click the triangle to the left of Opacity to open the Opacity control in the Viewer, and add a keyframe.**

13. **Move the Playhead to 01:00:07;05, which is one second into the clip, and add another keyframe.**

14. **Drag the Opacity control slider to 0.**

    Final Cut Pro fades the clip from opaque to invisible, revealing the travel matte beneath it.

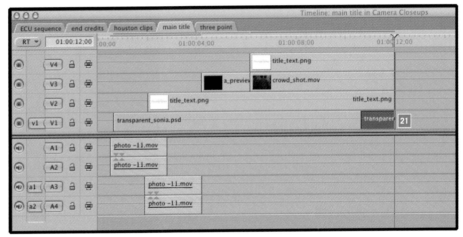

15. Use the arrow keys to scroll through the sequence.

The solid title text gently fades away to reveal the full-motion video in the travel matte below. To fully polish and complete the main title sequence, the last step is to add a transition to the introductory video sequence. First, you need to extend the still image of the photographer on Track V1.

16. Click the transparent_sonia.psd **clip in the Timeline to select it.**

The clip already appears in the sequence for its full duration. Rather than adding a second clip from the Browser and resizing it again to fit the Title Safe boundary, just copy and paste the clip you're currently using.

17. Press ⌘+C to copy the clip.

18. Align Source Control v1 to Destination Track V1.

19. Position the playhead at the first frame after the transparent_sonia.psd **clip ends in the Timeline (01:00:10;19).**

20. Press ⌘+V to paste a copy of the clip into the Timeline, extending the still image of the photographer on a transparent background.

21. Click the tail of the clip you just added, and drag it to the left so that it aligns with the end of the three clips above it.

> **261**

22. **Double-click the** `soho_opening.mov` **clip in the Browser to open the clip in the Viewer.**
    This fast-paced series of shots establishes Sonia Williams as a photographer working in SoHo. It also allows you to add a snazzy transition to the end of the main title sequence.

23. **Add an In point in the Viewer 15 frames after the clip starts.**
    Placing a shortened version of the clip in the Timeline leaves room for you to add a transition.

24. **Align Source Controls a1 and a2 with Destination Tracks A1 and A2.**

25. **Make sure the playhead is positioned at the end of the last clip in the Timeline, and click the Insert Edit button in the Canvas.**
    Final Cut Pro adds the video of `soho_opening.mov` to Track V1 and the audio to Tracks A1 and A2. Now you add the transition.

26. **Select the point where the** `transparent_sonia.psd` **clip meets the** `soho_opening.mov` **clip in the Timeline.**

27. **Choose Effects→Video Transitions→3D Simulation→Cube Spin.**

28. **Use the arrow keys to scroll through the transition.**

Final Cut Pro scales and distorts the outgoing clip (the photographer) and the incoming clip (the street signs) to make it look as if each is on one side of a spinning cube.

29. **Render the sequence.**

30. **Click the Play In to Out button in the Canvas.**

Looks good, doesn't it?

31. **Save the project.**

In this tutorial, you created a complex travel matte that plays full-motion video through a selected area of the frame in the shape of the title. You eased the matte into view and then added a transition to simulate three-dimensional movement. You now have a powerful opening sequence for your preview and have thoroughly explored Final Cut Pro's compositing and Digital Video Effects capabilities.

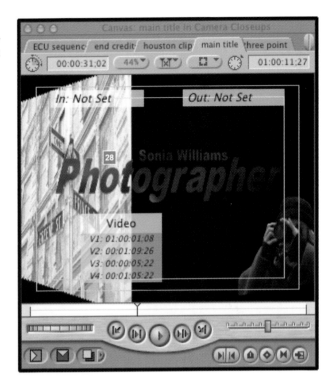

Discussion

Understanding Legal, Broadcast-Safe Levels and Color Correction

When you work with the color information in your project, your goal is twofold: to make sure your color levels are "legal," and to make sure the colors in each shot work together the way you want them to. Video clips contain color information that can be measured and adjusted. Managing the color information in your clips is similar to managing the audio levels in your project. Just as audio levels must fall within a certain range to reproduce sound without distortion, video levels must also fit a specific broadcast standard to display crisp, problem-free images on your audience's television sets. In addition, when the color information in each shot aligns properly, the shot works at its best, just as properly aligned audio levels combine to create a good sound mix.

Legal, broadcast-safe color

The range of color information that can be reliably reproduced through a television broadcast is called *broadcast-safe*. This color range is also referred to as being *legal,* so making a project's colors fit the broadcast-safe standard is also called making a project legal. There's no law or statute governing the use of color on television. If your project doesn't fit a broadcast-safe standard, you won't face criminal penalties. However, your images may reproduce poorly enough that the white and gray areas of the frame distort into an abstract shape and the black areas blend together into an unidentifiable dark form, rendering your project unwatchable. Problem video levels can also cause colors to bleed into one another, and even worse, to bleed into the audio of a broadcast program. To prevent this, broadcast organizations review a project's technical specifications before accepting the master tape. If the tape doesn't pass the technical evaluation, it goes back to the producer. PBS has exceptionally high technical standards, and its broadcast agreements can contain late delivery fines for tapes that aren't properly submitted.

The broadcast world takes color levels seriously. Even if you never expect your project to air on television, levels are still something to be concerned with. You don't need to set the color levels for the material that ships with the CD for this book, but this discussion provides a general overview of the process.

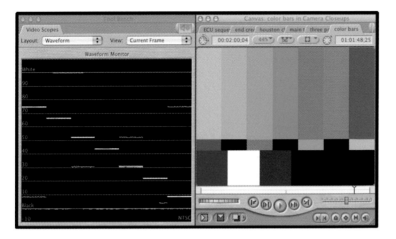

A waveform monitor measures the luminance, or brightness levels, in a video clip. In Final Cut Pro's waveform monitor, the reference level for white is 100 (the top of the scale), and the reference for black is 0 (the bottom). When the white and black levels fall within this acceptable range of the scale, the clip is broadcast-safe. If black levels fall below 0, details in the dark areas of the image become harder to distinguish. For example, the edges of a dark object on-screen may blend into the shadows behind it. If white levels rise above 100, bright areas lose detail, creating, for example, an unintentional glow around letters in a credit sequence and can even bleed into the audio tracks. Have you ever noticed a hum on your TV set when the screen gets too bright? When this happens information from the video signal is mixing with audio information to create an annoying sound on your television, because the color levels fall outside a legal range. At the end of this session, you apply a filter to the end credit sequence to make sure the whites don't get too "hot" and everything stays broadcast-safe.

Balancing color and making shots match

An editor uses a vectorscope to measure color hue and saturation, which are called *chrominance,* and to ensure proper color balance. *Hue* refers to the specific color (for example, green or red), and *saturation* refers to the intensity of the color in a given clip. By adjusting the color balance, an editor can make the color range of two adjacent clips more similar so they match more closely. Editors also adjust color balance to correct mistakes or to achieve a desired visual effect.

Keep in mind that different cameras record color differently. If you have a multiple-camera shoot, you may notice that the color looks remarkably different on the tape from one camera compared to the tape from another, particularly if you're using

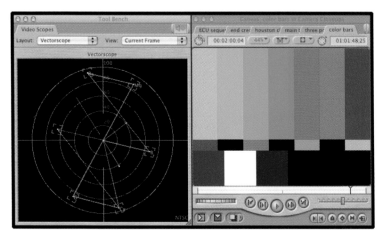

two different camera models. A skilled editor can work with the color balance to smooth out the difference. Even clips from a single camera shoot may contain drastic color differences due to lighting. Natural light has a blue tint, while artificial, or tungsten, light has a yellow tint. Depending on your lighting situation, you may need some color correction, especially if someone made a mistake such as forgetting to adjust the white balance on the camera.

People have emotional associations with color, and editors sometimes shift a color balance to create an emotional effect. Red, a warm color, is often associated with love scenes that involve champagne by the fire. If you drain the red from a clip, you're left with blue. In the late 1990s, a series of action movies came out with a distinctly blue tint. *Payback,* which was released in 1999, is a good example. Mel Gibson sets out to get even with the people who did him wrong, and the blue overtones of just about every shot give the film an intentionally cold, vindictive visual feel.

Discussion
Appreciating the Value of a Good Colorist

Final Cut Pro provides a full suite of color correction tools, from the waveform monitor and vectorscope pictured in the preceding discussion to a variety of color correction filters. The trick is turning access to the tools into effective use of color in your project.

Color correction is more than a mathematical process of defining color range and distribution. Color correction is the art of making color work for you on-screen, and that art can take years of practice to develop. Anyone can pick up a camera and record an image, but a cinematographer earns a living because he or she knows how to capture an image that looks good to an audience. Likewise, an audio editor knows how things should sound, and a professional colorist knows how things should look.

Adjusting the flesh tones of the people who appear on-screen is an important function of color correction and can highlight the talents of a colorist. People have an instinctive understanding of what a person should look like, and if the skin tones of the people on-screen don't match that expectation, the audience doesn't respond well. Even if people don't consciously make the connection, they register that something in the image just isn't right. Years ago, I watched a student project that the filmmaker had color-corrected himself, and in one interview after the next, all the faces had a purple tint to them. The tint was slight—no one looked like a beet—but it was noticeable enough that I couldn't concentrate on what anyone was saying because I was distracted by a mistake in the color balance. The filmmaker had succeeded in making everything broadcast-safe, but the project still didn't look right.

Making each shot work requires not only an understanding of video scopes and color correction tools, but it also requires the proper equipment as well as solid experience with the color correction process. The computer monitor attached to your editing system functions differently than an NTSC video monitor. As a result, the color in images that you see in the Canvas and Viewer windows displays differently than it appears on your audience's television screens. Final Cut Pro's documentation advises against using the Canvas or Viewer for color correction, because the image in those windows just isn't the same as what your audience will see. The documentation also advises against using a consumer television set for color correction, because televisions use filters to improve the appearance of broadcast images and can provide misleading information about the quality of your video.

A professional color correction suite contains a collection of high-quality monitors that provide accurate information about each image in your project (these monitors are often outside the purchase price range of an independent producer). Most importantly, professional facilities are staffed by professional colorists who know how to put the equipment to use. These professional services are not cheap, an old rule of thumb is to budget $100 for each minute of video in your finished project, but it may well be worth it.

I recently moved into a new apartment and paid someone to install two air conditioners. I could have saved some money by installing them myself, but I calculated that the expense was far less than the cost of potential problems that would arise if I accidentally dropped one from my 14th-floor living room window. When you finish a film or video project, you have it for the rest of your life. If you've already spent significant amounts of time and money to make your project something that you really feel good about, color correction may not be the time to cut corners.

Tutorial
» Using the Range Check Overlay and Broadcast Safe Filter

Final Cut Pro's Range Check overlay lets you easily determine if any of the clips in your project fall outside the broadcast-safe range. In this tutorial you use the Range Check overlay to test the levels of the main title and end credits sequences, and you apply the Broadcast Safe filter to ensure that all your levels fall where they should.

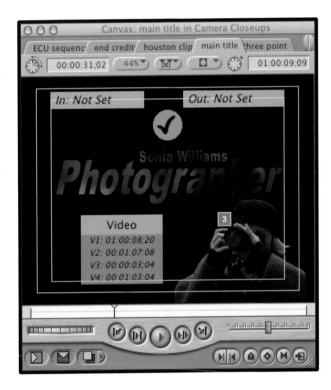

1. **Click the main title sequence tab in the Timeline to ensure the sequence you worked on in the last tutorial is open and selected.**

2. **Choose View→Range Check→Both.**
   The Range Check overlay determines whether the image in the frame that's currently displayed in the Canvas contains any levels outside the broadcast-safe range. You can set the feature to check for excess luminance or chrominance levels, or both.

3. **Use the arrow keys to scroll through the clip.**
   Because the Range Check overlay only evaluates the images in a single frame of video at a time, it's important to scroll through an entire clip, or better yet, an entire sequence. Frames with legal levels display with a check mark inside a green circle.

4. **Bring the playhead to 01:00:20;00.**

   The Range Check overlay displays a warning symbol (an exclamation point inside a yellow triangle), indicating levels that
   are not broadcast-safe. The overlay also displays animated red
   "zebra lines" over the bright spots on the two vans behind the
   photographer—these areas contain nonbroadcast-safe color.
   The red zebra lines may not be very large, because the problem areas appear only in small parts of the frame, but if you
   don't fix them, parts of your image will appear "blown out," or
   too bright. Using the arrow keys, scroll through the surrounding frames to observe how subtle shifts in the on-screen material can mean the difference between being broadcast-safe
   and unsuitable.

5. **Click the** soho_opening.mov **clip in the Timeline to select it.**

6. **Choose Effects→Video Filters→Color Correction→Broadcast Safe.**

   Final Cut Pro applies the Broadcast Safe filter to the selected
   clip, lowering—or *clamping*—color levels so that they fall
   within a legal range. The Range Check overlay changes to display a check mark inside a green circle, indicating that the
   image displayed in the Canvas is now broadcast-safe.

   < T I P >

   The Broadcast Safe filter contains a set of parameters you can control and adjust, just like any other filter in Final Cut Pro. To access
   the parameter controls, double-click the clip to open it in the
   Viewer window, and click the Filters tab.

7. **Render the sequence.**

8. **Click the end credits tab to display the sequence in the Timeline.**

9. **Choose View→Range Check→Both to evaluate the clips in this
   sequence.**

10. **Use the arrow keys to scroll through the sequence.**

The Range Check overlay displays a warning symbol and red zebra lines in frames that contain the scrolling and crawling text clips. The white text in the credits can easily extend beyond color-safe levels, but because you created the credits in Final Cut Pro, they're probably broadcast-safe. It's time to investigate.

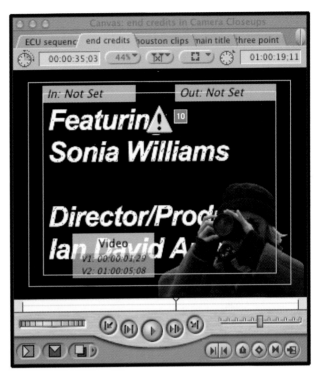

11. **Choose View→Range Check→Excess Chroma.**

This sets the Range Check feature to evaluate only for excess chroma levels. The Range Check overlay changes to indicate that the chroma levels are legal. This means that the color itself is broadcast-safe, but there may still be a problem with the brightness level.

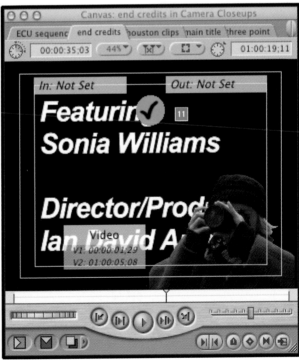

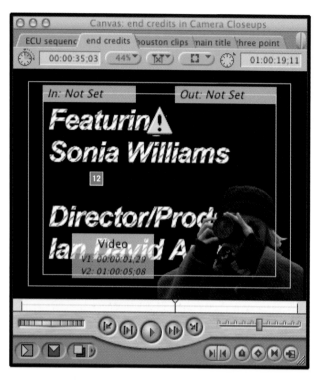

12. **Choose View→Range Check→Excess Luma.**

    The Range Check overlay changes to display a warning accompanied by a combination of red and green zebra lines. The green lines indicate acceptable luminance levels; the combination of red and green lines indicates that parts of the text are too hot. The solution? The Broadcast Safe filter.

13. **Shift+click the Scrolling Text and Crawl clips in the Timeline to select both together.**

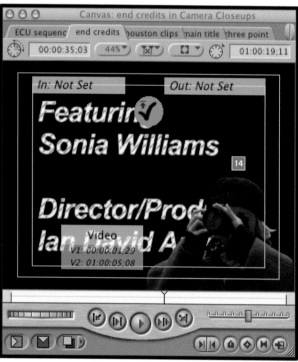

14. **Choose Effects→Video Filters→Color Correction→Broadcast Safe.**

    Final Cut Pro applies the Broadcast Safe filter to both clips. The Range Check overlay changes to a check mark, and green zebra lines have fully replaced the red. The clips are now broadcast-safe.

15. **Render the sequence.**

16. **Save the project.**

    In this tutorial, you used Final Cut Pro's Range Check overlay feature to evaluate which parts of your project are broadcast-safe and which needed work. You then applied the Broadcast Safe filter to ensure that your color levels fit an acceptable range.

» Session Review

At the start of this session, you reworked the main title sequence using a travel matte to display video through the outline of the title text. You refined the travel matte to fade in gradually, and you added a 3D transition into the next sequence. This session also addressed legal color levels and the importance of color correction, which can ultimately make the difference between a professional-looking project and a series of problematic images. In the final tutorial, you worked with the Range Check overlay and the Broadcast Safe filter to make sure that all your levels fell into place.

The following questions are presented to help you better understand the material in this part of the book. Answers for each question are found in the tutorial noted in parentheses.

1. What did you modify to make the `crowd_shot.mov` clip visible through the text outline in the first tutorial? (See Tutorial: Compositing a Travel Matte)

2. Which channel determines what is visible and invisible in the `title_text.png` clip? (See Tutorial: Compositing a Travel Matte)

3. How did you fade the travel matte in and out? (See Tutorial: Fine-tuning the Travel Matte and Adding a Cube Spin Transition)

4. How did you set the top layer of the `title_text.png` clip to the same size as the clip on Track V2? (See Tutorial: Fine-tuning the Travel Matte and Adding a Cube Spin Transition)

5. When you copied and pasted the `transparent_sonia.psd` clip, did you need to resize it again? (See Tutorial: Fine-tuning the Travel Matte and Adding a Cube Spin Transition)

6. The term *legal* refers to what? (See Discussion: Understanding Legal, Broadcast-Safe Levels and Color Correction)

7. What's the difference between luminance and chrominance? (See Discussion: Understanding Legal, Broadcast-Safe Levels and Color Correction)

8. What does the waveform monitor measure? (See Discussion: Understanding Legal, Broadcast-Safe Levels and Color Correction)

9. How do natural light and tungsten light color a shot differently? (See Discussion: Understanding Legal, Broadcast-Safe Levels and Color Correction)

10. Why is using a computer monitor or home television set as your primary color correction reference a bad idea? (See Discussion: Appreciating the Value of a Good Colorist)

11. What does an exclamation point in a yellow triangle represent in the Range Check overlay? (See Tutorial: Using the Range Check Overlay and Broadcast Safe Filter)

12. Which lines mean luminance levels are legal: red or green? (See Tutorial: Using the Range Check Overlay and Broadcast Safe Filter)

13. Which filter can you apply to clamp the levels in a clip? (See Tutorial: Using the Range Check Overlay and Broadcast Safe Filter)

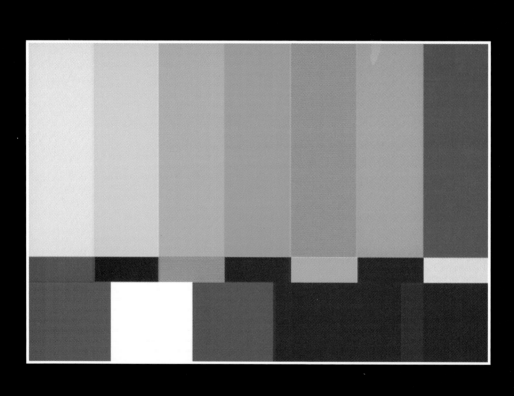

Part VII:
Final Edits and Exporting

Putting It All Together

Session Introduction

In this session, you combine the various sequences you've created into a finished product. You also create and archive different versions of the Camera Closeups project so that, if need be, you can return some day in the future to make changes. This session also contains tutorials on adding time effects to your project, enabling you to slow down or speed up clips at constant or variable speeds. In the following tutorials, you also save different versions of the project at different stages. At the end of this session, you add music to your project, making it fully refined and ready to export.

TOOLS YOU'LL USE
Timeline window, Viewer window, Browser window, Speed dialog box,
Time Remap tool, Insert Edit button, Overwrite Edit button

MATERIALS NEEDED
Session 11 project file you created (or the `session11.ppj` file from
the CD-ROM) and `raise_camera.mov`, `sonia_theme.aif`, and
`walk_through_frame.mov` from the Session 12 folder

TIME REQUIRED
90 minutes

Tutorial
» Creating a Constant-Speed Time Effect

In addition to changing the speed of a clip to accommodate a specific space in your sequence by using a fit to fill edit, as you've done more than once already, you can set a clip to a particular speed to create various effects. An editor may increase the speed of a clip to create a fast-motion or time-lapse effect, or slow a clip to create a dramatic action movie effect. (Think of the openings of *Reservoir Dogs* or *Con Air*—the cool bad guys always walk in slow motion.) In this tutorial, you add a slow-motion effect to Sonia as she walks across the screen from right to left, changing the entire feel of the shot.

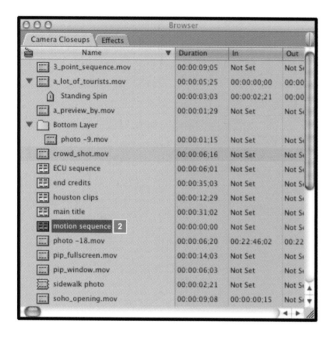

1. **Choose File→New→Sequence.**
   Final Cut Pro adds a new, untitled sequence to the Browser.

2. **Name the sequence** motion sequence.

3. **Double-click motion sequence in the Browser to open it in the Timeline.**

4. **Create a Part VII subfolder in the Final Cut Pro Complete Course folder on your hard drive.**

5. **Drag the Session 12 folder from the CD-ROM into the Part VII folder you just created.**

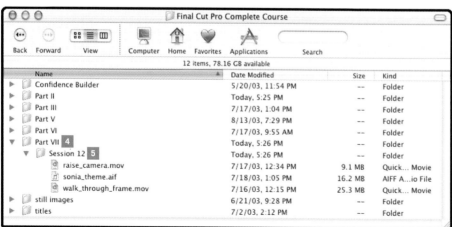

6. **Choose File→Import→Files.**

7. **Open Session 12 in the Choose a File dialog box, and then Shift+click** raise_camera.mov, sonia_theme.aif, **and** walk_through_frame.mov **to select all three files.**

8. **Click Choose.**
   Final Cut Pro imports the files.

9. **Double-click the** walk_through_frame.mov **clip in the Browser to open the clip in the Viewer.**

10. **Set an In point in the clip at 00:00:03;18.**

11. **Set an Out point at 00:00:06;02, and place the clip at the beginning of the Timeline.**

12. **Click the clip in the Timeline to select it (be sure to select the video and audio tracks).**

13. **Choose Modify→Speed to open the Speed dialog box.**

<TIP>
You can also open the Speed dialog box by pressing ⌘+J.

14. **Enter** 50 **in the Speed field.**
   This slows the video in the clip to play back at half speed.

15. **Click OK.**
   Final Cut Pro closes the dialog box and applies the speed effect.

16. **Click the Play In to Out button.**
   Sonia walks across the screen at half speed, creating a noticeably more dramatic feeling than the clip had without the time effect. (Play the master clip in the Viewer to compare.)

17. **Save the project.**
   In this tutorial, you added a constant-speed motion effect, changing a clip from normal-speed playback to half-speed. The clip now occupies twice as much space in the Timeline but does not include any additional material—the clip has simply been stretched to play back slowly. In the following tutorial, you add a variable-speed time effect to make the clip even more dramatic.

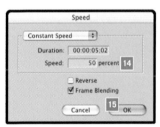

Tutorial

» Creating a Variable-Speed Time Effect

In the past, Final Cut Pro only allowed an editor to make constant-speed changes to a clip. You could set a clip to play back at any speed that you wanted, but the entire clip had to play back at the same rate. Meanwhile, editors were using more expensive editing systems to create variable-speed effects, where images on-screen would slow down and speed up in the same clip. Final Cut Pro now provides the same level of speed control using a technique called *time remapping*. Time remapping enables you to move a particular frame of video to an earlier or later point in the Timeline, stretching and compressing the video around that frame to speed up and slow down. In this tutorial, you remap a frame in the sequence that you created in the last tutorial to produce a variable-speed time effect.

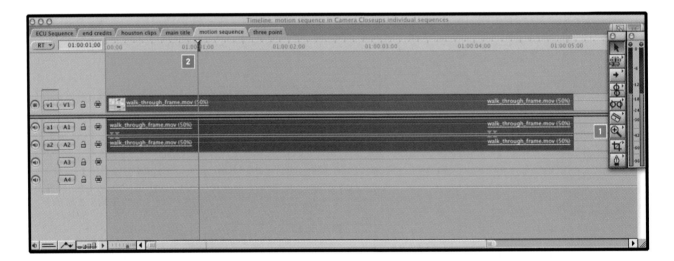

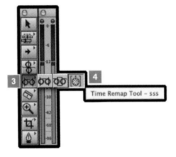

1. **Double click the Zoom tool so** `walk_through_frame.mov` **fills the Timeline.**

2. **Position the playhead at 01:00:01;00.**
   This is the first frame in which Sonia appears fully inside the Title Safe area. In the next step, you move this frame to an earlier point in the sequence, creating multiple playback speeds in the same shot.

3. **Click and hold down the Slip tool in the Tool palette.**

4. **Select the Time Remap tool (it looks like a clock) from the pop-up choices that appear.**

<TIP>
You can also access the Time Remap tool by pressing S three times.

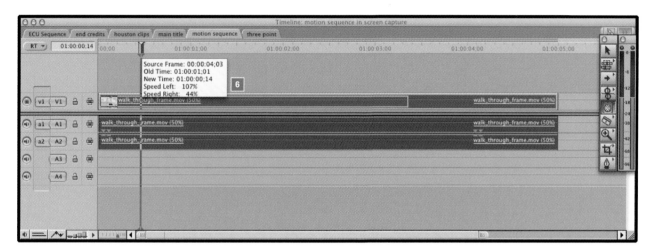

5. **Using the Time Remap tool, Option+click at the playhead's current location, hold the mouse down.**

6. **Drag the frame to the left until the Time Remap display indicates Speed Left: 107%, Speed Right: 44%.**

   In this action, you are moving the selected frame to a new point in the Timeline, and Final Cut Pro is remapping the frames around it to accommodate the change.

7. **Release the mouse.**

8. **Render the sequence.**

   If you have a fast system, your computer may display the effect as a real-time render preview. Either way, you need to render before you can output the final version of your project.

9. **Click the Play In to Out button.**

   Final Cut Pro speeds up the first part of the shot so that Sonia walks through slightly faster than full speed. At the point where you released the mouse, the clip slows dramatically to less than half of the clip's original speed.

10. **Save the project.**

    In this tutorial, you remapped a clip, moving a frame to an earlier location. To make the remapped clip fit the same space in the Timeline, Final Cut Pro sped up the frames before the clip and slowed down the frames after the clip to create a variable-speed time effect. Using the Time Remap parameter controls in the Motion tab, you could continue to reshape the clip in an infinite number of ways to fit your creative vision.

Modifying the Time Remap Effect

The Time Remap controls in the Viewer tab contain a graph of the speed effect, with a keyframe for each effect in the clip. The image here shows a graph of the effect you just created. The first and last keyframes denote the beginning and end of the clip; the second keyframe indicates your effect.

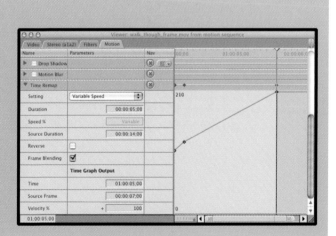

You can modify the effect by doing the following:

>> Clicking and dragging the keyframes to new locations.

>> Adding keyframes to the graph.

>> Smoothing the graph to create Bezier curves instead of straight lines between keyframes. (To create Bezier curves, Control+click a keyframe and choose Smooth from the pop-up menu that appears.)

Tutorial

» Creating an Archive Version

At this point, you've created a group of complete sequences that you are now ready to combine into a finished product. In the next tutorial, you edit the sequences together into a master sequence, but first it's a good idea to archive what you've done so far; you do the archiving in this tutorial. Archiving project files at various points in the development of a show affords you a level of safety—if you make a change that you don't like, or if you run into problems, you can go back to an earlier version that works. Archiving projects is more reliable than using the Undo feature, especially when you work on larger productions.

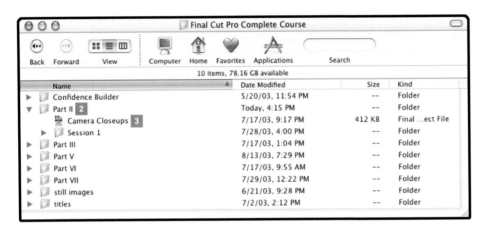

1. **Navigate to the Final Cut Pro Complete Course folder on your hard drive.**

2. **Double-click the Part II folder to open it.**
   The Camera Closeups file in the Part II folder is your Final Cut Pro project file. When you make changes to the *Sonia Williams: Photographer* preview, Final Cut Pro stores your work in this file.

3. **Click the Camera Closeups file once to select it.**

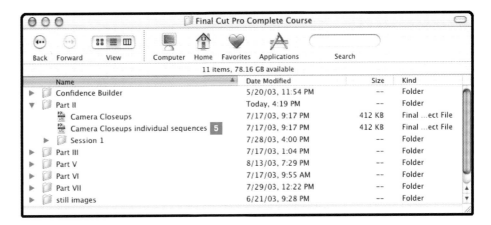

4. **Choose File→Duplicate.**

   Final Cut Pro creates a duplicate version of the project file. By default, the Finder names the file Camera Closeups copy.

5. **Rename the duplicate file** Camera Closeups individual sequences.

   You now have a working version, called Camera Closeups, and an archive version, called Camera Closeups individual sequences. You can continue to work on the original Camera Closeups file in Final Cut Pro, and the archive version remains unchanged, allowing you to return to it in the future if necessary.

Tutorial

» Combining Clips and Sequences into a Finished Project, Part I

At this point, you've worked with a full range of Final Cut Pro's effects and features. Now it's time to combine the different elements you've created into one master sequence. In this tutorial, you create a master sequence and place the main title, motion, and ECU sequences into the master sequence.

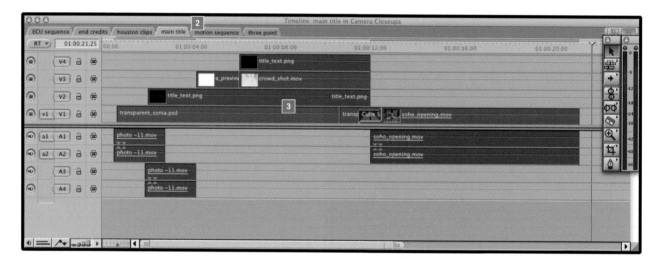

1. **Open the Camera Closeups file if you closed it earlier, and create a new sequence named master.**

2. **Click the main title sequence tab to open the sequence in the Timeline.**

3. **Press ⌘+A to select all the clips in the sequence, and then press ⌘+C.**

   Final Cut Pro copies the sequence.

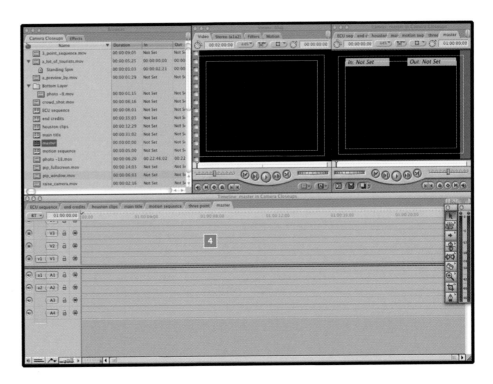

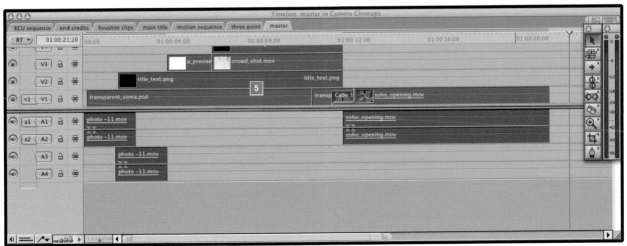

4. **Double-click the master sequence in the Browser.**

The blank master sequence opens in the Timeline. (The master sequence is blank because you haven't added anything yet.)

5. **Press ⌘+V to paste the clips from the main title sequence into the master sequence.**

Final Cut Pro adds the clips, on multiple tracks, to the master sequence Timeline. This enables you to build a complicated sequence using multiple tracks that work together.

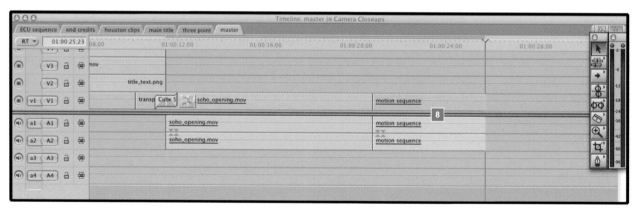

6. **Click motion sequence in the Browser window, and drag the icon from the Browser window into the Viewer.**

Final Cut Pro opens the sequence in the Browser window, as if it were a clip. Final Cut Pro also closes the motion sequence tab in the Timeline.

7. **In the Timeline, position the playhead in the first empty frame in the master sequence.**

8. **Click the Insert Edit button in the Canvas.**

Final Cut Pro adds the motion sequence to the Timeline as if it were a clip. You could have added the main title sequence the same way, but then everything in the sequence would have been compressed into one video track and two audio tracks (Final Cut Pro calls this *nesting*). However, the motion sequence consists of only one video and two audio tracks, so it's not a problem.

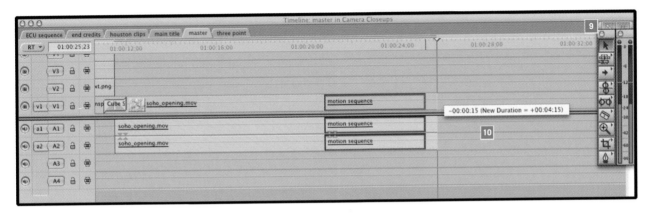

9. **Click the Linked Selection button in the upper-right corner of the Timeline.**
   If you click a video clip in the Timeline, Final Cut Pro selects the accompanying audio tracks.

<NOTE>
The Linked Selection button is the green button partially hidden by the Tool palette in the figure.

10. **Press A or click the black, upward-pointing arrow to use the Selection tool. Click the end of the motion sequence clip in the Timeline, and drag the clip to the left to trim the last 15 frames.**
    At the end of this tutorial, you add a dissolve effect between this clip and the next. Trimming 15 frames enables you to create the transition.

11. **Double-click the** `raise_camera.mov` **clip in the Browser to open the clip in the Viewer.**

12. **Add an In point to the clip 15 frames from the head.**

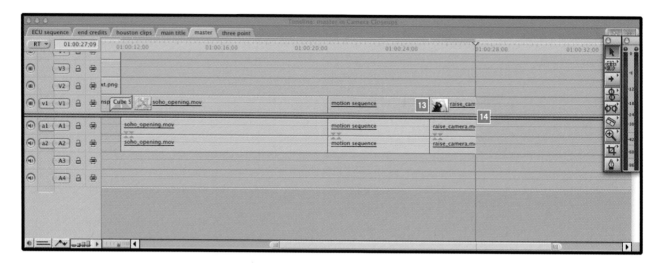

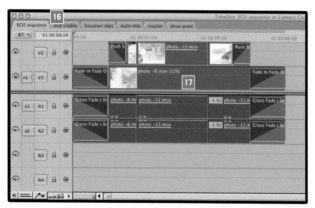

13. **Drag the clip from the Viewer into the Timeline, just after the motion sequence clip.**

14. **Select the end of the clip.**
    The next element you add to the Timeline is the ECU sequence. First, you add a transition to move the `raise_camera.mov` clip off-screen before the next sequence fades in. This helps the timing of the sequence and keeps the audience from feeling that too much is going on at one time.

15. **Choose Effects→Video Transitions→Slide→Push Slide.**
    Final Cut Pro adds a 1-second Push Slide to the end of the clip, moving it out of view to the top of the screen. This transition works particularly well combined with the Push Slides you added to the ECU sequence earlier.

16. **Click the ECU sequence tab to display the sequence in the Timeline.**

17. **Press ⌘+A to select all the clips in the sequence.**

18. **Press ⌘+C to copy the sequence.**

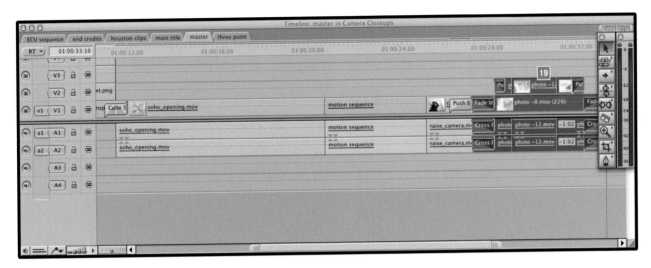

19. **Click the master tab to open the sequence, and then press ⌘+V to paste the ECU sequence into the master sequence Timeline.**

    The edited sequence, including transitions, appears in the Timeline.

20. **Drag the playhead through the sequence to preview what you've assembled so far.**

    The sequences are starting to come together nicely. Before you render the opening assembly to play it back at full speed, add the transition from the motion sequence clip to the `raise_camera.mov` clip.

21. **Click the transition between the motion sequence and the `raise_camera.mov` clips in the Timeline.**

22. **Choose Effects→Video Transitions→Dissolve→Dip to Color Dissolve.**

    The outgoing clip fades to black, and the incoming clip fades up from black. Now you're ready to render.

23. **Render the sequence so that you can see everything you've done so far.**

24. **Click the Play In to Out button.**

    The master sequence is starting to look like a finished product.

25. **Save the project.**

    In this tutorial, you added existing sequences to a new sequence timeline by using two different methods. You added two sequences by copying and pasting their contents, and you added a third sequence by dragging it into the Viewer and then inserting it into the Timeline as if it were a clip. Cutting and pasting a sequence enables you to re-create the exact placement of individual clips on separate layers, while adding a sequence as an insert or overwrite edit compresses the material into one video track and two audio tracks.

Tutorial
» Combining Clips and Sequences into a Finished Project, Part II

In this tutorial, you complete the master sequence, adding the remainder of the sequences that you've created so far and inserting transition effects. At the end of this tutorial, you have a complete and carefully crafted preview as evidence of your efforts.

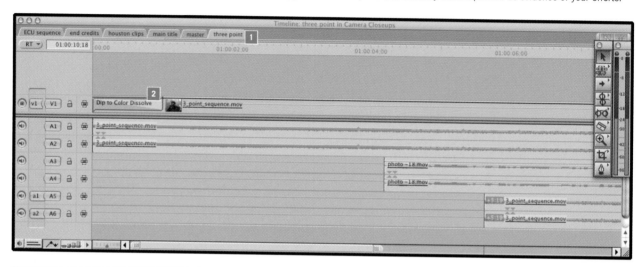

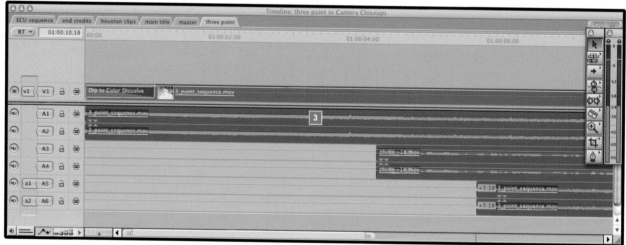

1. Click the three point sequence tab, and select the head of the first clip in the three point sequence.

2. Add a Dip to Color dissolve.
   This fades in the first shot of the three point sequence and creates a nice segue from one sequence to the next.

3. Press ⌘+A to select all the clips in the three point sequence, and then press ⌘+C to copy the sequence.

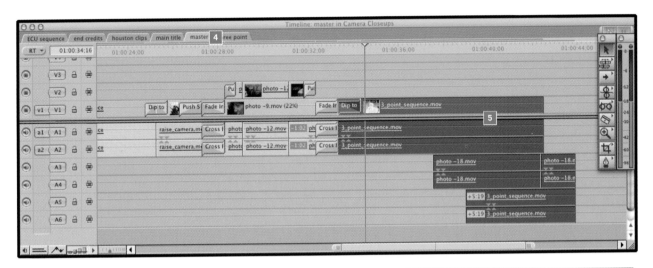

4. **Click the master tab to open the master sequence.**

5. **Position the playhead after the last frame in the Timeline, and choose Edit→Paste Insert.**
   The three point sequence now appears in the Timeline, complete with the Dip to Color transition you just added.

6. **Drag the houston clips sequence from the Browser into the Viewer window.**
   Final Cut Pro closes the houston clips sequence tab in the Timeline and opens the sequence as a clip in the Viewer.

7. **Position the playhead a few frames after the tail of the last clips on Tracks V1, A1, and A2.**

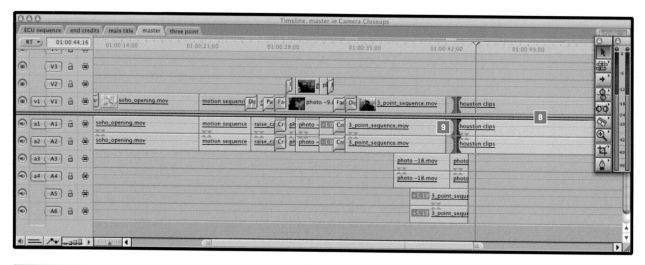

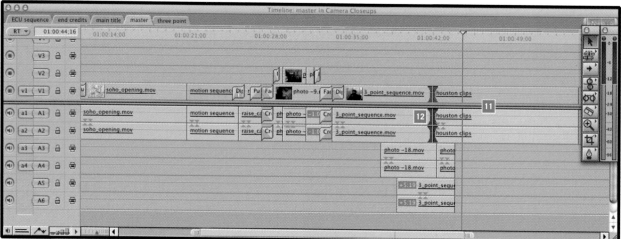

8. **Click the Overwrite Edit button in the Canvas.**
   Final Cut Pro adds the houston clips sequence to the Timeline.

9. **Trim the head of the houston clips sequence clip by 15 frames.**

10. **Trim the tail of the outgoing clips on Tracks V1, A1, and A2 by another 15 frames.**
    This makes room for a transition.

11. **Drag the houston clips sequence to the left so that there's no gap in the Timeline.**

12. **Shift+click Tracks V1, A1, and A2 where the three point sequence ends and the houston clips sequence begins.**

13. **Choose Effects→Video Transitions→Wipe→Edge Wipe.**

    Final Cut Pro adds an Edge Wipe transition to the sequence.
    The three-point sequence already contains an edge wipe at the
    end of the first shot —the photographer lowers her camera
    and a diagonal Edge Wipe eases the transition into the still
    images. This second Edge Wipe enables you to create a sym-
    metrical transition out of the still image.

14. **Double-click the Edge Wipe transition you just added to the
    Timeline.**

    The Edge Wipe transition's parameter controls open in the
    Viewer.

15. **Type** 320 **in the Angle field.**

    The sequence already contains an edge wipe that comes in
    from the bottom left of the frame, and ends at the upper right.
    Setting the edge wipe you add in this step to 320 means it
    will come in from the bottom right of the frame, and end in
    the upper left. This semeterical use of transitions marks a
    clear beginning and ending to the still image section of the
    preview.

16. **Select the Feather Edges check box.**

    This creates a soft edge to the transition, rather than a sharp
    line.

17. **Drag the Border slider all the way to the right to 100.**

    This makes the soft edge as wide as it can be, creating the
    smoothest possible transition effect.

18. **Render the sequence.**

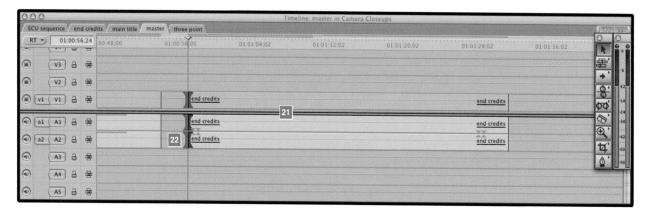

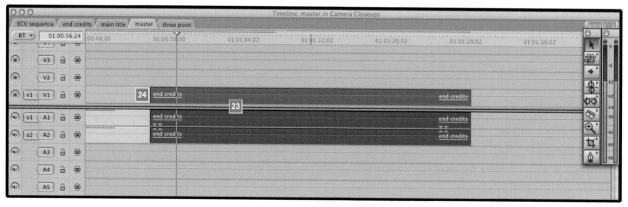

19. **Play back the three point and houston clips sequences you just added.**

    The two sequences work well together, especially with the voice-over on Tracks A5 and A6 that begins in one sequence and ends in the other. The Edge Wipe provides an especially smooth transition, as do the Dips to Color before and after the ECU sequence.

20. **Save the project.**

    All that remains to add is the end credit sequence.

21. **Drag the end credits sequence from the Browser into the Timeline a few frames after the end of the houston clips sequence.**

22. **Trim the tail of the houston clips sequence by 15 frames and the head of the end credits sequence by 15 frames.**

    This makes room for you to add the last transition of the project.

23. **Slide the end credits sequence to the left until it aligns with the end of the houston clips sequence.**

24. **Click the point where the two clips meet.**

25. **Choose Effects→Video Transitions→Dissolve→Cross Dissolve.**

    Final Cut Pro dissolves the end of one shot into the start of another to create a smooth visual transition.

26. **Render the master sequence.**

27. **Click the Play In to Out button.**

    You have created a fully functional preview for *Sonia Williams: Photographer*, with transitions, credits, and advanced effects.

28. **Save the project.**

    In this tutorial, you completed the master sequence, adjusting various clips and adding transitions to refine the finished product.

Tutorial

» Adding Music and Saving a New Version

One of the greatest advantages of digital editing is the ease of creating multiple versions of a single project. Editors often create one version for theatrical release, another shorter version for broadcast, and another for foreign distribution. In the past, creating multiple versions required an excessive amount of work, but with Final Cut Pro, you simply save another version of the file. In this tutorial, you add music to your master sequence and save a new version of the completed project.

1. **Bring the playhead back to the first frame of the master sequence.**

2. **Insert two new audio tracks after the last track.**

3. **Click the bar that separates the video and audio tracks, and drag it up so that all the audio tracks are visible in the Timeline at the same time.**

4. **Double-click the** `sonia_theme.aif` **clip in the Browser.**
   The clip's waveform displays in the Viewer window. Before you edit the music into the master sequence, lock the tracks you're not working on to prevent any unintended changes.

5. **Press Shift+F4 to lock all the video tracks in the sequence.**

6. **Press Shift+F5 to lock all the audio tracks.**

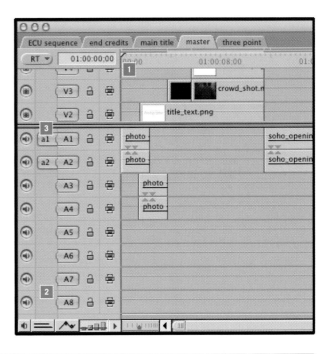

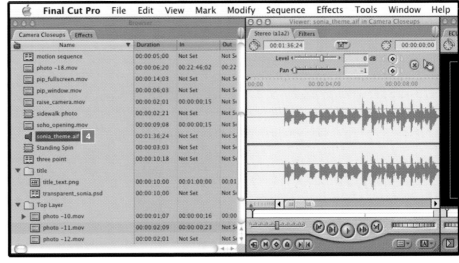

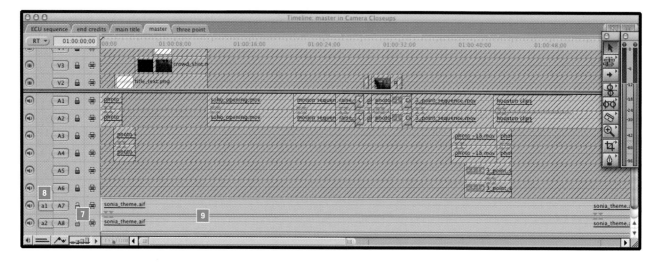

7. **Click the lock icons on Tracks A7 and A8 to unlock these tracks.**
   You can now work on the last two audio tracks in the sequence without damaging anything else in the sequence. An ounce of prevention is worth a pound of cure, especially this far into the project.

8. **Align Source Controls a1 and a2 with Destination Tracks A7 and A8.**

9. **Click the Overwrite Edit button in the Canvas to edit the music,** sonia_theme.aif**, into the sequence.**
   The music was composed specifically for this project—changes in the score fit the changes on-screen, and the levels are set to work with the interview and natural sound in the Timeline.

10. **Render the sequence.**

11. **Click the Play In to Out button.**
    The music builds during the main title and changes with each of the major visual changes on-screen—the split-screen ECU sequence, the picture-in-picture sequence, and the credit roll. The music bed also fades itself under Sonia's interview in the three point and houston clips sequences, and slows to a stop after the crawl. Your preview is good to go.

12. **Choose File➝Save Project As to open the Save dialog box.**
    This allows you to save a new version of the project without making changes to the existing version of Camera Closeups.

13. **Name the new version** Camera Closeups master with music**.**

14. **Click Save to close the window and create a new version of the project in the Part II folder on your hard drive.**

Final Cut Pro closes the last version of Camera Closeups without saving any changes to it, so the file exists just as it did at the start of this tutorial, before you added any music. The project open on your screen now is the new version, Camera Closeups master with music. The new name appears in the project's Timeline, Browser, Viewer, and Canvas windows. In this tutorial, you added music to the master sequence and saved the project as a new version. You now have the following versions of the project on your hard drive:

>> Camera Closeups individual sequences, which is the archive version you created in the early part of this session before combining the separate sequences into a completed master.

>> Camera Closeups, which contains an edited master sequence without music.

>> Camera Closeups master with music (the latest version), which contains an edited master sequence complete with music.

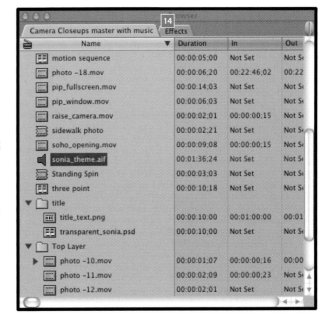

Discussion

A Film Is Never Finished; You Just Stop Working on It

Deciding when your film is finished may be one of the hardest parts of post production. Digital editing enables you to continually redo each edit and adjust each transition in an infinite number of ways. In this session, you learned how to create different versions of a project, which is great for backing up your work, but it can also lead to fruitlessly spinning your wheels as you try every possible combination of changes and revisions. At some point, you need to "fish or cut bait" if you have any hope of sharing your work with an audience.

The trick is to find a balance between being a perfectionist, which is your job as an editor, and being pragmatic enough to come up with a finished product. The accomplished documentary filmmaker and cinematographer Jon Else said, "No film is ever finished - you just stop working on it." He makes an excellent point— you can always find ways to improve a work that you care about.

When you work on a professional film, there's a clear deadline and you can't get around it. Films have specified postproduction periods written into their budgets and can run out of money to pay people if they don't finish on time. This creates an obvious incentive to finish. In the past, independent producers working on their own had to rent time on a digital editing system, which quickly added up to large sums of money and provided a clear reason to hurry.

If you're working on your own Final Cut Pro system and don't have to worry about money, setting an end point may be a bit more challenging (ironically, owning the editing system that so clearly increases productivity can also slow you down because you have no monetary incentive to stop editing). One strategy may be to set a timeline based on the entry dates of a film festival you'd like to be a part of. Another could be making a plan to finish your project by the date of a specific event at which you'd like to screen your work. In any case, there comes a day when it's time to finish. Regardless of how much you love editing, it's a lot more fun to show your work to a crowd of people—especially when they like it.

» Session Review

In this session, you completed the final edits for this project. You created a slow-motion clip using a constant-speed effect and using Final Cut Pro's new Time Remap tool. You also created a duplicate version of your project and built a single master sequence from the individual sequences you created in the course of this book. In the last tutorial of this session, you added an original score to the master sequence and saved a new version of the completed project. Your preview is now assembled, polished, and ready to present.

The following questions are provided to help you review the information in this session. Answers for each question are found in the tutorial noted in parentheses.

1. When you change the speed of a clip using the Speed dialog box, why does the length of the clip change in the Timeline? (See Tutorial: Creating a Constant-Speed Time Effect)

2. Why does the length of a clip in the Timeline stay the same when you apply a variable-speed effect? (See Tutorial: Creating a Variable-Speed Time Effect)

3. When you move a frame to another position in a clip, what does Final Cut Pro do to the frames around it? (See Tutorial: Creating a Variable-Speed Time Effect)

4. Once you've selected the project files for a work in progress on your computer's hard drive, how do you create an archive copy? (See Tutorial: Creating an Archive Version)

5. What is the value of saving an archive version? (See Tutorial: Creating an Archive Version)

6. What is the difference between copying and pasting clips from one sequence into another versus editing one sequence into another from the Viewer? (See Tutorial: Combining Clips and Sequences into a Finished Project, Part I)

7. If a sequence is open in the Timeline, what happens when you drag the sequence from the Browser into the Viewer? (See Tutorial: Combining Clips and Sequences into a Finished Project, Part I)

8. Other than copying and pasting the clips from one sequence into another, and instead of opening a sequence in the Viewer and editing it into the Timeline, how can you place one sequence into another? (See Tutorial: Combining Clips and Sequences into a Finished Project, Part II)

9. What is the keyboard shortcut to lock all the video tracks in a sequence? (See Tutorial: Adding Music and Saving a New Version)

10. If you open a project, make a series of changes, and then choose File→Save As, which of your changes are saved to the original project? (See Tutorial: Adding Music and Saving a New Version)

11. When you complete the Save As function, which version appears open on your monitor, the new one or the old one? (See Tutorial: Adding Music and Saving a New Version)

» Other Projects

The music that you added to the master sequence was created specifically for this project using Soundtrack, a music production application that ships with Final Cut Pro. Soundtrack is designed to integrate with Final Cut Pro and enables you to compose music for your project in the same way that LiveType enables you to create animated titles. Open the Soundtrack application and do some experimenting. You may soon find yourself creating new music beds for this and other projects.

Two areas in which you can improve the audio for the finished version of your master sequence are as follows:

» The shutter-click sound effects don't fade out smoothly under the opening title.

» There's some lightly audible discussion as the photographer walks out of the frame in the last shot.

Try using the audio mixer or keyframes in the Timeline to smooth out the audio and refine the sound mix.

Deciding on Your Method of Delivery

Discussion: **Distributing by Tape, Web, or DVD, and Why It Matters**

Tutorial: **Optimizing Your Movie for the Web**

Tutorial: **Encoding Your Movie for CD-ROM**

Tutorial: **Creating an MPEG-2 for DVD Production**

Tutorial: **Submitting a Batch**

Discussion: **Understanding Spatial versus Temporal Compression and Work Arounds for Web Streaming**

Session Introduction

Your preview is now complete and ready to share with an audience. Unless you plan on only inviting people to sit down in front of your computer to watch your film, you need to output a version of your project so that people can see it. The current version of Final Cut Pro offers a broad array of output choices, ranging from professional- and consumer-level videotapes to DVDs, CD-ROMs, and Web-based streaming video files. This session introduces a number of output options available to you, and walks you through the process of exporting different versions in a variety of media formats.

TOOLS YOU'LL USE
Timeline window, Batch window, Preview window, Presets window,
Preset menu, Destination menu, Output Filename field, Batch Monitor

MATERIALS NEEDED
Session 12 project files

TIME REQUIRED
90 minutes

ssion

Distributing by Tape, Web, or DVD, and Why It Matters

Once you edit a project in Final Cut Pro, you have a wide array of distribution choices and formats available. I always thought it was ironic that until recently, filmmakers could shoot and edit their work in a digital format but were forced to package the end product on an inferior analog tape to share it with an audience. Current digital technology frees you from the limitations of tape—you no longer have to distribute your project on a VHS cassette but instead can deliver your work as a digital product that audiences can view with no loss in quality. The key to success is choosing the right file format for your medium of delivery and optimizing your project to fit the strengths and weaknesses of the format you've chosen.

Web

The World Wide Web offers tremendous opportunities for you to share your work with people across the globe at a minimum of expense. The current limitation is bandwidth. Anyone with a computer, a modem, and access to a telephone line can connect to the Internet, and once your work is online, it's only a click away. The trouble is that only so much information can travel through any Internet connection at one time. This amount of information is referred to as *bandwidth,* and most of the time, bandwidth is very limited.

In Web terminology video files are "heavy," meaning they require significant amounts of memory and, as a result, require high-bandwidth connections. As you've seen when working with the media files for this project, video files take up significant amounts of space on your hard drive. Imagine trying to download the same video files over a dial-up modem connection—it wouldn't be fun.

To optimize video projects for online delivery, editors output the files at smaller image sizes and lower frame rates, similar to the way you output the video logo that you created in the Confidence Builder. Editors also lower the image quality of files they intend to distribute online, because lowered image quality means less information in the video file, which takes less time to download. The cost is a reduced-quality version of your product—the viewer sees a much smaller picture that doesn't look as good, and because of the lower frame rate, the motion isn't nearly as smooth. To compensate, people who know they're going to distribute via the Web shoot more closeups (a full-frame image of a person's face looks much better at a small size than a wide shot of a landscape) and shoot less motion. Pans and tilts look jerky at lower frame rates. Likewise, the shot of Sonia walking across the frame would lose its elegance at a reduced frame rate.

CD-ROM

CD-ROMs offer the opportunity to distribute your work in an interactive format, along with additional material such as a teacher's guide or behind-the-scenes images and text. The random-access features of a CD-ROM enable your audience to navigate in an order that they determine, at the speed of their choice. Because CD-ROM is a digital medium, you can produce an unlimited number of copies with no loss in quality. (There's no degradation from generation to generation when you work with digital material.) Because CDs are smaller and lighter than VHS tapes, they're also easier to send by mail and require less postage. For a while, people considered the CD to be the best thing since sliced bread. Of course, each format has inherent limitations.

When you distribute video on a CD, download time is not an issue because you provide the material on disc. Instead, the issue becomes the processor speed of your user's system. Video playback requires a powerful computer, which is part of the reason the system requirements for Final Cut Pro include large amounts of RAM and processor power. Most desktop computers cannot play back video effectively, so in addition to smaller frame sizes and lower playback rates, video producers generally compress CD-based video files with a codec to make them more accessible. The term *codec* means *compressor/decompressor.* Editors use codecs to compress files, making them lighter and easier for a user with the appropriate codec to decompress and play back. For example, The RealPlayer uses a codec to enable you to view files encoded with RealPlayer's proprietary technology. Apple's QuickTime player uses a variety of codecs to enable you to view multiple types of media formats.

Another limitation of CD-ROMs is the amount of data they can hold. A standard recordable CD holds 700MB of data, but as you may remember from earlier in this book, 5 minutes of DV-format video takes up more than a gigabyte of storage space. So, unless you plan on distributing very short projects exclusively to users with very powerful computers, you need to apply some type of compression. As you compress your video, you may face some of the same challenges as optimizing for the Web—small frame sizes, low frame rates, and poor image quality.

DVD

If you're looking to shoot, edit, and distribute your work digitally, DVD may be the route to take. DVDs look great, sound great, and fit in the mail just as easily as a CD—just look at the success of online DVD rental house NetFlix. The DVD format enables you to create interactive features similar to those on a CD-ROM if not more impressive, and the video and audio quality of the DVD format are noticeably superior because you can include more information on a DVD. A DVD holds slightly less than 5GB of information, which is approximately 7 times more than a CD, but considerably less than the storage space that 30 minutes of DV-format video would require (6.5GB). As a result, creating a DVD still requires compression—just not as much as some other formats.

You can compress full-screen video to fit on a DVD at standard broadcast frame rates, and with a certain amount of skill, you can even produce good-quality images from start to finish. Advanced compression programs enable you to apply different compression levels for different types of content. A static shot of a person standing still against a white background is relatively easy to compress, because there's very little motion and the background doesn't change from frame to frame. The shot would be harder to compress if the person was moving or if the background was finely detailed and constantly changing (for example, if the person was standing against a background of leaves rustling in the breeze). An even harder type of shot combines camera motion, motion inside the frame, and a detailed changing background (for example, if the camera panned across a background of moving leaves while a person walked through the frame). Interestingly enough, I took a break from writing this part of the book and watched *Far from Heaven* on DVD— the opening is a moving shot of leaves blowing in the breeze.

Some directors keep compression in mind when they're shooting and adapt their content accordingly. If you're not interested in compromising your artistic vision to make your work DVD compatible, good-quality compression becomes especially important.

Compressing high-quality video takes skill, experience, and expensive equipment. Much like color-correcting video, you may be able to do a good job on your own, but it may also help to work with a professional who does this for a living.

Once you've compressed your material into a DVD-ready format (MPEG-2), you still need to import the material into a DVD-creation program, such as DVD Studio Pro, to create a disc that can play on an audience's home DVD player. There's a fair amount of detail involved in this process as well, and a skilled professional can make it much more pleasant and may produce far better results than you could at home. You can often find a good compressionist at the same facility that you find a good colorist.

Tape

The VCR may not be elegant, fancy, or even new, but it works and it's a truly reliable format. Full-screen video is no problem, complex motion plays back just as easily as a static shot, and the videotape format is friendly to long pieces as well as short. Best of all, you can feel confident that all members of your potential audience have access to a VCR (schools often have older equipment and are generally slower to adopt new technologies such as a DVD player). Technical quality suffers a de facto loss when you dub to VHS because you lose a generation, but printing to tape is a straightforward process that you probably don't need professional assistance to do well.

I finished graduate school as the film world was moving from analog to digital technology. I finished editing my thesis documentary project on an Avid digital editing system in the spring of 1997. At the time, the Internet was beginning to explode all around me, and everyone was talking about new forms of media that would some day take over the world and forever change the way people watched television and movies. Since then, I've come to work in different distribution formats: VHS, Web-based, CD-ROM, and so on, for different projects. The following tutorials walk you through the process of compressing video for various formats so you can get a better idea of the strengths and weaknesses of each format. As you decide how you would like to distribute your projects in the future, think about how you want audiences to use your work. You can then choose the format that best matches what you have in mind.

Tutorial
» Optimizing Your Movie for the Web

Final Cut Pro ships with a powerful program called Compressor. Compressor is designed to integrate with Final Cut Pro (like Soundtrack and LiveType) and enables you to compress a video file for various playback formats, including each of the formats in the previous discussion. In this tutorial and the tutorials that follow, you use Compressor to output several different versions of the preview you created for this course.

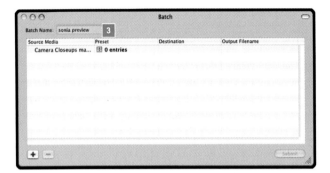

1. **Click the master sequence tab to ensure that the sequence is open and displayed in the Timeline.**

2. **Choose File→Export→Using Compressor.**
   Final Cut Pro launches the Compressor application. Because the master sequence was open when you chose File→Export, it becomes the sequence you work with in Compressor and is listed in the Batch window.

< N O T E >
Because Compressor and Final Cut Pro are designed to work together, you can easily work with an open sequence without having to first export a version of it as a QuickTime file. In the past, other compression applications forced editors to export a QuickTime version of the material they wanted to work with before compression could begin. The extra step of exporting a QuickTime file cost both time and hard drive space.

< T I P >
You can also import additional files into Compressor by choosing File→Import and selecting a file from your hard drive or by dragging a file into the Batch window.

3. **Enter** sonia preview **in the Batch Name field in the Batch window.**
   Each compression task you assign to Compressor is referred to as a *job*. In the following tutorials, you assign Compressor to output several different versions of the sequence at different compression settings. In the final tutorial, you have Compressor process all the jobs as one *batch*.

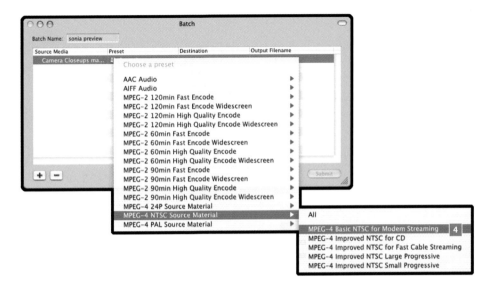

4. **Click the Preset pop-up menu, and choose MPEG-4 NTSC Source Material→MPEG-4 Basic NTSC for Modem Streaming.**

The Batch window changes to display the selected preset along with a destination and an output filename. MPEG-4 is a file format designed for use on the Web and by wireless devices such as advanced mobile phones and PDAs. The preset you selected—MPEG-4 Basic NTSC for Modem Streaming—is a collection of settings designed to optimize the master sequence for the Web at a file size and frame rate accessible to people with dial-up modem service.

<TIP>

You can also select other presets to optimize the file for users with higher-bandwidth Internet access.

5. **Click the Destination pop-up menu, and select Other.**

The destination dialog box opens. The destination is where Compressor saves the finished file. The default—Source—places the finished file in the same place as the original file. Creating a new destination folder makes it easier to find the compressed files later.

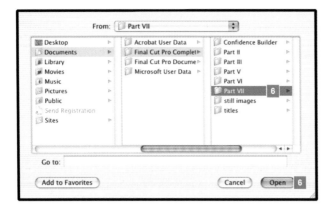

6. **Navigate to the Part VII folder in the Final Cut Pro Complete Course folder on your hard drive, and click Open.**

   The destination dialog box closes, and Compressor assigns the Part VII folder as the destination for your compressed file.

7. **Double-click the default name in the Output Filename column, and rename the file master_web.**

   Your file is now ready to process.

<NOTE>

Some Web servers cannot process filenames containing spaces or capital letters. Using an underscore and all lowercase letters in the filename master_web ensures people will be able to access your work when you put it online.

8. **Choose Window→Presets.**

   The Presets window opens, displaying a summary of the presets applied to the sequence. The compressed file will play at 160 × 120 pixels (reduced from the original 720 × 480) and a frame rate of 6 frames per second (fps) (reduced from the original 29.97).

<TIP>

You can also open the Presets window by pressing ⌘+2.

9. **Click the Preview button in the Presets window to open the Preview window.**

<TIP>

You can also open the Preview window by pressing ⌘+3.

10. **Click the Play button.**

    The master sequence plays, displaying the original, uncom-
    pressed version on the left and a preview of the compression
    settings that you have applied on the right. As you can see,
    this is not the most elegant presentation of your video. Once
    you gain an understanding of the way Compressor functions,
    you can come back and modify the settings to achieve more
    polished results.

11. **Close the Preview and Presets windows by clicking the red button
    in the upper-left corner of each window.**

    In this tutorial, you assigned Compressor to create a version of
    your master sequence for Web-based streaming. The preset
    you assigned is designed to deliver a file that uses smaller
    amounts of memory so that a user can download it quickly.
    The cost is reduced frame size and image quality. Using pre-
    sets designed for users with faster Internet connections
    enables you to output a file at a larger size and better quality.

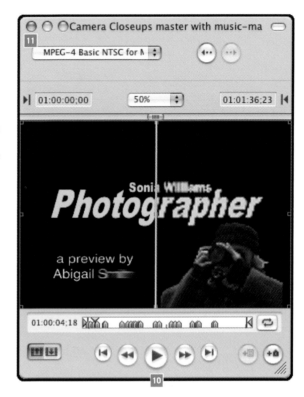

Tutorial
» Encoding Your Movie for CD-ROM

One of the benefits of working with Compressor is that you can apply more than one compression setting to the same source media file. Compressor then outputs one new compressed media file for each setting. This enables you to create several different output files at once, instead of having to adjust a group of settings and wait for each file to output before adjusting the next group of settings. In this tutorial, you add an additional preset to the master sequence and output a version for CD-ROM.

1. **In the Batch window, click the Preset pop-up menu, and choose MPEG-4 NTSC Source Material→MPEG-4 Improved NTSC for CD.** Compressor adds a second job to the Batch window. As you can guess from the name, MPEG-4 Improved NTSC for CD is a preset designed to compress NTSC video for CD-ROMs.

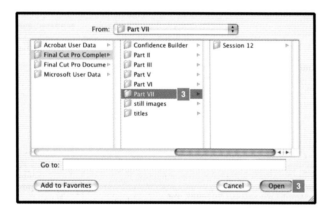

2. **Click the Destination pop-up menu, and select Other.** The destination dialog box opens.

3. **Navigate to the Part VII folder in the Final Cut Pro Complete Course folder on your hard drive, and click Open to save this version in the same location as the Web file.**

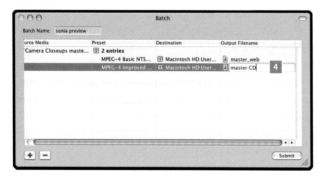

4. **Double-click the default name in the Output Filename column, and rename the file** master CD.

5. **Choose Window→Presets to open the Presets window.**

   The master CD version is set to display at 640 × 480 pixels, far larger than the Web version, and at a frame rate of 29.97 fps, which is the same as the original material. The video is also set to encode at a constant bit rate of 1000 Kbps. This means that playback requires 1000KB of information per second. This setting adjusts the quality to provide good playback on computers that may not be the fastest or the most powerful. Higher bit rates produce better-quality video but may be inaccessible to many computers. The bit rate of the Web file, in contrast, is set to only 32 Kbps to deliver a file that's easy to download, but it also may not have an acceptable level of image quality.

6. **Click the Preview button to open the Preview window.**

   The image quality in the preview frame is very good and, in fact, looks better than the preview image of the source material in the left half of the window.

< N O T E >

To see how the image plays back you can press the play button, but because the frame rate is set to a full 29.97 fps the motion will be very similar to the original master sequence.

7. **Press the Play button to watch the preview in the Preview window.**

8. **Click the red button in the upper-left corner of each window to close the Preview and Presets windows.**

   In this tutorial, you applied a preset to create a version of the master sequence for CD-ROM delivery. This version uses a higher frame rate, better image quality, and a larger size than the Web version but can still play back easily on commonly available desktop computers. The image size is still smaller than the original, because generating larger images requires greater processing power on a user's system.

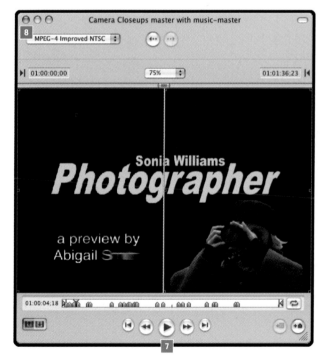

Tutorial

» Creating an MPEG-2 for DVD Production

With Compressor, you can easily export MPEG-2 files that you can use to create DVD versions of your work. DVDs offer the ability to create interactive video projects with stunning picture and sound quality. They also require a fair amount of technical understanding. The presets in Compressor can help get you off to a good start. In this tutorial, you create a third-version, DVD-quality output of the master sequence ready to import to a DVD-authoring program.

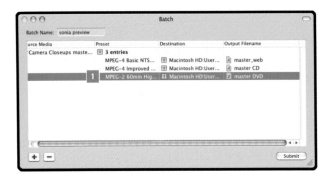

1. **Click the Preset pop-up menu, and choose MPEG-2 60min High Quality Encode→MPEG-2 60min High Quality Encode.**
   Compressor adds a new job to the Batch window. MPEG-2 is an older version of the MPEG file format that you used in the last two presets and is used as the standard for DVD production.

2. **Click the Destination pop-up menu, and repeat the steps that you took in the last two tutorials to set the destination to the Part VII folder.**

3. **Double-click the default name in the Output Filename column, and name the output file** master DVD.

4. **Choose Window→Presets to open the Presets window.**
   Compressor is set to encode this version of the master sequence to display full-frame video at 29.97 fps, just like the source material.

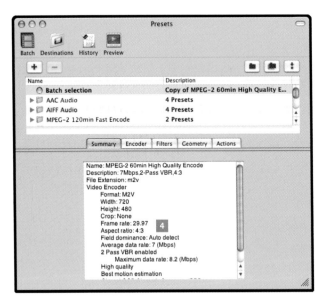

5. **Open the Preview window.**

   The preview of the encoded file in the right half of the window looks really good, and is in fact comparable in quality to the original source files that ship with this book.

6. **Press the Play button to watch the preview in the Preview window.**

7. **Close the Preview and Presets windows.**

   In this tutorial, you assigned a third preset to your source file, creating a third-version output of the master sequence. This version is DVD quality and ready to import into a DVD-authoring program such as DVD Studio Pro. You're now ready to submit the batch and have Compressor create three new files based on the presets you selected.

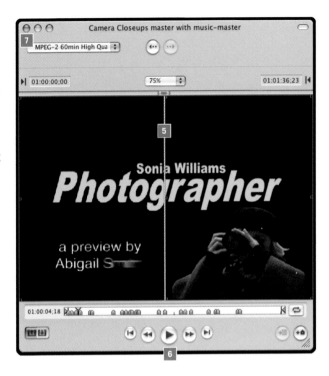

High Quality Presets

The High Quality presets use two-pass, variable-bit rate encoding, which means that the encoder reads through the file twice. In the first read, or *pass,* the encoder analyzes the video to determine which parts are easier to compress and which require more complicated processing. In the second pass, Compressor processes the video by applying greater compression to some areas and less to others. The result is a variable-bit rate, playing back more information where it's needed to produce better image quality, greater detail, and smoother motion. Two-pass processing takes longer than one-pass, which is used by the Fast Encode presets.

When you select the 60min High Quality preset, the average data rate is set to 7 Mbps, which uses approximately 7 times more information per second than the master CD clip and obviously produces better results. Because the preset uses variable bit rate encoding the entire file is not set to 7 Mbps — the "average data rate" is just that, an average. Higher bit rates provide better quality, but they also require more memory, which is an issue for DVD production as well as the Internet. A DVD holds a fixed amount of information (4.7GB), so shorter video files can use higher bit rates while longer video files require lower bit rates to fit on one DVD. That's why you can't just simply apply the highest quality setting to an entire DVD project—anything longer than a few minutes would result in a file too large for the disc. The 120min and 90min presets use significantly lower average bit rates so they can accommodate longer video files.

Tutorial
» Submitting a Batch

Now that you have applied three different presets to the source media file—your master sequence—you're ready to process the batch. Encoding three different types of files can take a while, even with the fastest of computers. Fortunately, Compressor works in the background, so you can continue to use your computer as it processes files. You can't work in Final Cut Pro until the processing is completed, because much of the processing is done in the Final Cut Pro application itself.

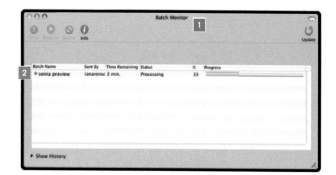

1. **Click the Submit button in the Batch window.**
   The Batch window closes, and the Batch Monitor opens. Batch Monitor is a separate program that, as the name implies, enables you to monitor the progress of the batch you've set Compressor and Final Cut Pro to encode.

2. **Click the triangle next to the sonia preview batch in the Batch Monitor window..**

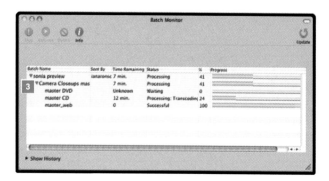

3. **Click the triangle next to Camera Closeups Master.**
   Batch Monitor displays each job in the batch and the time remaining.

<NOTE>
Video encoding takes a substantial amount of time, so the process may take a while, particularly encoding the DVD clip.

4. **Once the compression is complete, open the Part VII folder in the Final Cut Pro Complete Course folder on your hard drive.**
   Inside the folder are three files that were generated by Compressor: master CD.mp4, master_web.mp4, and master DVD.m2v. Compressor turned each preset you applied to the source file into a new compressed media file. The file that you output for the Web is the lightest, and the DVD-quality file is the most memory- and processor-intensive. In this tutorial, you created versions of your master sequence that you can easily distribute as complete digital files viewable by audiences around the world. The Web file is ready for you to upload to the Web server of your choice on the Internet, you can burn the CD file onto a disc, and the DVD file is ready for a DVD-authoring application such as DVD Studio Pro.

Discussion
Understanding Spatial versus Temporal Compression and Work Arounds for Web Streaming

When you compress a video clip using Compressor or another software package, the application applies a compression algorithm to the material. The algorithm is basically a mathematical formula that decides what data to leave in and what data to eliminate. Removing data from a clip makes the file size lighter and makes it easier for a computer to process.

Different codecs use a variety of algorithms to make files lighter. One of the compression algorithm's basic functions is to reduce redundant information in a video clip. Two fundamental methods of reducing redundant image information are spatial compression (also called intraframe compression) and temporal (or interframe) compression.

Spatial compression

Spatial compression examines one frame of video for information that appears in more than one part of the image (for example, a solid color background). Instead of having to create a detailed background image, a computer can simply apply the same color information to a large area of the screen. As a result, an image with a solid color background requires far less memory than an image with a detailed background, such as a landscape or a crowd shot, and is much easier for a computer to process. This is why a shot of a person standing in front of a white wall is easy to compress.

<NOTE>
If you've ever compressed a still image for the Web as a JPEG file, you've used spatial compression.

Temporal compression

Temporal compression compares images in one frame to the images in surrounding frames. Often the same image appears in more than one frame. For example, if a person walks across the screen from the left to the right, the background may not change at all and would be consistent in each frame of the shot. This consistent background is considered a *temporal redundancy.* When the compressed file is played back, the computer may not need to draw a new background for each frame of video; it can simply reuse the repeating background from frame to frame.

Even shots with a finely detailed background, such as a person standing in front of a Rousseau painting, are relatively easy to compress if the background appears unchanged in several frames of video. A constantly changing background (leaves blowing in the breeze) becomes difficult to compress because there's no redundancy.

If the video in your clip contains both temporal and spatial redundancies, it becomes particularly compression-friendly. As you apply higher compression settings, your image quality may start to degrade. If you start out with images that are easier to compress, it becomes that much easier to achieve quality results.

Web streaming and video compression work arounds

Streaming video means creating a file that a user can start to play back before the complete file has been loaded onto his or her computer. Instead of delivering one large chunk of information that the user must wait to download, the file arrives as a continuous stream of information. During the compression process, the file is broken into *packets,* which are then streamed, one at a time, to the user. If the file contains too much information, the packets can easily become too heavy to stream effectively. The Web file that you compressed in the previous tutorial uses approximately 1.2MB of memory, which will not be easy for a person using a dial-up modem connection to access. Even though you shrank the video, lowered the frame rate, and reduced the image quality to a marginally acceptable level, the file still remains outside the reach of people with commonly available Internet connections—as does most video.

An effective workaround is to stream a series of good-quality still images accompanied by good-quality audio. Compressor offers presets that create audio-only .aiff versions of your work as well as a still image sequence. Editing the resulting stills in a program such as Adobe Photoshop enables you to create a series of images that can be encoded using both spatial and temporal compression. You can then import these images and sound files into an animation program, such as Macromedia Flash, to create Web-ready streaming media. If you select one or two still images to use per second, and dissolve from one to the next, you can create elegant visual presentations accompanied by carefully crafted audio that easily streams to users with readily available dial-up modem service. For examples of this technique, visit www.digitaldocumentary.org.

» Session Review

In this session, you created three compressed versions of the master sequence, each for a different media format. Using the Compressor application that ships with Final Cut Pro, you created a version for the Web, another for distribution via CD-ROM, and a third for delivery as a DVD. In the process, you gained an understanding of the strengths and weaknesses of each media format. This session also provided an overview of the compression process and an explanation of compression technology. Now that you're familiar with Compressor, you can experiment using additional existing presets or by creating your own.

The following questions are designed to help you understand the information in this section of the book. You can find the answers in the discussions and tutorials listed next to each question.

1. What is bandwidth, and why does it matter? (See Discussion: Distributing by Tape, Web, or DVD, and Why It Matters)

2. What is the major concern when compressing video for a CD-ROM? (See Discussion: Distributing by Tape, Web, or DVD, and Why It Matters)

3. If a DVD holds so much more information than a CD-ROM, why do you still need to compress your video? (See Discussion: Distributing by Tape, Web, or DVD, and Why It Matters)

4. With all the digital media choices available, why would you still use VHS tape to distribute your project? (See Discussion: Distributing by Tape, Web, or DVD, and Why It Matters)

5. What is the advantage of using Compressor instead of another compression program that isn't designed to integrate with Final Cut Pro? (See Tutorial: Optimizing Your Movie for the Web)

6. What is the MPEG-4 file format designed for? (See Tutorial: Optimizing Your Movie for the Web)

7. When you apply more than one preset to a source media file, what happens? (See Tutorial: Encoding Your Movie for CD-ROM)

8. Which has a higher bit rate, the CD version or the Web version of your master sequence? (See Tutorial: Encoding Your Movie for a CD-ROM)

9. When you compress a file for delivery as a DVD, why can't you simply apply the highest quality setting to the entire video? (See Tutorial: Creating an MPEG-2 for DVD Production)

10. How does variable-bit-rate processing result in better picture quality? (See Tutorial: Creating an MPEG-2 for DVD Production)

11. What are the advantages of a two-pass encoding process and why does two-pass encoding take longer than one-pass? (See Tutorial: Creating an MPEG-2 for DVD Production)

12. Why do the 120min and 90min presets use significantly lower average bit rate settings than the 60-minute preset? (See Tutorial: Creating an MPEG-2 for DVD Production)

13. What is the advantage of batch-processing your files versus processing them one at a time? (See Tutorial: Submitting a Batch)

14. Why do the different file output types take different times to process, especially the DVD file type? (See Tutorial: Submitting a Batch)

15. What is the difference between spatial and temporal compression? (See Discussion: Understanding Spatial versus Temporal Compression and Workarounds for Web Streaming)

16. What is the difference between a file that streams and a file that downloads? (See Discussion: Understanding Spatial versus Temporal Compression and Workarounds for Web Streaming)

Exporting Your Movie Project

Session Introduction

It all comes down to this: You've spent countless hours adjusting and tweaking every last detail of your project, now it's time to send your work out into the world. This final session addresses the creation of your final master tape—probably the most important stage of your project and definitely not a time to take shortcuts. The master that you output is the final version of your project—it's what audiences see when they watch your film or video project. The discussions and tutorials in this part of the book aim to help you create flawless content that looks as good to everyone else as it does to you.

TOOLS YOU'LL USE
Timeline window, Easy Setup dialog box, Print to Video dialog box,
EDL Export Options dialog box, OMF Audio Export dialog box

MATERIALS NEEDED
Camera Closeups master with music

TIME REQUIRED
90 minutes

Discussion

The Second Set of Eyes: Showing a Test Audience

When you work on a project for a long time, it's easy to lose perspective. You can get used to things that don't look or sound so great and lower your standard of quality. You can also spend endless amounts of time obsessing over parts of the project that look fine to everyone else. Showing your work to an audience you trust may provide just the feedback that you need to refine the last bits of your work.

You have an infinite familiarity with every camera movement, dialog inflection, and editing decision in your project. You also have a significant emotional attachment to your work and the content of your project. Your audience, however, is seeing your film for the first time, and their response may be entirely different.

Have you ever listened to your favorite song with a group of people who don't know it? They may love it the same way you do, or they may not like it at all. Either way, their response can bring you an entirely new perspective on something you thought you knew inside out—they're likely to hear things that you don't, and you may walk away with an entirely new opinion. You can put the same dynamic to work for you before you create your master tape. Invite a group of people whose opinions you trust to take a look at your cut. Ask them what they think after they've seen it, but more importantly, pay attention to them while they're watching (especially when they think you're not looking). Do people laugh when you think they should? Does the mood in the room feel like you successfully engaged everyone in the events on-screen, or do you feel like people are shifting in their seats and are anxious to get up? The verbal feedback people give you is valuable, and their unselfconscious actions can tell you even more.

Analog post production involved many more people than just an editor sitting by himself or herself in front of a computer. This made things more expensive and sometimes made editing much slower, but it also established a collaborative process in which more than one person shaped each sequence. This collaboration, sometimes referred to as "working with a second set of eyes," results in considerably stronger end products because it takes more than one opinion into account. Learning to work with a good test audience becomes especially important when you edit by yourself. Once you finish your project and make a whole stack of copies, it becomes very difficult—and expensive—to make changes. Arranging a test screening takes time and effort, but you may find yourself happy enough with the results to make it an invaluable part of the process.

Discussion
Knowing When to Finish Your Project Yourself and When to Use a Post Production Facility

In the past, deciding whether you should finish a project yourself was easy—almost no one had access to the equipment needed to make a broadcast-quality master on his own. Before Final Cut Pro, video color correction was well outside the realm of desktop computing, and available editing systems worked with low-resolution media files that were fine for editing but just wouldn't work as a final product. As a result, creating a quality master meant spending the money to go to a post production facility for an online edit. In an online edit, a skilled editor uses a specialized and powerful computer system to create a finished version of your project with material taken directly from your source tapes. Using an Edit Decision List (EDL), which you provide, the editor re-creates each of your edits and transitions to form the highest-quality master output.

These days, technology has made high-quality output infinitely more accessible. Using Final Cut Pro, you have the ability to create an excellent finished product that you can proudly show at film festivals or confidently deliver to a client. As you saw in Session 12, you have all the tools available to conform your project to broadcast-safe levels, and as you learned in Session 13, you can output a high-quality digital version directly from Final Cut Pro.

So why spend money to go to a post production house? The answer depends on how you plan to use your master tape and what level of quality you're trying to achieve. Once you finalize your edits and fully color-correct your project, much of the quality of the master tape depends on the type of deck that you use. Using a higher-quality format for your master tape allows you to make higher-quality copies. Because there's a generational loss each time you make an analog copy of a tape, a higher-quality master can result in significantly better VHS dubs for distribution. Higher-end formats, such as digital Betacam, require exceptionally expensive decks. Instead of buying a new piece of equipment that may cost $70,000, you can finish your project at a post production facility for a lot less money and get the benefit of the staff's professional experience.

Additionally, some broadcast outlets, or clients, may have very strict technical requirements that you need to meet for them to accept your work. Even if finishing the project at a post production facility costs you a few thousand dollars, paying someone to help you make everything perfect the first time may be much less expensive than paying someone to fix mistakes that could have been avoided—especially if making mistakes means you might really annoy the person who's waiting for you to deliver a tape.

The tutorials in this session show you how to record your master sequence to tape using Final Cut Pro and show you how to output an EDL. Either way, it's your project, and this is the last step in post production. You've spent so much time and effort to make your film a reality; make that last push and make every last detail exceptionally good.

Tutorial

» Recording from the Timeline

Final Cut Pro allows you to make a recording of your sequence as it plays in the Timeline and provides the Print to Video function. Both result in the same level of quality, but Print to Video allows you more control. If you create the master tape yourself, instead of going for an online edit, you can play your sequence in the Timeline and record the sequence onto a connected deck to create your master. If you decide to bring your project to a post production house for an online edit, it's a good idea to record the sequence onto a tape to bring with you as a reference. In both cases, playing a sequence in the Timeline and recording the output is the easiest way to make a videotape copy of your project.

1. **Select Final Cut Pro→Easy Setup.**
   The Easy Setup dialog box opens displaying a summary of the current output settings. For a connected deck to record the sequence as it plays back in the Timeline, Final Cut Pro must be configured to output external audio and video to your equipment. In this case, Final Cut Pro is set to output both audio and video through the computer's FireWire interface. If your computer is configured differently, your Easy Setup dialog box displays different information.

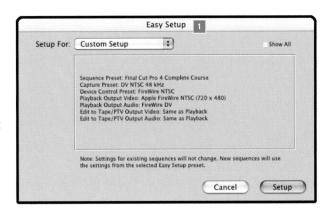

2. **Bring the playhead to the first frame in the sequence.**
   When you start recording, in the next step, the deck records whatever is in the frame of video in which the Timeline is currently located. In this case, you place the playhead in a blank frame, so the deck records black.

<NOTE>
Select View, and make sure that Looping is not selected. If it is, the sequence will not stop at the end of the Timeline, but will repeat.

<NOTE>
If you had an image in the first frame, the deck would record a still image of your first frame until you began playback in the Timeline. To avoid recording a still image of your first frame, you could either add a frame of black to the head of the Timeline or simply select the entire sequence in the Timeline and slide it to the right, creating a blank space at the head.

3. **Press Record on your deck or camcorder.**
   Wait a few seconds for your deck to come up to speed. Recording before the deck has reached full speed can result in technical problems.

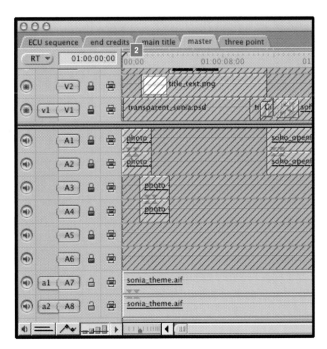

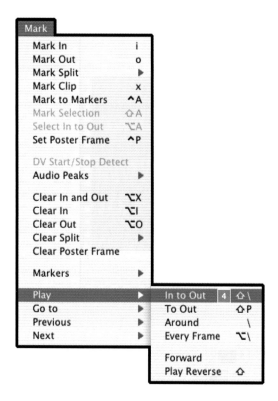

< N O T E >
If you use a camcorder to record your sequence, be sure you place it in VCR mode and properly connect all the cables first.

4. **Select Mark→Play→In to Out.**
   Final Cut Pro plays the sequence from the first frame to the last.

< N O T E >
If you set In and Out points in the Timeline, Final Cut Pro plays only what's between the two points instead of playing the entire sequence.

5. **When you reach the end of the sequence, stop your record deck.**
   The deck records the image in the last frame of your sequence until you stop the recording. In this case, the last frame of the sequence is blank, so just as in the beginning, the deck records black. If the frame contained an image, your deck would record a still of the image until you stopped the recording.

6. **Check your tape.**
   It's that simple. If you like the sequence you recorded, you're good to go. In this tutorial, you recorded your master sequence onto a tape as it played in the Timeline. You now have a perfectly functional tape you can use for reference in an online edit or bring to a duplication facility to have copies made.

Tutorial
» Using the Print to Video Feature

If you want a more controlled output than simply recording from the Timeline, you can use the Print to Video function. Printing to video allows you to output all or part of your sequence to tape, along with additional items, such as bars and tone or a countdown screen.

1. **Click the master sequence tab to display the sequence in the Timeline.**

2. **Choose File→Print to Video.**
   The Print to Video dialog box opens, displaying the options for your sequence. To perform this step, external video equipment must be connected to your computer and turned on; if it isn't, you get an error message.

3. **Select the Color Bars check box.**
   This adds 60 seconds of bars and tone to the head of your material. The bars and tone don't show in the Timeline but are added to the sequence when you print to tape. Your post production facility can use the bar and tone information to calibrate their equipment when they dub copies of your master.

4. **Select the Black check box to add 10 seconds of black between the color bars and the start of the sequence.**
   The Duration Calculator displays the length of your media as well as the total length of your media combined with the elements that you added to the head and tail of the sequence. If you work with a longer sequence, the Total duration field helps ensure that everything fits on the length of tape you've chosen.

5. **Click OK to close the window and apply the settings.**
   Final Cut Pro renders any material you added.

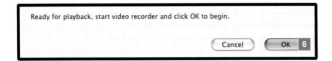

6. **A dialog box appears, instructing you to start recording. Set your deck to record, and click OK to start the process.**

7. **Once playback ends, stop the deck.**

   In this tutorial, you used the Print to Video function to output your master sequence to tape. The sequence was accompanied by bars and tone, 10 seconds of black at the head of the sequence, and 5 seconds of black at the end.

<NOTE>

You can set the sequence to loop if you want to record it to the same tape more than once. If you loop your sequence, the trailer plays after the final loop.

<TIP>

You can also set In and Out points in a sequence to print only part of the sequence to video.

<TIP>

You can change the length of any elements you add to the leader or trailer of the sequence by entering a new value in the appropriate field.

Discussion
Exporting an EDL for an Online Edit

Now that you printed a sequence directly to tape, you may decide the higher level of quality you gain from an online edit is worth the increase in cost. There's no need to online the project you edited for this book, but it's something to seriously consider for work you do in the future. The first step in an online edit, once you finish editing your sequence, is to create an Edit Decision List. When you generate an EDL in Final Cut Pro, the application assembles a list of all the edits that you made and the accompanying source timecode. The resulting EDL is a text document of the start and end timecode of each edit as well as the edit's location in your sequence. Final Cut Pro also records which tracks you placed each clip onto and any transitions you may have added. Each item in the EDL, called an *event,* represents some type of edit you applied to the material in your sequence.

When you bring the EDL to your postproduction facility, the editor uses the list to re-create your sequence directly from the source video tapes exactly as you created the sequence in Final Cut Pro. The editor can then output the finished product at the highest possible level of quality. If you export the EDL from Final Cut Pro as the proper type of electronic file, the editor can import it directly into his or her editing system, saving you considerable time and money. Each online system has it's own set of specifications, so be sure to consult with your online facility in advance so you know exactly what you need to bring to the edit.

To generate an EDL for your project in Final Cut Pro, choose File→Export→EDL. The EDL Export Options dialog box opens.

The settings you choose in this box determine the format of your EDL and how information in your sequence is organized. The Format drop-down menu is perhaps the most important item in this dialog box—different online editing systems use differently formatted EDLs. If you choose a format that doesn't work with the system at your post production facility, your EDL won't be useful.

In addition to formatting, the structure of your sequence is important when creating an EDL. If you have multiple layers of video, as you do in this sequence, the structure may not be suitable for an EDL. (Many EDLs allow only two video tracks and either two or four audio tracks.) If you find yourself with a sequence that

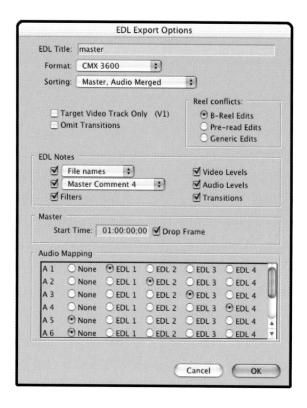

contains too many tracks, consult your online facility. Also, because the EDL was developed for older systems that generated a narrower array of video effects and transitions, many of the transitions available to you in Final Cut Pro are not supported in an EDL. If you use a transition that's not supported in the EDL format you choose, Final Cut Pro substitutes the most similar available transition. Even in cases where the same transition is available, it may look entirely different when created in an online system as opposed to in Final Cut Pro. Finally , online systems can be very particular about the types of media they accept. Depending on the system that your post production facility uses, you may need to deliver your EDL on a double-density floppy disk. That's right—a floppy disk. You may be working on the most powerful, dual-processor G5 computer available, but you still need to find yourself a 720K floppy disk to bring to the online edit. Some editing systems even require you to deliver your EDL on a DOS formatted disk. (I'm not kidding.) Check with your online facility in advance. A good post production studio can answer all your questions before you show up.

Tutorial

» Exporting OMF Audio Files for a Professional Mix

If you go to the effort and expense of bringing your project to a postproduction facility, you may want to consider working with a professional sound engineer. An engineer can hear things in the mix that you don't, and he or she most likely has access to specialized audio equipment that's outside your purchase price range. The post production facility that you use for your online edit may have an audio editor on staff, and if it doesn't, it can surely recommend one.

To prepare for your audio mix, it's a good idea to export OMF audio files. OMF (Open Media Framework) is an audio file format used by video editing applications such as Final Cut Pro, and by professional audio editing applications as well. The benefit of OMF audio is it allows an editor to individually work with each audio element in your mix. Unlike an EDL, which contains a description of the audio (its source timecode In and Out points), an OMF contains a description of the audio as well as the audio itself. An audio editor can then open the OMF in an audio-editing application, such as Pro Tools, and perfect each fade, transition, and edit—and even rework the entire mix. Because each element retains a separate identity in an OMF export, the audio editor is not constrained by the edits and mix you created in the Timeline, but instead can make changes and additions as needed. One of the greatest benefits of working with OMF audio is Final Cut Pro allows you to export all your audio tracks together, not just the two or four you're limited to with an EDL.

1. **Select File→Export→Audio to OMF.**
   The OMF Audio Export dialog box opens.

<NOTE>
Another option in the Export menu is Export to AIFF. Like OMF, the AIFF file type is recognized by many audio applications. Exporting your mix to AIFF, however, creates one long clip from your entire mix and, as a result, does not provide an editor with the flexibility of an OMF.

2. **Leave the Sample Rate drop-down menu set to 48 kHz and the Sample Size drop-down menu set to 16-bit.**
   It's generally a good idea to export the audio at the same settings at which it was imported, which in this case is 16/48. Check with your audio editor in advance to make sure your output is compatible with the post production facility's equipment.

3. **Leave the Handle Length field set to 1 second.**
   A *handle* is the amount of extra media that is exported before and after each edit. Handles give editors room to breathe—the editor may decide a fade should be slightly longer, and if you provide handles, he can make changes. Again, ask your editor what length he prefers; he will probably be impressed you even thought to ask.

4. **Click OK to close the dialog box.**
   The Save dialog box opens.

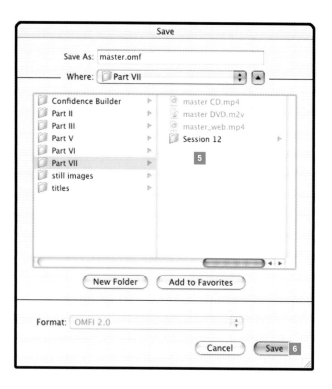

5. Navigate to a location on your hard drive where you want to save the file.

In the figure, the `master.omf` file is being saved in the Part VII folder.

6. Click Save to output the OMF.

In this tutorial, you created an OMF output of your project's audio. OMF is a very flexible format. Not only can you export all the audio in your project, but because the file format allows each sound element to retain its own identity, you can also polish and reshape your sound mix with great precision.

Tutorial

» Backing Up and Saving Your Files for the Future

Before you pack up and go home for the night, the last thing that you need to do is back up your files. Once you create your final edited master and output to tape, you probably won't need your project files again, but if you do, you'll be glad that you made a backup copy.

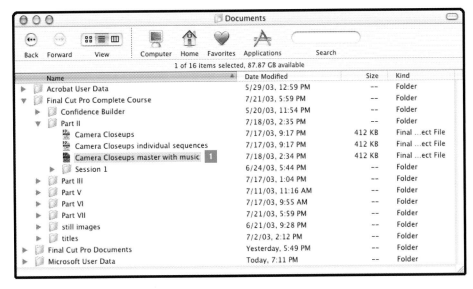

1. **Navigate to the latest version of your project files on your hard drive, and select the file.**

2. **Press ⌘+D to duplicate the project files.**

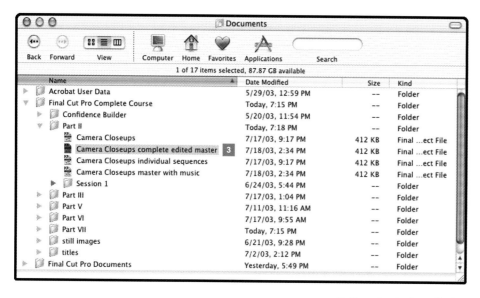

3. **Name the duplicate file** Camera Closeups complete edited master.

4. **Copy the file to removable storage media, such as a Zip disk, to archive it.**

   If you don't have a Zip drive attached to your computer, you can burn a copy of the project file to a CD. The benefit of storing your backup project files in a location other than your computer's hard drive is that if your system ever suffers a catastrophic crash, your project files remain unharmed. In this tutorial, you created a backup version of your completed project, and you saved the file on removable media so the project is not stored only on your computer's hard drive.

Discussion
Editing Film in Final Cut Pro and Outputting to a Professional Format

At some point, you may decide that you want to work with film, rather than video, as your source material or your final output medium. In either case, you can work with Final Cut Pro to edit your film digitally. Once you finish your film project, you can output to video, DVD, or higher-end formats such as high-definition video. You can also create a film copy of your finished Final Cut Pro project, called a *release print,* which you use to screen your work in theaters.

Film captures a wider range of colors than video and, in the hands of a talented cinematographer, can produce images that are significantly higher in quality. Working in film is a more expensive and often a more time-consuming process than video. To achieve the higher image quality, filmmakers often shoot on film and then transfer to video so they can edit on a digital editing system, such as Final Cut Pro. When the transfer is done properly, the images retain their high quality, and bringing the material into the digital video format allows an editor a greater degree of control.

In the spring of 2003, filmmakers Ferne Pearlstein and Robert Edwards completed *Sumo East and West,* a documentary about the art and culture of sumo wrestling. They shot the documentary in film and edited it in Final Cut Pro. When film footage is transferred to videotape for editing, a technician creates a database that shows the relationship between the timecode on the videotape and keycode numbers on the negative. Once the editor has finished cutting the project together, he or she can then work with a negative cutter to conform the original negative into an edited film print. Rather than following the traditional path of working with a film laboratory to create an edited print, Pearlstein and Edwards decided to finish digitally. They transferred selected sections of the negative to high-definition video instead of creating a master film print first and then transferring the completed print to video. Pearlstein and Edwards needed to create a broadcast master of their finished product for television, and they wanted a film print to show in theaters. Working in high definition allowed them to do both and to retain an exceptional level of quality.

"I'm glad we did it this way because you have so much control in the digital world," Edwards said. Using an EDL that was generated in Final Cut Pro, their negative cutter pulled the shots that appear in the documentary. They then assembled the selected shots at an online postproduction facility to create a high-definition master, which they color-corrected and carefully fine-tuned to make sure everything worked exactly the way they wanted. Adjusting film color is an imprecise process, while digital color correction is "incredibly precise—you have so much control it's almost too much control," Edwards said. As you've seen with Final Cut Pro, every last detail is within the control of the filmmaker. The same holds true for film when you bring it into a digital postproduction environment.

Sumo East and West premiered at the TriBeCa Film Festival in New York City and screened as a high-definition videotape. "It looked so great, people thought they were looking at a 35mm film print," Edwards said. Pearlstein and Edwards have also screened a digital Betacam copy of the film at other festivals, which audiences have responded to equally well.

In the past, filmmakers shied away from finishing film productions on video, fearing they would lose quality. With current technology, when the process is done properly, finishing on video is no longer an issue. According to Edwards, "very soon it will be the standard, if it isn't already."

For more information about *Sumo East and West,* visit www.sumoeastandwest.com.

» Session Review

In this session, you learned how to output your master sequence to video, either on your own or by creating an EDL to bring to a postproduction facility. The session also showed you how to export OMF audio to bring to a professional sound editor, and it showed you how to back up your project files and store them somewhere other than on your computer's hard drive. This final part of the book also addressed the importance of screening your work to a test audience before it's too late to make changes, and it raised the question of when you should finish a project yourself and when you should bring your work to a professional facility. Creating your final output is the last step in the postproduction process and one of the most tangible—at the end of the day, you have a finished product that you can hold in your hand. Finishing a project is a great feeling; the only better feeling in filmmaking comes from people telling you how much they like your work. Now that you've edited a project from start to finish in Final Cut Pro, you're ready to go out and cut together some projects on your own. Let's go to the videotape.

The following questions are provided to help you process what you learned in this final session of the book. You can find the answers in the tutorials and discussions listed in parentheses.

1. When you record from the Timeline, does recording start when you play the sequence or before? (See Tutorial: Recording from the Timeline)

2. If you have an image in the first frame of your sequence, what does your deck record before you start playback? (See Tutorial: Recording from the Timeline)

3. What is the difference between recording from the Timeline and using the Print to Video feature? (See Tutorial: Using the Print to Video Feature)

4. When you set the Print to Video dialog box to add items such as color bars or black to your sequence, do they appear in the Timeline? (See Tutorial: Using the Print to Video Feature)

5. When you add color bars or black to a sequence, can you adjust their length? (See Tutorial: Using the Print to Video Feature)

6. If you export an EDL in Final Cut Pro, is it compatible with all types of editing systems? (See Discussion: Exporting an EDL for an Online Edit)

7. Are all of Final Cut Pro's transitions compatible with an EDL? (See Discussion: Exporting an EDL for an Online Edit)

8. What is the maximum number of audio tracks an EDL can contain? (See Discussion: Exporting an EDL for an Online Edit)

9. To export all the audio tracks in a sequence, what format would you use? (See Tutorial: Exporting OMF Audio Files for a Professional Mix)

10. What is the difference between the menu choices Export to OMF and Export to AIFF? (See Tutorial: Exporting OMF Audio Files for a Professional Mix)

11. Why should you back up files to removable media after you finish with a project? (See Tutorial: Backing Up and Saving Your Files for the Future)

Appendix

What's on the CD-ROM

This appendix provides you with information on the contents of the CD-ROM that accompanies this book. For the latest and greatest information, please refer to the ReadMe file located at the root of the CD-ROM. Here is what you will find:

>> System Requirements

>> Using the CD-ROM

>> What's on the CD-ROM

>> Troubleshooting

System Requirements

Make sure that your computer meets the minimum system requirements listed in this section. If your computer doesn't match up to most of these requirements, you may have a problem using the contents of the CD-ROM.

For Macintosh

>> Minimum PowerPC with G4 350 MHz processor, or faster

>> AGP (Accelerated Graphics Port) graphics card

>> 384MB of RAM; 512 recommended

>> DVD drive

» 6GB Audio/Video rated disk drive; 20GB or larger recommended

» Mac OS X v10.2.5 or later

» QuickTime 6.1 or later

» Color monitor with at least 1024 x 768 resolution

» CD-ROM drive

Using the CD-ROM with the Macintosh OS

To install the items from the CD-ROM to your hard drive, follow these steps:

1. Insert the CD-ROM into your CD-ROM drive.

2. Double-click the icon for the CD-ROM after it appears on the desktop.

3. Double-click the License Agreement icon. This is the license that you are agreeing to by using the CD. You can close this window once you've looked over the agreement.

Please note: To open a file from the Project Files folder and work with it in a tutorial, you must first drag the project file from the CD onto your computer's hard drive. You must also drag the media files for that session onto your computer's hard drive.

When you first open a project file that you've dragged onto your hard drive, Final Cut Pro alerts you that media files must be reconnected. This is so Final Cut can establish links to the files it needs. Click "Reconnect" and follow the prompts to reconnect the project files to the media on your hard drive. If you work on a session more than once, you won't have to identify file locations after the first time.

What's on the CD-ROM

The following sections provide a summary of the software and other materials you'll find on the CD.

Author-created materials

This CD contains all the media files you need to complete the exercises in this book, and also contains Final Cut Pro project files for each completed session. The CD also contains an example of the completed project for you to refer to.

The file complete project `sample.mov` is a demonstration version of the project you complete for this course. Media files, video and audio, are organized into folders labeled with the part of the book they correspond to (for example Confidence

Builder, Part III, etc). The sample project files are all in one folder, labeled
Project Files.

The contents of this CD are as follows:

» complete project sample.mov

» Confidence Builder

» Part II

» Part III

» Part V

» Part VI

» Part VII

Project Files

The Confidence Builder folder, and the folders for Part II through Part VII, contain
the media files needed to complete the tutorials in this book. The media files con-
sist of professionally recorded audio and video for you to edit, along with original
music created especially for this book. The tutorials contain specific instuctions
on how to import media from the CD onto your hard drive, and where to place
each file you import. The Project Files folder contains Final Cut Pro project files
for each session in this book.

To use one of the project files on the CD as a reference to see what a completed
session should look like, all you need to do is double click on the file's icon. Each
session has its own project file.

Troubleshooting

If you have difficulty installing or using any of the materials on the companion
CD-ROM, try the following solutions:

» **Turn off any antivirus software that you may have running.** Installers sometimes
mimic virus activity and can make your computer incorrectly believe that it is
being infected by a virus. (Be sure to turn the antivirus software back on later.)

» **Close all running programs.** The more programs you're running, the less memory is
available to other programs. Installers also typically update files and programs; if
you keep other programs running, the installation may not work properly.

» **Reference the ReadMe:** Please refer to the ReadMe file located at the root of
the CD-ROM for the latest product information at the time of publication.

If you still have trouble with the CD-ROM, please call the Wiley Product Technical Support phone number: (800) 762-2974. Outside the United States, call 1(317) 572-3994. You can also contact Wiley Product Technical Support at www. wiley.com/techsupport. Wiley Publishing will provide technical support only for installation and other general quality control items; for technical support on the applications themselves, consult the program's vendor or author.

To place additional orders or to request information about other Wiley products, please call (800) 225-5945.

Index

Workflow
Media Te
Creation C
Manageme
Digital As
Fonts an
Digital M
Content N
Manageme
Workflow
Media Te
Creation C
Manageme
Digital As
Fonts an
Digital M
Content N
Manageme
Workflow
Media Te
Creation C
Manageme

About Seybold Seminars and Publications

Seybold Seminars and Publications is your complete guide

to the publishing industry. For more than 30 years it

has been the most trusted source for technology events,

news, and insider intelligence.

SEYBOLD
SEMINARS

PUBLICATIONS

Today, Seybold Publications and Consulting continues to guide publishing professionals around the world in their purchasing decisions and business strategies through newsletters, online resources, consulting, and custom corporate services.

○ **The Seybold Report: Analyzing Publishing Technologies**
The Seybold Report analyzes the cross-media tools, technologies, and trends shaping professional publishing today. Each in-depth newsletter delves into the topics changing the marketplace. *The Seybold Report* covers critical analyses of the business issues and market conditions that determine the success of new products, technologies, and companies. Read about the latest developments in mission-critical topic areas, including content and asset management, color management and proofing, industry standards, and cross-media workflows. A subscription to *The Seybold Report* (24 issues per year) includes our weekly email news service, *The Bulletin,* and full access to the seyboldreports.com archives.

○ **The Bulletin: Seybold News & Views on Electronic Publishing**
The Bulletin: Seybold News & Views on Electronic Publishing is Seybold Publications' weekly email news service covering all aspects of electronic publishing. Every week *The Bulletin* brings you all the important news in a concise, easy-to-read format.

For more information on **NEWSLETTER SUBSCRIPTIONS,**
please visit **seyboldreports.com**.

CUSTOM SERVICES

In addition to newsletters and online information resources, Seybold
Publications and Consulting offers a variety of custom corporate services
designed to meet your organization's specific needs.

○ **Strategic Technology Advisory Research Service (STARS)**
The STARS program includes a group license to *The Seybold Report* and
The Bulletin, phone access to our analysts, access to online archives at
seyboldreports.com, an on-site visit by one of our analysts, and much more.

○ **Personalized Seminars**
Our team of skilled consultants and subject experts work with you to create a
custom presentation that gets your employees up to speed on topics spanning
the full spectrum of prepress and publishing technologies covered in our publications. Full-day and half-day seminars are available.

○ **Site Licenses**
Our electronic licensing program keeps everyone in your organization, sales
force, or marketing department up to date at a fraction of the cost of buying
individual subscriptions. One hard copy of *The Seybold Report* is included with
each electronic license.

For more information on **CUSTOM CORPORATE SERVICES,**
please visit **seyboldreports.com**.

SEYBOLD SEMINARS

EVENTS

Seybold Seminars facilitates exchange and discussion within the high-tech publishing community several times a year. A hard-hitting lineup of conferences, an opportunity to meet leading media technology vendors, and special events bring innovators and leaders together to share ideas and experiences.

Conferences

Our diverse educational programs are designed to tackle the full range of the latest developments in publishing technology. Topics include:

- Print publishing
- Web publishing
- Design
- Creative tools and standards
- Best practices

- Multimedia
- Content management
- Technology standards
- Security
- Digital rights management

In addition to the conferences, you'll have the opportunity to meet representatives from companies that bring you the newest products and technologies in the publishing marketplace. Test tools, evaluate products, and take free classes from the experts.

For more information on **SEYBOLD SEMINARS EVENTS**, please visit **seyboldseminars.com**.

Wiley Publishing, Inc.
End-User License Agreement